Fleet Street Fox has been a tabloid reporter for more than a decade, and started a blog three years ago revealing the inside story of her divorce and chronicling a trade in decline.

More recently she has started a news comment blog at www.fleetstreetfox.com, which gets 100,000 hits a month (and growing) and has seen her invited on to Radio 4's *Woman's Hour* and *Charlie Brooker's Screenwipe*.

This book is the first instalment in her diaries, a blend of her own true story and internal scandals of Fleet Street, with much more to come . . .

THE DIARIES OF A FLEET STREET FOX

CONSTABLE • LONDON

Constable & Robinson Ltd
55–56 Russell Square
London WC1B 4HP
www.constablerobinson.com

First published in the UK by Constable,
an imprint of Constable & Robinson, 2013

A copy of the British Library Cataloguing in Publication
Data is available from the British Library

ISBN 978-1-78033-656-5 (paperback)
ISBN 978-1-178033-813-2 (ebook)

Printed in Great Britain by
Clays Ltd, St Ives plc

1 3 5 7 9 10 8 6 4 2

MIX
Paper from
responsible sources
FSC
www.fsc.org   FSC® C018072

DEDICATION

THIS story is as close to the truth as I can get without being sued, served with an injunction, or never spoken to again by some of my friends.

In places identities and chronology have been fudged to deny the bad guys an opportunity for revenge, and to prevent the good guys from getting big heads.

Other parts are raw and unvarnished, and I reckon you'll be able to spot when I'm writing from the heart.

As a consequence this book is a blend of fact and fiction, and you'll have to work out for yourself which bits are which.

I owe thanks to too many people to list here, but mainly to my inspiring and brilliant Mum and Dad, the two best friends anyone could ever have.

Finally, this book is dedicated to the feral beasts of Fleet Street – I'm proud to be one of you.

To my friends – enjoy. And to my enemies – read it and weep.

PS I am not a real fox.

DAY ONE

TODAY is the worst day of the rest of my life. I mean, it can't get much worse.

So far I have attempted double murder, been in police custody, had several of the all-time Worst Conversations of my Life, and suffered a nervous breakdown at the 'Baskets Only' checkout in Sainsbury's.

All that and it's only just gone noon. I suppose something more awful could happen in the next twelve hours, but unless I'm the sole victim of a tiny but well-aimed nuclear strike it's simply not going to register.

When today began, at 12.01 a.m, I was in a prison cell contemplating the ruin of everything I know and uncomfortably aware that I had broken the first rule of journalism. As a trainee reporter you are always told to practise your shorthand, stay away from the TV cameras, and above all things 'never become the story'. But now not only was I the story, it was one my Fleet Street colleagues would cheerfully kill each other to find out about, and one which I have written so many times about other people that I knew all too well where it would lead. I could almost hear the knives being sharpened for me.

I was also experiencing the world's worst cup of tea, which the nice custody sergeant had got me out of a machine, the first ominous twinges of stress-induced diarrhoea, and the realization that my cell possessed just one tiny square of toilet paper.

On top of that my shoes, laces and belt had been taken away – 'just to be sure' – and the only foot-coverings available in the high-security nick, more often used to house suspected terrorists, were size fourteen plimsolls. Pacing up and down the urine-scented ten-foot cell under the unblinking eye of a CCTV camera, I resembled not so much a desperate criminal as a woman trying to walk in flippers.

Slap, slap, slap. Turn. Slap, slap, slap.

And all the time sipping the undrinkable tea, grimacing, and thinking to myself: 'I do hope I'm not in front of that camera when the squits arrive.'

It would have been bearable had I been drunk. Then I could have found the whole thing wildly funny, burbled to myself for a bit and lapsed into a deep, dreamless sleep, thinking I would have a great yarn for my mates when I sobered up. Unfortunately I was stone-cold sober and chillingly aware of my surroundings, the failings which had led me there, and all of the possible, uniformly grim and painful outcomes. As I stared at the tiled wall all I could think was: 'I am twenty-nine years old, my heart is broken, and my life is over.'

That was twelve hours ago, and then I was numb, if a little weepy. Now the sun is high in the sky and I'm feeling a pain so great it's a physical agony. It's as though my heart is being torn to pieces, like there's a knife behind my ribcage, and my lungs are filled with burning rocks. Even my blood hurts, as if there's ground glass in every vein and capillary, each corpuscle sharpened to a series of lethal points bowling crazily around my insides, cutting, slashing, tearing. I've cried so much my throat is raw, but the tears still pour out of my eyes. Hell could not hold the pain I feel.

But journalists are never off-duty, and even today I'm a news reporter, which means I cannot help but question things that seem unusual. The amount of snot I am producing, for one. Where's it all coming from? Why won't it stop? Why haven't my eyes fallen out? And now that I have failed at both murder and marriage, what's left?

Another nagging worry is that I'm trying to hide, but the car park at Sainsbury's may not be the best place to do it. Everyone who walks past the car can see me sitting in it sobbing like a mad woman. But all hacks know it's easy to hide in a crowd, comforting even, and anything is better than being at home. My husband's there with my parents, and they want A Word with him. God knows how much of him will be left when I go back. *If* I go back.

I did not expect to be here on a sunny day in June. I should be at work, gazing out of the newsroom window wishing something interesting would happen, emailing my mates, and spending the lunch hour gazing in the windows of Baby Gap while telling myself it's far too early to be buying bootees.

Instead my chest seems to have been ripped open by a rocket, and my best friend is a parking space. Why is the sun shining? Where are the glowering storm clouds you're supposed to get at times like this? The torrential, end-of-the-world rain? Why does everything look the same, when everything's changed? How can people still be walking around and smiling?

I can never smile again. I feel powerless, adrift, buffeted about like a twig in a torrent, swept towards a

3

sewer's gaping mouth, where the best I can hope for is a different *kind* of shit. Or maybe it is more like being a clown who tripped over his stupid giant shoes in the hall of mirrors and is now sat, uncomprehending, amid the dying tinkly noises, thinking: 'Whathafu . . . ?'

But it's spilt milk now. Everything I knew and loved has been torn up, thrown out, ripped away, and all that's left is me. Somehow I have to work out what to do and press on, surrounded by 10,000 shards of glass, about a billion years of bad luck and frankly astonishing amounts of mucus.

This is not a task to undertake lightly or without some kind of specialist equipment. After an hour or so wandering the supermarket aisles, crying quietly, picking things up and putting them down again, I am back in the car post-breakdown with the most useful items I could find.

One giant 1.5 litre bottle of screw-top white wine (normal-sized bottle will not be enough), one double pack custard creams, one triple pack Cadbury's Dairy Milk chocolate, a copy of *Hair Ideas* magazine and today's edition of the *Scum*, front page screamer: 'JEN AND ANGELINA – CONFRONTATION!!'

'Oh God, I am absolutely *buggered*,' I think, banging my forehead on the steering wheel as the memory of everything that happened the night before triggers a new wave of pain that fountains up through my chest and geysers out of my swollen eyes.

Mum said she would ring when it was safe for me to go home but I am fed up of waiting. This day has been very long, not least because I have been awake for all of it. At 1 a.m. the sympathetic constables released me into my parents' shocked custody; at 2 a.m. I was still trying to explain recent events to them (Third Worst Conversation of my Life); at 3 a.m. I went to bed, and at 3.07 a.m. I got back up again; at 4 a.m. I was logged on to the computer torturing myself with emails and waiting for daylight so I could talk to someone; at 5 a.m. I realized daylight had arrived but the only other creature awake was the cat from next door, who wages a malicious war with me over her perceived right to shit in my flowerbeds. I spotted her squatting, yelled 'geddowdervityerdamncat', watched the bloody animal bolt over the fence, and then realized I was on my own again.

At 6 a.m. I emailed some things to work, and at 8 a.m. rang my boss, the news editor, Bill Bishop. He's known to all as 'Bish' – an old school newspaperman, the last of a breed. He's as northern as chips with gravy, and of indeterminate late-middle-age; there are unconfirmed rumours that he used to file his copy on tablets of stone and once bollocked Noah for missing a deadline.

'What fookin' time d'yer call this? Has the Queen died or summat?' he said when I rang. I said: 'Not that I know of. Um. I'm afraid I've had a spot of bother.'

There was a pause of one beat, and Bish said: 'What'd yer get arrested fer?' I told him the story, explaining I was now a hardened but crap criminal. He listened quietly and sighed. 'Well, tek the rest o'the week off, we'll manage wi'out yer. Chin oop, lass.'

At 9 a.m. I woke up Mum and Dad, who had stayed overnight, and we drank tea while staring silently at the walls. At 11 a.m. I went to see a solicitor, who said I could change the locks for my safety so long as I didn't bar Twatface from the house. Then I wandered the supermarket, getting concerned looks from the shelf-stackers. They whispered to each other while looking at me, not bothering to hide their curiosity any more than I tried to hide my tears, until eventually I went back to the car where I could cry without upsetting anyone. Ah, the phone . . .

Dad is at the front door putting a new lock in. Mum's in the kitchen switching the kettle on. I don't say anything to either of them, just unscrew the wine and walk into the garden to sit under my tree. It's got huge twisty roots to sit on, and I lean against the trunk and take in the garden I've worked so hard to make nice. It's one of my favourite spots in the world, a place where I always feel fulfilled and at peace. I don't even notice it now – I just sit on my root, swig from the bottle, and cry. It's like breathing, I can't seem to stop doing it.

Mum and Dad come out to sit with me. They speak quietly and with long pauses, like they're in a library or a funeral home. Mum talks about my husband. She says he was sad, unshaven, unwashed, wearing yesterday's suit. He told them he cared about me and was stricken by conscience. He promised to be honest. Then he packed a couple of bags and left. Dad said he wanted to thump him. Mum said she was optimistic. They want to take me back home for a few days. They pack a bag and steer me like a sleepwalker to their car.

The clock radio in my old bedroom says it's 23.37. When it said 20.30 I went to bed exhausted and just switched off, immediately unconscious. Now I am awake again. That means my total amount of sleep in the past forty hours has been three hours and seven minutes. It's kind of interesting to know that is all my mind and body need to function at a basic level, but I'm now alert as a field mouse that has seen the shadow of a hawk – panicking, worrying, fretting over all this rubbish – and I am on my own for the nine hours it will take for the rest of the world to wake up and give me someone to talk to. I quietly pace the house for a few hours, trying not to wake my parents, and then return to bed to bury my face in the pillow and muffle the great, gasping sobs I heave up until dawn.

Perhaps I will evolve to become completely nocturnal, terrified of daylight and noise, venturing out only in darkness. Long, fine hairs will grow all over my body, my eyes will bulge to enormous proportions and I will be targeted by documentary-makers . . . 'and here, our infra-red cameras have captured for the first time this elusive creature as it comes out of its burrow to forage. It may once have shared a common ancestor with humans, but, after many years' isolation, it is nervous of man and survives on a diet of stale Pringles, cold tea and custard creams . . .'

One good thing happened today though – The Editor rang. Now, newspaper editors are a strange bunch: former reporters of one kind or another who spend years politicking to get to the top of a very greasy pole, and live in a rarefied world of power, chauffeur-driven cars and never having to carry cash. Some editors are nice and some are mean, and they are all a little bit bonkers. I've always thought mine was all right compared to others, pretty decent, but no more or less than that. Anyway The Editor rang, and as I answered the call and realized who it was my first thought was that I'd get a rollocking for not being at work.

Instead I was asked: 'How are you?' I stumbled, surprised, through the story of the past twenty-four hours.

7

The Editor mmmed and uh-huhed and said: 'She didn't? He what? Well no, I don't blame you.'

The Editor listened as I brought the tale up to date, said nothing when I wept a little at the end, and then told me: 'Well, the phones have gone mad. Every hack in Fleet Street seems to know something happened, but not exactly what. And as far as I'm concerned, that's how it's going to stay. No one here will breathe a word about it and the gossip will soon die down. The good news is that I hear she's REALLY fat.'

That's when I cracked a smile for the first time. 'Ha,' I said, snuffle-snorting through the snot.

Then The Editor said: 'He's a wanker. You're a great reporter, a gorgeous girl, brilliant and young. In six months this will look totally different. You'll be fine. Don't let this beat you.'

The Editor rang off, telling me to take as much time as I liked and not to come back to work until I was ready to face everyone. I looked at my watch and realized the newsroom would be right on deadline for first edition, and The Editor had spent half an hour listening to me, even with a paper to get out. It made me feel that all was not lost. Even better, it had made me laugh. It was half-hysterical and painful and I was crying at the same time, but a laugh's a laugh, and in the current circumstances something to be grateful for.

Alone here in my childhood bed, I counted up the things I'd gained in a day. A £125 bill for seeing a solicitor I never thought I'd need, for one; entry into the national DNA database for another; and thousands of unanswered questions, most of which were a form of 'is he with her?'

But also, better, some knowledge too: that I am probably not capable of murder, having failed so miserably on my first attempt; The Editor's not that bonkers; a lot of the Worst Conversations of my Life are now out of the way; and if I can laugh a bit today, then one day I'll laugh a LOT. It might be when I'm locked away for the safety of myself and others, but a day will come when I will laugh at all of this.

Maybe tomorrow.

THE DAY BEFORE

IT'S 4 a.m. and I can't sleep. At times like this things play on your mind.

Like how on earth I married such a twat, for example. Or why I stayed. And what's so wrong with me that he seriously thinks some big bird is more attractive?

Maybe she has a lovely personality? Or maybe she is even more stupid than I am?

My mobile's been going mad and in normal circumstances I'd have a right ear that looked like it had been left on a radiator – journalists spread gossip quicker than butter. Instead I've left the phone to ring and beep to itself, unable to bear the kindly concern, the worried friends and the incorrigible gossips fishing for a good line. Now and again I've picked it up and flicked through the messages to delete them, and have managed to notice something of a theme developing.

The Editor heard she was fat. The crime girl says, 'She's a porker.' The sports reporters have been spluttering about needing, 'Twelve pints and a packet of scratchings' before they'd go near her. The showbiz columnist was told she resembled a kraken.

Seeing as these people are friends – and spiteful bastards all – it's to be expected and I would dismiss the remarks as normal bitching if it weren't for the fact that I've seen the woman myself.

Now, I'm no oil painting. Normal hair, normal face, normal height, reasonable legs I suppose. Normal levels of female insecurity too, which led me to assume my rival had to be a gorgeous little thing capable of drawing the attention of any red-blooded male.

A few things raised my suspicions – a nonchalant mention of a name I didn't recognize, a missed dinner, a sudden need to work late. The kind of thing that would be ignored by most people but in a hack gets your nose sniffing. The average person would be surprised at the amount of information a reporter can find about them through perfectly legal means – electoral roll, social networks, Google – like who lived where and at what time with whom. The most common thing people say when I knock on their doors is a shocked, 'How did you get this address?' As though it's a state secret I could only have found out by torturing their granny. When I tell them they're in the voters' register, the phone book, or left their Faceache open, they deflate and say, 'Oh, yeah.'

In my case I came home from work one day and he'd left his work emails wide open on the computer. I went to turn it off, the screen came to life, and everything imploded.

I remember some screaming, but it wasn't that high-pitched female kind you get with spiders or mice. They were low, guttural, they came from my stomach. They sounded like a gorilla was being tortured. And of course then I knew her name.

After five minutes' work on the computer I also had her home address in a rich bit of town, date of birth, family history, workplace, friends' details and her phone number. Not many wives could have done that – this job is a blessing at times, as well as a curse.

She's posh and she's young, and her name – Hattie, short for Henrietta – makes her sound like a consumptive Victorian damsel in a swoon. She probably has a collection of stuffed toys, too.

I also knew from the emails that my husband was with her and not, as he'd claimed when saying he suddenly wouldn't be home for dinner, with friends in Highgate.

There is only one thing any reporter – hell, any woman – would do in this situation. Front them up on the doorstep, of course; stand the story up or get it knocked down. I had to know for sure.

I drove there, although I couldn't tell you how. At one point I realized I was doing 80 m.p.h. in a bus lane, and decided I didn't care. There was no answer to my knocks at her door so I thought maybe they were out. I walked around some of the local pubs to see if I could spot them – no doubt scaring the customers who saw a demented, wild-eyed woman doing laps of the bar – and then went back to her flat, in the basement of a big Georgian house.

As I went down the steps to her door a second time I saw one of the net curtains twitch, and realized they were inside, looking out at me and probably laughing. So I knocked on the door, then thumped on it, and as my anger built started to use my feet as well, anything to make them open up and talk to me. As they continued to hide I started roundhouse-kicking, which as I was in heeled boots just hurt my foot. After ten minutes or so the doorknocker fell off, and in my screwed-up thought processes it seemed the politest thing to do to post it through the letterbox, in case it got stolen. Then I carried on kicking for a bit, with some yelling thrown in. Some of the neighbours looked out of their windows, and

I took great delight in shouting, 'WHORE!' at the top of my voice so they could all hear.

Eventually I realized that my targets were prepared to wait it out until I got tired. I went back to my car, where I'd left my phone, and rang my husband. I can only imagine the scene inside the flat, but after ten or more rings he finally answered, in the jolliest high-pitched voice you've ever heard.

'Hello! How are you? I'm in Highgate!'

'I know exactly where you are. I read your emails,' I said, quite calmly. 'Get out here.'

'Y-you read my emails? H-h-how did you . . .'

'Least of your problems. Get out here NOW.'

I hung up and as I walked back down the steps to her door, he opened it and stepped outside. He looked sheepish, and was doing up his shirt buttons.

I had not really thought about what I was going to do, but it wouldn't have been anything more than a shout and a scene. Seeing him having to get dressed when he left her made me furious, and from the top of the steps I launched myself at him, my hands outstretched. I didn't have any intent in mind beyond trying to stop the thing that was hurting me. He caught my hands and when I tried to break free he threw me against the concrete wall next to the steps. I fought and yelled, and as I pushed off the wall we spun around and I was thrown against the wall opposite as I struggled and screamed. A neighbour came outside, and a passer-by tried to push between us, and told my husband to stop.

'It's all right,' replied my husband, with one of his charming smiles, as though it was a reasonable explanation for a street fight. 'She's my wife.'

The bystander looked at me.

'It's true,' I said. 'And that WHORE in there is going to explain what she's doing with my husband!'

The stranger backed away, the neighbour stared with his mouth open, and my husband smiled reassuringly at them both. While he looked away I grabbed the chance to deliver two solid kicks to my husband's testicles. As he bent over I whirled and ran back to Hattie's door, which was as shut as it had ever been. Next to it was a window and a dozen pots and troughs filled with dead plants she'd obviously never bothered to water, on the sill and on the ground.

Without any thought, I picked up a rectangular trough about a foot long and six inches wide. My husband reappeared and tried to grab it from me, and we wrestled over the terracotta for a few seconds before it flew from our grasp – intentionally or otherwise, I honestly don't know – and smashed through the window.

For some reason I followed it, as frenzied and set on killing as a zombie in a film, with my eyes out on stalks and spittle flying everywhere.

I came to my senses somewhere in the middle of Hattie's broken window, my head and shoulders swathed in a net curtain, hands and knees in broken glass, nails dug into the wooden sill like a lioness' claws in a gazelle, and with my husband trying to pull me out by the ankles.

Somehow it dawned on me that the police were coming – I think he told me – and I realized that being arrested inside the building was technically burglary, and a lot more serious than being arrested outside, which was an entirely different kind of crime. Terrorism of some sort, perhaps. The homicidal rage ebbed away and I reversed gingerly back on to the pavement.

Immediately I heard approaching sirens, and my husband said: 'You'd better go.'

'I'm not going anywhere,' I replied, folding my arms and planting myself facing the door. 'I've nothing to hide, and when the police turn up she's going to have to open that door and look me in the eye.'

Two constables appeared in great haste and there was an unpleasant conversation in which my husband explained to the officers that *this* was his wife and in *there* was his girlfriend.

One of the officers stood next to me while the other knocked on the door, which did not open. 'Can you open the door, please?' he said. There was a pause, while he listened to someone squeaking in terror on the other side. 'No, you have to open the door or we'll break it down. You called us, and we have to verify that you're safe.'

There was another moment before the door opened a crack. The officer pushed it open further, then stepped inside and shut it behind him.

During the journey my brain had whirred with put-downs, witty remarks, catty one-liners that would have left her a quivering wreck and him begging for my forgiveness. But when I had that brief glimpse as she opened the door all I could do was stand there like a guppy fish, mouth open, eyes wide, brain reading 'Error 404: Witty remarks could not be found.'

She was in silhouette with the summer evening sun coming in a window behind her. I saw a bob haircut, an A-line fifties-style dress, and flat shoes.

She had very sturdy calves, I noticed abstractedly as my eyes passed over them, and while logic told me she had to have ankles there was no obvious sign of any.

15

My husband was stood next to me. I looked at him, pointed at the now-closed door, and said: 'Are you serious . . . ? But . . . she's FAT.'

The policeman next to us made a coughing noise.

My husband took a drag on his cigarette – he had only lit it because he knew I hated them – and said: 'She's not that big.'

'Not that big? She's got calves the size of my *torso*! She's fucking HUGE!'

The policeman spluttered, then clamped his lips tight.

'We haven't had sex yet,' muttered my husband.

'I'm not bloody surprised! You'll probably have to send off for a small stepladder and some kind of pulley system. Fuck ME!' I exclaimed, hands on hips, shaking my head in disbelief.

The policeman turned to face the wall and compose himself as his colleague came out of the flat. The first officer told me I was being arrested and my husband stood and watched as they led me away to the patrol car.

I sat on the back seat and caught sight of the computer display on the dashboard, which read: 'Caller says partner's ex-wife has turned up and is causing a disturbance.'

EX-wife?

PARTNER?

WTF?

Then it was off to the cells, to wait for a lawyer, to call my parents from the custody suite, asking them to come and get me, to pace and cry and be interviewed on tape and have my fingerprints taken, before accepting a formal warning, get given my shoes back and be released.

My state of mind has not improved much since then. I've since found out that Hattie's a reporter, too – only she hates the tabloids, which are where the most successful and well-paid journalists end up, because they sell more and it's harder work. She told one friend of mine: 'Oh, I simply couldn't bear to work for the popular press. I only want to work for serious papers.'

So, the *unpopular* press, then? I see.

Yet she's having an affair with a married newspaper executive who works on one of the country's biggest tabloids. She obviously doesn't mind the popular press when they're buying her dinner.

And what was he thinking? A journo married to a journo and shagging a journo who expects not to be found out by all the other journos they both know? I spend half my life catching people having affairs. It took me less than a fortnight after they had met to realize what was going on, and mere minutes to prove it was true. Fleet Street is a tiny, incestuous little world – everybody knows everybody else, or at least someone who met them in a bar once. He was always going to get busted, if not by me then by any one of two dozen other people.

Well, I know what he was thinking. He was thinking: 'She's not that big.'

Hattie's a nice, girly name, and it suits her about as well as I suit hot pants. She's not nice, and while I'm prepared to take someone's word for it that she is a girl, there's no obvious external clue. And if you think I'm being vindictive – she had the bloody cheek to press charges, which is pretty nasty considering it's *my* husband she's stealing. In her shoes I would have had some sympathy for the wronged wife, and something approaching a sense of shame.

And all over a flowerpot through a window. Although I admit, had I got inside the flat I've no idea what I might have done. Part of me wishes the police had found me cackling over their dismembered corpses with a power tool in each hand. A flowerpot and a broken window sound pathetic.

Bollocks to nice Victorian names – she is Fatty to me for evermore! If she ever walks into my newsroom I shan't be responsible for my actions.

(Except in the next 365 days, which is the period during which I must not get arrested for anything else, according to the police caution she has so thoughtfully arranged for me.)

18

DAY TWO

OH, it's morning. Quick check – yep, just as rubbish as yesterday. Fab.

The days are becoming circular, a constant spiral of hurt as though I have been strapped to a Catherine wheel and tortured by a cackling hag. Today is just as painful as yesterday, and I am just as broken.

I tossed and turned for hours last night, reliving the fight, and in the darkest hours I simply buried my face in the pillow and cried, horrible stabbing pains tearing through me. The physical agony is very real, although it must be purely in my head – who knew that love could be this bad? Even when the grief recedes, it still feels like my skin's being slowly sliced off from the inside.

Eventually, exhausted and desperate for a few hours of unconsciousness, I decided to search my parents' bathroom cabinet for anything that might bring sleep.

Milk of magnesia won't do it. Nor will thirty-year-old Strepsils, crusty tubes of Germolene, or ancient cotton buds. Why do they never throw anything away? That old bottle of cough syrup has probably fermented long enough to be a type of whisky, but I am too young to die.

Instead I settled on a cup of warm milk, and ended up stumbling around the house trying not to wake the folks up. This is quite difficult when your teenage bedroom has been turned into a geriatric gymnasium and you don't want to turn any lights on. It's not my familiar smelly pit any more; the giant Daniel Day-Lewis poster is long gone. It's all treadmills and exercise bikes, and my poor limp teddy bear sitting on the bed, with worn paws and a face faded in the sun.

I managed to fumble my way to the kitchen, but coming back crashed into a door frame, spilt hot milk all down myself and swore. I don't know if it was the thump or the swearing that woke her, but mums are attuned to the tiniest instance of either, so mine put on her dressing gown and came to sit with me for a while.

She's sleeping as little as I am, and it made me feel even worse to see the worry she feels for me. I simply cannot go on without sleep, I told her, and it doesn't feel like I will find it any time soon. It could be weeks before any kind of calm returns, and in the meantime, after three nights of being awake, it feels like my mind is going. My vision swims, my head throbs, and my hands shake. 'We have to go to the doctor to get something,' I said. At first she refuses, worried what I'll do with a handful of sleeping pills. 'I'm not going to do anything stupid,' I said. 'Dish me out one a night if you like; but I cannot go on like this.'

She tucked me into bed just as she used to, sat with me and stroked my cheek softly with her knuckles like she did when I was a little girl, until my eyes finally drifted shut and for a while the thoughts ceased their constant circle.

I woke up at 6.14 a.m., and waited for sounds of movement before I went to talk to the elders. Seeing them sitting up in bed, the morning sun on their faces, it was shocking to realize how old they have become. Perhaps it was only the events of the past few days, or maybe I just hadn't noticed before, but Dad's hair seemed suddenly grey, and his laughing blue eyes were dull. Mum's unlined face appeared to sag as she sipped her tea and asked if I had managed to sleep.

Dad is keen on the idea of brisk, vigorous exercise as a cure-all for heartbreak and mental anguish. At his insistence I nibbled half a Weetabix and was dragged out to the garden to help him prune a tree, but after a few minutes I started to shiver and tremble and he sent me indoors.

I rang Cee, my oldest friend. She said: 'You're probably better off without him.' Mum, who was quite positive yesterday and saying things like, 'All is not lost,' changed her tune, too, and said: 'Maybe it's for the best.'

The upshot is I am considering starting a game of cliché bingo. Others still to collect in the set include: 'It's not you, it's me,' 'It'll all come out in the wash,' and 'We can work it out,' plus many, many more. 'You've still got your health,' is the gold-star clincher.

We went to the chemist and got some herbal sleeping pills, then because I had nothing else to do I checked my husband's emails – he used to tell me his password, the plonker. There was a receipt for an Interflora order, and I was getting irritated by his pathetic apology when I noticed they weren't for me. They were for Tania Banks.

Now, Tania Banks has been a friend of both of ours for years. Another reporter, she had sat next to me in the newsroom for a while, and through me met my husband. Lately I had begun to be annoyed by her: there were rumours among the photographers that half her stories were made up, although for some reason she seemed able to dodge the usual consequences. She was always banging on about her latest diet, and wore a bra that was too small in the mistaken belief that it made her boobs look bigger, when in fact it just gave her back-fat. But we still shared gossip and mutual friends, and I always covered for her when she disappeared for two-hour manicures.

Anyway, Tania came to our wedding, made a catty comment about my shoes which I chose to overlook, drank vast amounts of champagne and in return gave us, oh, all right, a quite nice set of saucepans. Tania, during the few weeks since Fatty's name was first mentioned, has been a shoulder for me to cry on while I've wondered where he is, been confused by his suddenly-offhand treatment and caught him out in silly lies which now, finally, make a dreadful sense. I told her all my suspicions while they were still forming in my head, and she told me I must be wrong.

Tania is also friends with Fatty. She introduced her to my husband at a dinner party which I was going to go to until he said: 'No, boo, you're tired after a long day at work. You go home, and I'll see you later.'

He's been staying with Tania for the past few days. And Tania, apparently, deserves flowers. But I don't.

So I emailed her and begged her to tell me anything, anything at all.

This is her reply:

<To Foxy, 11.32 a.m.
From: Banks, Tania
Oh, my love – I cannot begin to imagine how dreadful you must feel, poor thing. It is simply awful, and you've all my sympathy. Obviously, as their friend my first loyalty is to the other two parties, who I should

say are wretched. Anything I could tell you about their relationship would just cause you more pain. We are all concerned for you, so if you need anything, just let me know.

Tania

PS I imagine you won't be able to show your face at work so let me have the number of your Cheryl Tweedy contact and I'll crack on with that toilet story.>

My. Bloody. GOD. *All* her sympathy? What, both grains? *Their* friend? Wretched? RELATIONSHIP? And now she wants my Cheryl contact, too? Christ on a bike, is there anything life won't take off me?

After the spluttering ceased I wrote a reply which hopefully, like poison, will find its way to Fatty's ear.

<To: Banks, Tania, 11.40 a.m.

From: Foxy

Tania – I don't blame you for wanting to stay out of it, but I'm sure you can understand my need for answers, considering that in the space of ten days my husband was capable of trying for a baby with me and then watching calmly as I was led away to the cells.

PS I've already filed copy on Cheryl.>

Ha. Bet he didn't tell Fatty the baby stuff. It's not strictly true, it's more that we weren't *not* trying for a baby, but it'll get him in trouble and throw a spanner in their works. I think it's the least they deserve after the anvil it feels like they've dropped on my head.

23

For most of today I've been numb, which I suppose is an improvement on crying and screaming. The only thing that makes me feel better is this – writing it down, no nearer making sense of it all, but just a way of marking the time, separating one day from the next. All day and night the thoughts flutter around my head like butterflies, and setting them down in words is like pinning them to a board, so they are finally under control. Like filing a story for the paper.

So now I've started this diary I think I'll keep on writing it. It makes me feel better, and as Bish always says if a reporter's overthinking a story too much, 'Jus' get it off yer notebook, for fook's sake. Don't let the ale get warm.'

But is it a good idea to be reporting on your own insides?

DAY THREE

THE clock says 1.42 a.m. It's official, herbal sleeping pills are shit.

Maybe it's just me. Maybe herbal stuff doesn't work if you're a criminal and a rubbish wife. The label on the bottle ought to read: 'WARNING: May make you drowsy, but probably won't because they're only herbal. Do not attempt to operate heavy machinery, drive, eat or make a cup of tea because simple tasks are beyond you. If you feel side-effects just be grateful you're feeling something. None of the above applies in cases of heartbreak, recriminations and/or betrayal. Will definitely not work if taken by idiot who obsessively rereads emails between Scarlet Woman and Cheating Husband into small hours of the night. No refunds possible.'

2.19 a.m. Ah, hell – next week's our anniversary! Not our wedding anniversary, our getting-together one. Does that count?

3.41 a.m. I might be pregnant. Or maybe she's pregnant?

6.42 a.m. Am I ever going to sleep again?

About lunchtime Cee rang in a combative mood. We've known each other all our lives and normally I'm the tough one and she's the soft one. But today she just asked how I was, and when I said I still wasn't sleeping, didn't know what to do, and felt broken, she said: 'Ditch him.'

'Just like that? Just "ditch him"? It's that easy, is it?'

'What would you say to me in the same position? If I'd rung you a year ago and said I'd left my husband because I'd found out something but refused to say what because I didn't want you to think bad things about him, then gone back when he'd promised never to do whatever it was again, and a year later all this had kicked off, what would you tell me?'

I paused and thought, and then said quietly: 'I'd tell you to cut your losses and run.'

Her voice softened, and she said: 'And that's why I'm saying it. You don't have kids, you can start again. I know you, you'd never be able to forget this. What would you do if he did it again? Could you live with that?'

No, I don't think I could. For the first time I think about my husband objectively rather than as the man I have loved for so long. All that we had, once the rains came, held as much water as a rusty sieve. Being *in* love doesn't matter a damn – that feeling comes and goes with time, like the tide. What remains while you wait is the respect you have for each other, your friendship – your character, your principles, your core. The corners get rubbed off over the years, but what you basically are, deep down, remains the same. I try my best, I have rights and wrongs, and he . . . he has weaknesses. Now I think about it, I couldn't tell you one thing that he would never do, a single line that he would not cross. He didn't care enough to try to be better than he was. He put himself before us, and that's not the deal I thought we'd struck.

I dug out my mobile. He was still saved in the memory as 'Scooby' – after the face he pulled and noise that he

26

made, when . . . well, you know. I renamed him 'Twat-face'. I recorded a new ringtone too, so that instead of playing 'Scooby dooby doo, where are you . . .' it will now screech out 'What a wanker!' when he rings. *If* he rings.

Three days at the homestead is enough for me, and for my folks. I decided to go home because there were plenty of things there to keep me busy, whereas at their house I was just moping about avoiding well-intentioned requests to, 'Come and help wash the car,' or questions like: 'Do you want to turn the compost heap?' They felt as useless as I did, but at least if I was at home we'd stop being useless at each other.

I packed my stuff up and went outside to find my dad and say goodbye. He was at the bottom of the garden, guarding the bonfire in that way dads do, wearing oil-stained jeans and an old shirt, and he walked up to meet me. We met in the middle, and I said: 'I'm off now.'

He said: 'Oh, right. Well, keep your chin up.'

'Yes, I'll try.'

'Things will look better in a bit.'

'Yes, I expect so.'

I obviously looked like I didn't believe him, because he took a step closer, put an arm around my shoulders and spoke more earnestly.

Looking intently at me, he said: 'I know it doesn't seem it, but one day it will be much better. It cannot stay like this for ever. Every day that passes will be a tiny bit better than the one before. Maybe not much, but it will be just a little bit better, I promise.'

And then he started to cry. My dad – my big, tall, strong and always-has-an-answer Dad – put his head on my shoulder and sobbed like a baby. I cuddled him and stroked his back as it trembled, and it was the strangest, most alien thing. He smelled of cut grass and two-stroke oil and soap, just as he always does, but for a moment he was a little boy again, bewildered and sad, in need of someone to hug him and say it would all be OK.

It lasted for ten seconds or so, then he lifted his head and sniffed, gave me a squeeze around the shoulders and said: 'Let your mum know when you're home safe, then.' I promised I would, said goodbye and drove home.

I rang to let them know I'd arrived. Mum answered, and I said: 'Is Dad there?'

'No, he's in the bath. Why?'

I told her what had happened, word for word. She was speechless for a moment.

'I haven't seen your father cry in forty-five years,' she said. 'Not once.'

Lying in bed, waiting fruitlessly for sleep, I felt the roiling hurt and pain inside me begin to solidify around a cold, clinical anger. What Twatface has done to me was because I decided to marry him: *my* pain, *my* choice, and *my* problem. But as a result of that he had also been invited into my parents' home and family, and now they feel the same betrayal. Because of me.

So I cry every day and every night – so what? That was my own stupid fault. My mum is worried, but much as I wish she wasn't that is what mums do. To make my father cry, to make the strongest and tallest and handsomest and funniest and most wonderful man in the whole world, who has never *ever* cried, break down and sob because for the first time in his life he cannot help his little girl – that is something I will never forgive. The thought makes me furious. I wanted to kill Twatface for that alone.

I lay there, my hands balling into fists at my sides, and realized that even if I decide to take him back, and run the risk of being hurt again, there is no way I will risk my parents' heartbreak. He might hurt me again, but I could never allow him to do that to them.

The more I think about it, the more I can see only one way out.

DAY FOUR

ANOTHER night of zero sleep, only this time I thought a bit of music might help to take my mind off its never-ending circle. So the iPod – the only useful present Twatface ever bought me – went on.

Now, I am superstitious about the shuffle function. I think that whatever comes up means something, or helps to make sense of the events of the day. It's about as logical as astrology, with the added bonus that if you don't like what the Shuffle Gods tell you it is perfectly acceptable to flick to the next random track, and flick again, until you hear something you do like.

Sometimes the Shuffle Gods are kind, and you get just the right song to make you tap your feet and sing at the steering wheel. Then there are the days when they are cruel and harsh, when you press 'shuffle' and sit, poleaxed, as some far-off singer sums up your life in three short, painful minutes.

And that's what happened to me, as an anonymous man read out a speech given to some high-school kids years ago. Over gospel music.

It shouldn't work, but somehow it does.

As I sat on the side of the bed and stared at the wall, the deep-voiced man told me the real troubles in my life would be the things that never crossed my worried mind, the kind that blindside you at 4 p.m. on an idle Tuesday.

It was 4 p.m. last Tuesday when it happened: 4 p.m. when I was just bored with nothing much to do; 4 p.m. when I first found out there might be a problem in my marriage; 4 p.m. when I realized there was another woman. My world crumpled at 4 p.m. last Tuesday. My heart contracted into a tiny point of darkness, and then exploded into everything that has happened since.

I was just telling myself that everything can be fixed, if you try hard enough, when the gravelly man went on: 'Don't be reckless with other people's hearts, don't put up with people who are reckless with yours.'

And that was the moment – the point of clarity, of no return. I saw for the first time that was exactly what had happened. My husband, the father of my unborn children, my best friend and person I love above all others, had held my heart and had recklessly dropped it. He'd stopped loving me.

Once it was light I pulled myself together and went to the supermarket to stock up on meals for one. (Oh, that was depressing. Standing in front of the freezer compartment, looking at a selection of individual microwaveable packets, and realizing I might as well fill the trolley. Then waiting at the checkout, looking at the shop assistant as she glanced at the food, then back at me, and thought to herself: 'Single'.). I got some veg too, for the look of the thing, and ice cream, of course. Back home I emptied the fridge of everything that was dead or dying, chucked in the new stuff, and then grabbed some black bin bags.

I toured the house and everything that was Twatface's went in – shoes, clothes, bags, coats, CDs. (Almost all of them Nick Cave or Bob Bloody Dylan, including the 'B' sides and stuff no one knows – I am never going to listen to that crap again.) I piled it up in the living room for him to collect. Other bags I filled up with papers and junk to chuck out, like the interminable bloody lists he used to write about everything and never complete. If he had a day off he would always have a list of things to do, starting with 'groceries', 'buy papers' and 'walk in park', and finish up, two sides of A4 and six hours later, with 'learn Mandarin' and 'drink less'– both equally unlikely.

In the bureau were a bunch of bank statements I seized to shove in a bag, but then something caught my eye – cash taken from an ATM in Sloane Square, round the corner from her house, the previous week. I looked through the papers and saw there were trips to restaurants I'd never visited, and receipts for takeaway pizzas I hadn't eaten. Then, and this was the kicker, £120 spent in Maggie Jones in Kensington. *Our* restaurant. The place where we'd had our first date, and where the manager used to greet us with open arms saying, 'Hello, you two lovebirds!' and give us free champagne.

He'd taken her to Maggie Jones. I could barely believe it. Although it was the least important thing, it seemed like the biggest betrayal. Was it so he could always remember it as 'our' restaurant whichever woman he was with?

Then, somehow, I found myself standing over my jewellery box and taking off my wedding ring. He had left his on my dressing table. He was always taking it on and off and was never really comfortable with it – should have seen it coming, I suppose – and I put them both in a ring box with my engagement ring, and shoved it into my sock drawer where I wouldn't have to see it.

I hunted through my stuff and took out every necklace, bracelet and pair of earrings he'd bought me – not many – and on top of the wardrobe found my wedding handbag and shoes, and at the back of a drawer the posh underwear I'd worn. I looked at my wedding dress hanging in the wardrobe; it was too painful to touch. I took down the picture of our happy day, which had pride of place in the living room, and my dried bouquet, which was stuck in a vase, and packed most of it in a box along with the wedding album. I closed it up with several layers of duct tape, carried it up to the loft, and shoved it into the furthest corner. I never wanted to see any of it again, but I couldn't bear to throw it away.

Just as I was piling the rest of his crap in an angry corner of the living room, I suddenly heard a woman shout: 'What a wanker! What a wanker! What a WANKER!'

I was scared for a moment, wondering how some screechy loon had got into the house, before I remembered it was my new ringtone, and laughed in relief. Then I stopped, because it meant Twatface was on the phone.

He didn't say much, except that he was coming round tomorrow 'for a talk'. Can't wait.

DAY FIVE

AT 6 a.m. I woke up – well, I didn't, but morning arrived and there didn't seem any point in staring at the ceiling any more – and heaved myself upright simply out of boredom.

The bedroom seemed empty, with conspicuous spaces where Twatface's pants would usually have spent the night on the floor, his lists drifted under the chest of drawers and his watch sat on my dressing table.

The empty side of the bed sprawled mockingly behind me, but I could not look.

I pulled on a pair of jeans, which seemed to be a lot roomier through lack of eating anything, and wandered into the hall.

We'd bought the house a year ago from an elderly couple as a renovation project – it was the only way we could afford to buy in Greenwich, a nice part of town near the river. The wallpaper, carpets, plaster, wiring – everything – needed changing. We'd chucked our cruddy collection of loaned furniture into it and were coping until we could afford to do the work.

The previous occupants had not held with normal decorating practices. The wallpaper was stapled up rather than pasted, gaping holes in the walls were covered with strange wicker hats stuck on with double-sided Sellotape, and nasty vinyl floor tiles had been superglued to the kitchen ceiling.

Twatface and I had stood in the hallway on our first viewing, looked around, and held hands as we imagined our children running down the stairs and into the garden. After we'd moved in we'd agreed that a sunny yellow would be best for the nursery. We'd decided we'd get a cat called Fang for him and a dog called Dave for me. I'd thought it was a shared dream we'd built together, but now it felt as if I had been muttering to myself in a mirror.

Clearing the garden cost nothing, but he couldn't be bothered to help me much. He got comfortable with the interior, vile as it was, and if I so much as picked at a bit of wallpaper to see what was behind it he would shout that I was 'destroying' the house and tell me to leave it to an expert.

'Well,' I thought, 'he's not here any more.'

Standing in the hallway, I slowly pulled at a piece of pink-and-yellow-striped hairy (yes, really) wallpaper, stapled top and bottom to the wall and billowing loosely in the middle. Off it came. Then another, and another. It wasn't long before the halls and stairs were stripped of their disgusting coverings, back to the bare plaster, and I was up to my knees in swathes of crusty, dusty wallpaper.

I bought an industrial-sized tub of the most boring magnolia paint I could find, slapped it over the walls, and was stood at the top of a stepladder with the radio on when I began to feel happy.

My body was busy, and my mind was occupied, calculating how much wall was left, and telling myself that if I did that bit next I'd be 60 per cent, no, call it three quarters, of the way through one wall, and then, when

I'd done that, maybe I'd have enough appetite for a sandwich . . .

Then the tinny sound of the radio penetrated the happy humming in my head, and the grating Welsh vowels of Bonnie Tyler fell through my ears like acid rain.

She sang about listening to the sound of her tears and wondering if the best years had passed, and when she fell apart so did I.

I collapsed like a paper hat in a rainstorm, slumped on the top step of the ladder, and wailed as the pain washed over me again. Head dropped on to my hands, I sat on my perch and screamed until I tasted blood.

Then I realized that one of those hands still held a paint roller, and I'd wiped magnolia over most of my hair. Instead of being an attractive, grief-stricken, wronged woman when Twatface came round I was going to be a paint-smeared loon covered in snot and coughing blood. Making a conscious effort to pull myself together, I doused my face in cold water and carried on – but changed radio stations. Soft rock is not your friend in times of emotional crisis.

My mobile rang, and I checked who it was before rejecting the call, but stopped when I saw it was Buff Arnold. A lovely fellow and a good friend, but shallow as a puddle when it comes to women. He's a news reporter like me, with a natural tendency towards lapdancers and hookers so tends to do the sleazy stuff. We're mates and he doesn't usually ring unless he wants something, so the call was odd. I decided to answer it.

'Hello, Buff,' I said.

'Babe, am I bothering you?'

'Nah, I've got a few days off. To what do I owe the honour?'

He spoke very carefully and slowly. 'Well, I've heard something dreadful I really hope's not true, but I wanted to make sure you were OK . . .'

My heart sank. If Buff – who's rarely in the office – had heard the news of my zombie-frenzy then I'd made the rounds very thoroughly indeed.

'Depends what you've heard, mate,' I sighed.

'There are rumours that you've split up with your man. It can't be true?'

'It is, I'm afraid.'

'Shit, babe. He's a twat.'

'That much I know. What else do the rumours say?'

'Well, apparently she's fatter than you. People at other papers are all talking about it, and ringing me asking if I know you. I haven't discussed it with anyone, but as soon as I heard the rumours I rang Harry Porter. And he wouldn't tell me.'

'Really?' Harry's our political reporter, knows all the gossip, and has lips looser than a whore's drawers.

'Yeah. He said The Editor had told everyone in the office that it wasn't to be discussed, and that you were to be protected at all costs, but that he was sure you'd appreciate a phone call from a friend.'

I was stunned, for the umpteenth time. For journalists not to gossip is like, well, not breathing. Like a fish not swimming or a footballer asking for a pay cut. It's the world gone mad, it's the sun orbiting the moon, it's very, very odd. I felt a very tiny glow inside and thought to myself: 'Maybe not everyone hates me.'

I must have done something right, somewhere, to have caused a group of journalists – who would even describe themselves as an aggressive, self-interested and paranoid bunch of sociopaths and con-artists – to form a protective ring around me, effectively folding their arms and insisting there was nothing to see. I felt almost cared for, and strangely humbled.

I wiped a tear away and said to Buff: 'How did it get out, then?'

'Looks like your husband told his news desk – who thought it was so funny they told everyone else. But you know what they're like at his place, they're a bunch of children. Worse than the rest of us.'

Buff said he'd take me for a drink when I was back at work, and rang off. Twatface was already living up to his new name, it seemed. At least my lot had protected me – his had hung him out to dry.

It was only half an hour until showdown, so I washed, put some clean clothes on, and bit my nails until there was a knock at the door.

I opened it and there he stood, sheepish and covered in shaving cuts.

'Hi,' he said.

Speech was beyond me, so I simply opened the door wide for him to walk in.

We sat in the living room, he in his normal chair by the fire, and me on our scutty sofa. He asked how I was, and I shook my head. He said he was sorry, and I said nothing. All I could do was sit, my face turned away from him, as tears poured silently down. I concentrated on not making any noise, because if anything came out it would be a scream.

'Please, say something,' he said. 'Shout at me, anything. I do care about you.'

I turned and looked at him, and said haltingly, gasping for breath between sobs like a child: 'What is there to say? You've killed us. You've killed our future, every dream that we had. You've killed our babies. I'm not sleeping, not eating. You broke your promises to me, you stood and watched while I was taken off to the cells, and now suddenly you care?'

He stared at his feet. 'I'm so sorry. I do care about you. I've made a mess of everything. I want to change my ways. What can we do? Is there any way we can work it out?'

'Have you thought about the fact I might be pregnant? And what if she's pregnant?'

'I told you, we're not having sex.'

Silence for a bit. 'She's bloody stupid too if she's going out with you,' I said.

He laughed and said: 'Yes, all right. You're thinner, and cleverer. You are my wife, after all. Mum and Dad were horrified, and told me to sort things out with you. They said Hattie was stupid, too.'

'FATTY.'

He laughed again. 'All right, then, Fatty.'

He said he was still staying with Tania. Fatty had refused to let him move in, which made my heart leap briefly. He said he wanted to come back and see me, to talk things over, to see what we could do, and then went upstairs to get his passport and a few other things.

Five minutes later I wandered, sniffling, into the kitchen to see him putting several wine bottles into his rucksack.

'Hitting the bottle? Aren't you supposed to be changing your ways?'

'It's my wine and I like it, and I think people deserve it for letting me sleep on their sofa. By the way, I wanted to ask you. Do you remember last year, when we went to the States to visit my cousins?'

39

'Of course I remember.' His cousin Alice is marrying her girlfriend in a couple of months, maybe we'd still be able to go together . . .

'Well, is it best for us to fly to Boston and drive to Washington, or should we get a connecting flight? And do you know any good websites for hotels and things?'

I looked at him, confused. *We?*

He went on: 'Only I'm going back for the wedding, and Fatty wants to visit the Smithsonian and stuff. Obviously the wedding's in Boston, but it would be nice to see other bits if we're there for a week or so.'

I blinked. And blinked again.

'Are you seriously asking me to arrange a holiday for you and Fatty?'

'You used to do all this stuff. You're much better at organizing than me. And like you said, she is a bit stupid.'

Another blink. 'Are you fucking *mad*?'

If I hadn't been so weak for lack of food I might have had a second attempt at murder. As it was I just spluttered for a bit, and he said she might not go, and he'd love it if I could go with him, the cousins would much rather see me, and let's see, yeah?

He's gone now. The house smells of paint, but he didn't notice it. It's only 9 p.m. but I'm ready to fall into bed. I've got more serious sleeping pills now, and will take one of them, but it looks like my dear old dad was right about one thing at least – physical exercise does help. It's the only thing I managed today with any success, and it did me good to see the change a lick of paint made. It's not much, but the house is better than it was yesterday, even if I'm not.

DAY TEN

TWATFACE texted at 7 a.m. 'Hi, I forgot my electric toothbrush last week. Can I pick it up on my way to work? Oh, and more wine.'

I heaved myself up, every bone and muscle aching after days of painting and climbing ladders, and staggered to the bathroom. Located toothbrush, and was about to dump it by the front door when I stopped and looked at the toilet.

I looked at the bowl. Looked at the brush. Looked at the bowl again.

I thought: 'I can't.'

Then: 'I really, really can't.'

No solid food has passed my lips for nearly two weeks. Not wishing to draw you any diagrams, my bathroom visits were at first pretty unpleasant (stress chemicals do strange things to your digestive system), and then very infrequent and unpleasant. I've barely bothered to wash my hair for the past fortnight; I certainly haven't cleaned the bog.

I looked at the toothbrush again. The annoying git never washed it, just used it and put it back on the charger. Dribbly toothpaste and spit would ooze down the handle and dry, building up layers like rock strata until, even though I never used the stupid thing, I felt

41

compelled to chip the hardened grey mass off. It had a couple of days' worth of icky tooth sludge on it, I noticed.

Lifting up the toilet seat, I touched the bristles, briefly, against the rim, and quickly pulled it away. No lightning bolts shot out of the sky, and outside the window birds continued to sing. I held the brush against the rim a little longer. Still nothing. Next I wiped it around the edge of the seat for a couple of inches. Then, gingerly at first, and with increasing force, I shoved the end under the inner lip of the pan, right up into the gunky horrible bits where even bleach doesn't reach, and had a good dig around.

Then I turned it on.

Before I knew it that brush had been used to polish the entire bowl, inside and out, and under the rim, at least twice. By the end I was bent over the bog, cackling like a witch with two children in the oven.

I looked at the end of the brush – no sign of any abuse, at least not with the naked eye. Under a microscope it was probably *alive*.

When Twatface turned up an hour later I opened the door and grinned delightedly at him, and he looked confusedly back. He had brought a couple of wine boxes but was further disorientated when he went into the cellar to load up.

'How long ago did we go to Calais?' he shouted up to me.

'About a month,' I replied from the kitchen. 'Why?'

'I spent £300 on booze,' he said. 'Where's it all gone?'

'You've probably guzzled it,' I said, making sure the oven door was shut and wouldn't suddenly swing open to display the ten bottles I'd hidden.

'I have not,' he called up, outrage in his voice. 'This is really important!'

Muffling a giggle, I double-checked the washing machine was still holding a dozen bottles, and prayed he would have no reason to go upstairs and check in my knicker drawer, under the bed or behind the computer desk, where another fifty or so had been secreted.

'Well, I did have some friends over,' I lied. 'And it's our booze, because I paid for half of it.'

'Have you wasted it on bloody Fifi and Porter and that lot?' He paused, and there was angry clinking from the cellar. 'You've been spanking the Mâcon Villages, haven't you?'

Knowing it was his favourite, I twisted the knife. 'Is that the one with the yellow label? It tasted a bit funny. I might have poured it away,' I said as innocently as possible.

His face was purple with rage as he peered into the kitchen in disbelief. *'You threw it away?'* he shouted, in the same tone you might say, *'You killed a baby?'*

'I might have. Don't really remember,' I said, breezily, and wandered into the living room nonchalantly to bury my face in a cushion and stifle the laughter.

He saw himself out, in shaky alcoholic dudgeon, with six bottles and his faecal toothbrush.

Halfway through the afternoon the phone beeped and it was 'bloody' Fifi Jenkins, the world's tiniest and most Welsh showbiz reporter. 'Come to Bar du Musée at the weekend – my brother Beamy's having drinks with the lads, do you good, it will.'

Now most journos are only friends with other journos because normal people don't talk to us. Even if they do, we don't know how to handle it and prefer to stick to our own kind. Fifi, inexplicably for someone who pirouettes through a world of PRs, WAGS, wannabes and celebs both major and minor, has friends who buy a newspaper only occasionally, watch the TV news when they can be bothered and have no idea who's in the latest *Big Brother*.

Normal people, in other words.

The lie to Twatface about having a party had just been another way to hit him where he hurt – the booze nodule. But it played on my mind. I'd spent nearly a fortnight nursing the pain and licking my wounds. It was time I at least cleaned my armpits and emerged, blinking, into the sunlight. A night out would do me good, I thought.

I told Fifi I'd see her there, and wandered into the bathroom, thinking I should probably wash my hair. Then I caught sight of myself in the mirror over the sink.

There hadn't been any point in washing my hair because it only got more paint in it. It had also been pointless wearing make-up, or anything other than yesterday's tattered, stained jeans. I could still barely eat, so there had been no reason for breakfasts, either.

The creature looking back at me was someone I didn't even recognize. It had greasy hair scraped back into a ponytail, grey hairs springing free, sallow skin, a downturned mouth in a gaunt, lined face and dead, misery-filled eyes. And it smelled truly awful.

I leaned in and looked closer. Squeezed a couple of spots, then gave up because I only noticed more. Stuck out my tongue and put it away again in horror. There were new lines across my forehead that I swear hadn't been there a week earlier, and fresh wrinkles around my eyes. I was looking at a woman who, despite being only twenty-nine, appeared to have had fifteen tearaway children and a hard life somewhere with a low life expectancy – like Croydon or Zimbabwe. I half-expected my teeth to have fallen out.

It had been just under three years earlier that I'd walked down the aisle a blushing bride, a healthy size ten, with glossy hair and a happy glow. A thousand days at Twatface's mercy and I'd become a haggard crone. I looked like the 'after' pictures of crystal meth addiction. How could I possibly go out in public again? I felt old, I felt barren, and I felt I was over.

Trying to work out how those lines had appeared so suddenly, I frowned. Nope, the wrinkles went across my forehead, not between the brows. I contorted my mouth, squidged my eyes, wiggled every muscle there was, until finally I hit the one expression which deepened the new furrows.

Staring into the mirror, I saw my eyebrows raised and my cheeks pushed up and out as my eyes crinkled. Beneath it my lips were separated, and lifted at the ends. It was a look of surprise, of laughter – the expression of a woman who had got through three decades, and had smiled more than she'd scowled.

'Well,' I told the mirror. 'That's something, at least. They're not wrinkles, they're laughter lines.' I might end up with a face like a walnut, but if it's from spending my life laughing I'll say bugger to Botox.

Then I looked at the rest of it: the grey hairs and the thin, gaunt face. A spot of hair dye'd fix those, and good Lord, were those cheekbones?

The shop at the end of the road produced some dye, and while it was on I had a bath, a face pack, and shaved my legs – then did it all again because I had been so filthy. At the back of the wardrobe I found a pair of tight white trousers I had never been able to fit into and a slinky top.

When I looked once more in the mirror, I saw a girl with big worried eyes surrounded by black kohl, translucent skin, long legs and an arse which could finally, after years of failed struggle, be legitimately described as tiny.

Inside I was empty, and as scared as if I was on my first day at school.

But the boys wouldn't see that.

DAY TWELVE

THE boys didn't notice a thing.

Partly because Bar du Musée is heaving with totty of all sorts on a Saturday night, and partly because for most of the time I hid in a corner like an MP who's just been told a reporter wants a word about their expenses.

When I arrived Fifi was nowhere to be seen. Like much of Greenwich the place was packed with students and tourists, but weaving through the bottlenecking crowds I eventually picked up a barely believable Welsh lilt over the music.

'You've got FABerluss arms, you 'av, izzeht?'

Looking across, I saw tiny Fi – five-foot nothing in her socks – gripping a bicep bigger than her leg and grinning flirtatiously up at a blond beefcake who must have been six feet five inches tall, and about the same across the chest. In fact, Fi was stood in a pack of guys all of similar heights and girth, who had gathered around her in a circle like men always do with tiny, cute, big-boobed flirts. She glanced up, saw me, and burst through the pack. Holding a large glass of white wine out in one hand and an unlit cigarette in the other, she threw her arms around me, and said: 'Ow the devilll ah you, my lovellly? Av some wine and come and meet the boys. Thur all friends of Beamy. Thez is my friend, 'er 'usban's a rrrright little

47

shet. Thurs some wine for you, lovely. Getoutovvit you! Now 'ow have you been?'

This last was said more quietly, after she had shoved a couple of boys out of the way, pushed me into a seat at a table, thrust a glass of wine into my hand and looked at me kindly.

'Pretty shit, to be honest, Fi,' I sighed. 'I'm not sure I should be here.'

'You can't stay a'tome on yer own. I know things are all over the place at the moment, but that doesn't mean you can't lev a little.'

I told her everything Twatface had said and done, and she cackled loudly at the bits about hiding his wine and cleaning the bog with his toothbrush. She hugged me when I told her about the cell, and my dad, and got me another glass of wine. She laughed until she cried when I said: 'Her calves were the size of my *torso!*' Then, after three large glasses, and finally bored of my own dramas, I looked around and asked her who everyone was.

Beamy's her brother, and he's a member of an unofficial club which supposedly plays cricket and limps through some local leagues, but is really a drinking society for misfits. I'd met Beamy a few times before, and he's aptly nicknamed for having a constant smile on his face – but the rest of the fraternity were new to me.

The big blond beefcake, said Fi, was 'Bazzo' (surname Barraclough), another was known as 'Slappim' because he had wandering hands. There was a smaller one called 'Boney' (some kind of Napoleon complex), a skinny one called 'Porky', and another couple of tall ones called 'Gammy' and 'Raffles'. They were all drinking beer and joking, and there were more male hormones surging around me than I'd been within sniffing distance of since school.

'You should get talkin' to them,' said Fi. 'Your next man's out thur somewhur, izzeht.'

'I think it's a bit soon for all that, Fi,' I said uneasily. 'Twatface wants to see me again and talk about things.'

'Ooh, I'm not sayin' do anythen. Just get back on the bike, izzeht? 'Av a flurt. Come on, there must be one you fancy. Which one do you like?'

Starting to feel trapped, I looked around and randomly pointed out one with dark hair. 'That one.'

'Say 'ello, then! Come on.' And she pulled me to my feet, pushed another glass in my hand, and marched me up to the poor sod. 'Thez is Foxy,' said Fi, before nudging me in the back and walking away.

Christ. He stood and looked at me.

'Um, er. Hi,' I stammered. It had been nearly six years since I'd last had to flirt with anyone, and I hadn't been any good at it then. How the hell did this work?

'Hello,' he said.

We stared at each other as someone turned the music up.

He held his hand out. 'I'm Spacker.'

Oh, well done. What a brilliant choice you've made. Again.

'Spacker?'

'No, Spicker.'

'Bicker?' I said, with a hand around one ear.

'SPRITZER.'

'Splitsy?'

He rolled his eyes, leaned in and shouted in my ear. 'Steve. Steve Packer. They call me Spacker.'

'Oh, Spacker. I see.'

49

Luckily Beamy came over to talk to us, and I was rescued from having to make scintillating conversation while he engaged Spacker in chat about who'd had how many runs that afternoon. With attention diverted from me, I had time to look at my target. He was not that tall, but well-muscled under a tight white T-shirt, with very red lips and long coal-coloured eyelashes. Maybe not such a bad pick after all.

As the wine wore on it was a relief to be with people who had never met Twatface and didn't want to talk to me about him. They wanted to know about my job, how long I'd known Fi, and what bra size did I take, 34B or C? It had been a long time since anyone had tried to chat me up, and I found their oafishness amusing. They were as unlike Twatface – who prided himself on being a metrosexual and having sensitive skin – as it was possible to be. It was a big sea of testosterone, laced with white wine, and I threw myself in.

Which is how I found myself at 2 a.m., sat on a plastic bench at a shiny Formica table in the chip shop, singing along to some rude song I can't remember, sandwiched between Bazzo and Spacker.

Spacker's tanned arm rested against mine, and I could smell a slight hint of fresh sweat through his tight white T-shirt in the humid night. As I looked at the muscles of his bicep, it flexed and he turned towards me. He bent his head and kissed me with those red lips, which tasted like raspberries. Oh, all right then, raspberries dipped in beer.

A cheer went up around us, and someone shouted: 'Go on, son!' I looked up and saw Fi on the other side of the table, dipping a chip in some ketchup and winking at me. Spacker grabbed my hand and pulled me out of the shop into the cool air, and walking to the corner he drew me into his arms and kissed me again.

It occurred to me that I was kissing a man called Spacker on a street corner while drunk and smelling like a chip shop – a journalist's ability to sum up situations succinctly is not always welcome – and I pulled away.

'So where's your place?' he said, smiling and lowering those eyelashes at me.

Suddenly my husband loomed, even though he was scowling and saying, '*You threw it away?*' Much as I fancied him, I knew Spacker was going no further. Twatface might be with Fatty, he might have finally found a ladder and climbed up to do the deed, he might be doing it right this instant, but I was married and that was kind of that. The kiss made me feel better, but anything more would make me feel worse.

'My place is this way. And the taxi rank is that way,' I told him, smiling. 'Goodnight.'

I reached up to kiss him on the cheek, breathing in the scent of his clean sweat one last time, then turned and walked away. I felt him stand and watch me go, toying with the idea of following me for a second before deciding it wasn't worth it. But still, as I walked back home in those tight white jeans, I felt as though my heart had just restarted.

DAY FOURTEEN

THERE was only one way to survive going back to the office – getting to the pub as soon as humanly possible.

But first, the newsroom. I was nearly as scared as on my first day at a local paper years ago, when I'd been a nervous eighteen-year-old who'd turned down university for the offer of a job covering one country town and a dozen villages. I didn't know what the hell I was doing, forgot to bring a notebook or ask the right questions, made a mess of covering a parish council meeting on my patch, and crashed the borrowed office car. Going back to work the second day was more nerve-racking than the first, but after a quick bollocking it was business as usual, and with the glory of seeing my first bylines I realized I was born for the job – a person who observes more than they take part, who asks questions you don't want to answer and notices things no one else sees.

Now I do the same sort of thing for a national tabloid. My patch is a whole country, and sometimes others, too, but the questions I ask are of national statesmen rather than local councillors, TV and film stars instead of the carnival queen, and I've learned always to have a notebook and pen and never, EVER, admit it was my fault when I crash a car.

I'm still a person who notices too much, and when I walked into the newsroom at 10 a.m. I was dreading the silences, sympathy and crinkly, concerned foreheads of my friends.

'Thank FUCK you're back,' said Harry Porter, the gayest straight man you'll ever meet. 'I need a cup of tea and someone to answer my phone while I go for a dump.'

He sashayed off to the bogs with a copy of the *Daily Wail*, leaving me in the clutches of crime reporter Bridget Jones and a work-experience boy called Tom.

Bridget isn't her real name, that's Nicola; but she's blonde and single, so what does she expect? She is also Australian, and so chippy you wouldn't be surprised to hear she'd picked a fight with the entire world.

'Abaht bloody time,' she said, with her feet up on the desk while she read a copy of the *Glimmer*. 'It's been so boring round here I was thinking of smashing a winder to get arrested, or something equally *insane*.' She folded down a corner of the paper and looked over it at me, raising an eyebrow like Columbo used to when he puffed on his cigar; poor Tom just looked confused.

'Sympathetic as ever, Bridge,' I said, dumping my bag and shifting a load of old newspapers that had drifted on to my desk. 'Missed me, then?'

'Not had the chance, mate. Sky News have been filing updates on you every twenty minutes,' she said drily. I must have looked worried, because she added: 'Oim jokin'. Although we have had a team tailing your ex.'

My interest was piqued. 'Tell me you're making it up?'

'Ha, not really. As it happens I was meeting some of the crime pack down at the Stab in the Back last night, and he walked right in on us.'

All journalists gather together for warmth and friendship, more so when they specialize in one subject like Bridget and Harry do. Specialists usually end up talking and acting like the people they write about, so a defence reporter will have shiny shoes and a regimental tie, health writers tend to be hypochondriacs, and political types are fond of telling you they know best. Crime guys, generally, have grubby macs and drink in pubs no one else would patronize. Bridge is no exception.

'And oi'm sorry about this, but you probably ought to know – she was with him.'

If I hadn't already been sitting down I'd have fallen over. For Twatface to take Fatty into a pub where all of Fleet Street's crime reporters hang out is like him paying for a billboard on the M25. It means they're public. So much for his 'talking things over'.

Bridget was still speaking: 'I asked him what the hell he thought he was doin', and he mumbled something. Then Toxic Tim from the *Sunday Person* came up. Anyway he's never met you, has he? He knew Twatface, and said hello, then turned to her, all oozy, and said: "You must be Foxy, I've heard sooo much about you."'

I'd been told Tim was a decent enough chap out of work but one of those guys you wouldn't trust not to nick your contacts book or sell his own mother for a story. He'd been in Fleet Street nearly as long as Bish, certainly longer than computers, and possibly longer than photographs. Hearing that he'd presumed I was Fatty I didn't know whether to be outraged or laugh out loud – I settled for a snort and an eye-roll.

Bridge took a deep breath. 'Well, she had a face like a slapped arse. It was the funniest thing I've ever seen. Twatface went white and started stuttering, and then she grabbed him by the arm and dragged him into a corner to give him a bollocking. The crime pack pissed themselves.'

At that moment Bish lumbered up like an old tank. He

is firmly of the belief that a decent reporter is one who can file flawless copy while three sheets to the wind and taking enemy fire, and that the only place for emotion is in the top six pars of copy about a grieving widow. He has survived fifty years on the street with an unending supply of dreadful jokes, a regular Woodbine and only the most limited personal involvement with any of the weirdos he works with.

'Ooh, yer back, then. How's that coont of 'usband o'yours? What a wanker! Still, never mind. Park yer broomstick and go through this,' he said, dropping four hundred pages of A4 on my keyboard. 'It's the most recent list of party political donations. Find us summat no one else has had yet, can yer? It'll keep yer mind off things.' Then he turned and trundled back to the news desk.

Porter stamped back from the loos, saying: 'Bridget filled you in, has she? Apparently this girl's much bigger than you. What's your bloke thinking? Anyway, this is Tom. Say hello, Tom.' Tom said hello. He looked shell-shocked, as everyone does after ten minutes of listening to journalists speak to each other.

'Tom is the nephew of the managing editor,' said Porter, adding more quietly: 'I only found that out after I called the managing editor a dickless wanker for throwing back my expenses.'

Tom had the grace to look ashamed. I felt an affinity for another lost soul adrift on a sea of journalistic bullishness, got him a cup of tea, and showed him how to get the news wires up on his computer.

'Oh, and have you heard?' asked Porter. 'There was an email went round. Apparently half the staff are being made redundant.'

'What? Really?' This was the last thing I needed. Was I going to lose my job, too?

''Fraid so. Aforementioned executive says they want to slice a few million off the wage bill. It's across the board, apparently – journos, snappers, subs, everyone.' Porter grimaced sympathetically. 'Don't worry, we'll probably be fine. They have these culls now and again, and the staff usually ends up looking much the same as it did before. It's just how newspapers are these days, shrinking budgets and all that. The worst that can happen is they'll have to re-employ us all as freelancers on twice the money.'

I knew he was right – an industry which has been around for three hundred years hasn't found a way to make the internet pay yet, and although it's run by two students the website is the only bit of the organization gaining readers. People will always want journalists, but I suppose the way we deliver what we do has to change. It's a shame – and I know this is me being overly romantic – but a warm computer screen does not compare to the smell of hot ink on a fresh front page.

Still, it's not what someone whose life has just been turned upside down needs to hear on their first day back at work. I tried to put it to the back of my mind and got on with deleting the spam emails which had choked my inbox.

As the day passed, the rest of the staff floated past my desk in dribs and drabs. Fifi came in late from a film premiere the night before, gave me a squeeze, lit a cigarette and got on with writing her showbiz column. Cubby Fox, the health reporter, popped into the office briefly between 'appointments', which were probably with his doctor or a fine wine. Our best feature writer, Valentine

Lush, wandered in at lunchtime to write 1,500 words on a big interview with the wife of a cheating footballer and file his expenses, tossing me a £50 drinks receipt with the words, 'I hear you're a little down in the mouth. Have this one on me.' Meanwhile Sophia (who writes about handbags and rich people for the magazine and is so posh Bish calls her 'Princess Flashy Knickers') and the newsroom's token ethnic minority, Nancy, were out on the road, but said they'd be back to take me for a drink after work.

While I juggled emails, phone calls and political donations there was an unending supply of jokes about flowerpots, and I began to find my feet.

It was comforting to be surrounded by the black humour with which all journalists protect themselves from the outside world, even if I was the butt of the remarks. Whether covering a brutal child murder, a political scandal, or a cat stuck up a tree, we'd soon break down and weep from the sheer onslaught of human ineptitude and cruelty we witness every day if it weren't for jokes told in the poorest of taste. The one about missing toddler Maddie McCann, the Fritzls and the European hide-and-seek championships should never be told to her parents, but it still makes us snigger.

By the time 7 p.m. rolled around I'd managed successfully to avoid any serious work, bashed out a couple of picture captions and even raised a rueful smile when Porter suggested I have an extra pie for lunch to entice my husband back. Then Princess Flashy Knickers swung past my desk to drag me to the Gipsy Moth on the river for a catch-up with her and Nancy.

We'd all got married within a few weeks of each other, nearly three years ago. Sophia is quite girly, while Nancy is so hardened a news reporter that she makes Kate Adie look like a wet blanket. Both are much posher and a bit older than me, and I've always felt like the junior member of the trio, running to catch up with their exploits and capacity for Pinot Grigio.

Tonight was different: they listened as I told them everything that had happened in the past few weeks. They could not believe that Twatface had met and fallen for Fatty so quickly, but his emails don't lie, so I knew the dates were right. They'd met him plenty of times, and were stunned to hear of his casual cruelty when we had seemed so happy together in public.

Then Nancy asked if we'd had problems before, and for the first time I told my friends the things I'd found out a year earlier, how I'd left and how he'd begged me to give him a second chance.

'I can't believe you didn't tell us this,' said Nancy after I described the past 18 months. 'It must have been horrible for you.'

I shrugged. 'It made things quite unpleasant for a while.'

'How do you mean?'

'Well . . . it's difficult to say. We used to get on perfectly, and our arguments were always good-natured. But more recently every little thing seemed to escalate into a huge row and I didn't understand why. He never had any money to put towards the groceries, and if I asked him for some he'd scream at me and say I was lying or trying to steal from him. I bought new sheets once, put them on the bed, and he wouldn't let them touch his skin until they'd been washed in case they gave him cancer. When

58

he was out he would say he'd be home at 10 p.m., I'd be sleeping with one eye open for a couple of hours, then I'd get worried, and he'd wander in at 4 a.m., by which point I'd be about to ring the hospitals. Sometimes he was drunk and sometimes he'd come home at 4 a.m. apparently sober, and they were the times I worried most.

'He was always worse a couple of days after he'd been out on a bender. Sometimes he scratched at his skin in his sleep until his arms bled. Other times he'd fly into a rage at the least thing. He told me I made everything worse when all I wanted to do was help him.

'He was under a lot of stress at work, and it got bad around the time we moved house about a year ago. That was why it happened.'

Princess Flashy Knickers frowned at her wine, then asked quietly: 'Did he ever hit you?'

I was shocked. 'God, no! He'd never hurt me. I mean, all right, a couple of times the rows were a bit heated but he never *hit* me. He was just angry with me. I suppose it was my fault for arguing back. He said it was, anyway. I can't even remember what we rowed about now. There were quite a few times I was scared, when I thought we were both unsafe, and afterwards I would curl up in a ball and cry and he'd make me apologize to him.

'Once or twice, when he came home, I locked the bedroom door. He didn't like that,' I laughed awkwardly, and there was a heavy pause.

There is a journalistic trick in interviews of asking no questions at all, just letting someone witter to fill the silence and thereby reveal more than they were willing. It's a bit like digging a hole in front of someone and watching them fall in. As we sat there none of us said anything, while I gazed into my glass to avoid their eyes and

59

they listened to the things I didn't say. Couldn't say, and don't want to remember.

'It was just silly rows and stuff, it was the stress. A difficult time.'

I shrugged, having long ago accepted those as the facts, and took a drink of my wine. They both stared at me. Nancy sat with her mouth open. Princess, with sad eyes, said: 'Why didn't you tell anyone?'

I replied: 'He said I shouldn't tell any of my friends because you were all journalists and it might affect his career. I was so worried I did whatever he said. I just wanted everything to be better.'

Princess sighed. 'My ex used to tell me it was my fault.'

'What? Your ex?'

'I was with this guy for ten years. Before my husband. Everything was great, and then after a while he started taking cocaine. He would burst in, late at night, make up a row about something, and start a fight. At first he pushed me. Then he slapped me. Then he hit me. Each time it happened, he had to hurt me more than the time before. Eventually there came a night when he had me on the floor and was kicking me in the face and body. He broke my arm and smashed my jaw – look.'

She rolled up a sleeve and pointed out a nasty four-inch scar near her elbow, then pulled her long hair back and turned her face to the light so we could see for the first time a misshapen bump between her cheekbone and her ear, and another scar under her jaw. Nancy and I stared at them silently. We had never heard this story before either.

'I had loads of operations, and had to be wired back together. I'd told myself for years it was the drugs, and because he was nice some of the time I hoped he'd go back to how he was. It all happened so gradually, so slowly, while he told me it was my fault, that I learned if I said sorry to him and changed my behaviour he would be happy for a bit. But it didn't last, he just got worse. Whatever I did was never quite enough, so I changed more and more. He cut me off from my friends, and my family despaired. When I finally realized what was happening and left he tried to find me. I moved so many times, changed my phone, everything. I'm still scared that one day he'll turn up.'

Drugs aren't my thing – never have been. But I'm realistic enough to know they're common in all walks of life, and that cocaine is rife in Fleet Street.

As a rule of thumb news reporters like me don't indulge – or not much – because our lives are exciting enough and we get to see the unpleasant consequences first-hand: the inquests, the court hearings, trying to get reliable information out of someone who will tell you anything for £20 and a fix. Also we don't get paid very much, and you can't get a receipt for drugs. Showbiz types are sort of expected to dabble – their job is to party with the rich and famous, and drugs are always going to be part of that. Some even get to claim expenses for it, and most have at least a moment where the fact they can stand next to money and fame makes them think they can be rock 'n' roll too. The sensible ones know when to stop, and that no story is worth killing yourself for, but most showbiz journos at some point have needed someone to sit them down and straighten them out. Those who don't listen don't last.

Then there's the executives, the ones with a lot of money and stress. The steadier ones stick to drinking, but those who spend too much time sitting at a desk wishing they were still on the road can develop a problem. They crave excitement and have been trained, over years of ordering reporters around and the ups and downs of a twenty-four-hour news cycle, to expect instant gratification. They have too much money, too much stress, and too few people telling them they're wrong.

When it comes to the inevitable point that they have to choose between their careers and their fun, most find that an addiction to news is more powerful, with better rewards and bigger highs.

I honestly can't tell you what Twatface did or didn't do for sure, and I'm not sure I ever really want to know. When I'm working on a story and something just doesn't smell right I ask a question, and if I think I'm being lied to, I ask it again and again and again. When you do that in a relationship you become a nag, and although he never told me the reasons for his late nights, the money that disappeared, the way my kind and loving husband seemed to turn overnight into an angry, evasive stranger, I'd be a pretty poor journalist if I couldn't work out the most likely explanation was something he didn't want me to know.

Princess looked hard at me. 'We don't know what Twatface was doing, but I can tell you that if he never tried to fix things when they went wrong, if he always put himself before your relationship, then it was always going to go wrong. Maybe one day he would have done to you what my ex did to me. It might have taken thirty years, but it would have got worse. You're lucky you're out of it.'

Her words fluttered through my ears and dropped like lead into my skull. I struggled with the thought that my husband – my Scooby, who I thought I knew as well as the lines on my own hand – could possibly be in the same

62

category as the vicious thug who had almost killed my friend. Could it really be that I was at one end of the spectrum and she was at the other?

It was impossible to comprehend, but at the same time made perfect sense – like that optical illusion where you look at a picture of a young woman with her face turned away, and suddenly realize it's an old crone with a hooked nose. I remembered the time Twatface had made me get down on my knees and beg, in tears, for it all to stop. I did it because I just wanted things to be better.

Remembering it now, I was appalled at my own denigration in a way I had not been at the time. He broke me and I hadn't even noticed.

Princess could be wrong, of course. Twatface might, right now, be out there feeling dreadful about everything and desperate to find a way to fix it.

But even if he did – even if we had help, I took him back and gave him another chance – what would happen the next time things were stressful or imperfect? What if in five years' time we had a kid and it fell ill? Or his parents died, or mine did, or one of us lost a job? The answer, I knew, was that he'd try to escape the problems again and then what would I do? He might learn to deal with it, or he might hurt me properly the next time. I couldn't spend my life waiting for that. I wanted a husband who was on my team and would stand by me, not leave me on my tod while he went off down the pub, saying it was all too much to deal with, or who I would have to carry on my back through everything life threw at us. That's not the way our marriage was meant to be.

I kissed the girls goodbye and wandered home along the river. I remembered the nights spent waiting for him to come home, the tears, the rows. The things he had done to me and which I'd apologized for. For a year or eighteen months – half our marriage – I had cried most nights. What the hell had I been thinking about babies for? Was I insane? Sophia was right – it had ended just in time.

Then a thought occurred to me: my period was late. By a week.

DAY EIGHTEEN

PREGNANT? I can't possibly be pregnant.

I could be pregnant. I mean, it's biologically possible. But very unlikely. Twatface rarely if ever wanted to have sex with me. And I must admit that repeatedly asking your husband why he doesn't want to have sex with you, and please could he have sex with you, and, 'Look, I bought new knickers, what do you think?' could be construed as nagging and thus a turn-off.

Or so he said.

Anyway, that aside we did manage it occasionally. And we hadn't been that careful. It's been six weeks since my last period.

There are none of the normal signs of pregnancy – my boobs are smaller not bigger, my tummy is flatter not rounder – although my moods are all over the shop. And it's been so long since I ate solid food I am probably incapable of carrying a child. On a diet of custard creams, white wine and tea you can't even shit straight. If there was a foetus in there it would call Social Services and demand to be rehomed.

For a week or so I've avoided buying a test and finding out for sure, for the simple reason that being pregnant right now would be a very bad thing and I don't want to know.

So when, this morning, a half-hearted period finally arrived, I should have been relieved. Instead I sat on the loo and cried.

If there had been a baby, maybe Twatface would have come back. Maybe he would have behaved better. Even if he hadn't the marriage could not have been written off as a total dismal failure: it would still have produced something wonderful. And at nearly thirty, with a divorce looming, I might never have another chance.

But as I sat there and sniffled, I also realized that, had I been up the stick, I would inevitably have had other problems. Taking Twatface back 'for the baby's sake', for one. Handing over said baby, once a week, to a bad husband for another. Having a child so young that it might even call the other woman it saw at the weekends 'Mummy'. Having to stop work, sell the house, move in with my parents. All bad, all awful.

Far better, overall, simply to decide I had wasted several years of my life with an idiot, chalk it up, build a bridge and get over it. The logic was completely inarguable, but did nothing to stop the little wail in my heart that I didn't have my baby. None of this was going to get me anywhere. So I did what I've learned to do: put the sadness away, packed it up in a little box, and got on with the things I could change. I went back to see the solicitor.

Maurice's firm is near where I live, and he was the cheapest and kindest on the phone. He was short, portly, and middle-aged, and seemed a jolly chap considering he must spend his life dealing with other people's irreconcilable differences. He couldn't stop grinning when I first told him about the arrest, the adultery, the size of her arse. I sat in his office and told him what had happened since then, while he took notes and smiled. He said if I

66

went ahead with the divorce I'd need to pay £600 up front, which as Twatface had promised to pay costs I'd get refunded at the end.

'Six hundred pounds?' I said. 'It only cost £60 for the marriage licence!'

Even better, he saw no reason why I couldn't keep the house. I had put all the deposit down, I could probably manage the payments on my own, and as it was still in dire need of renovation the value wouldn't have increased, which meant I wouldn't have to pay Twatface off. Fatty might have my husband, and my future, and the babies I'd never have, but she was not having my house, too. Bollocks to that! I had to keep one thing, hold on to something for my future, to prove it wasn't all pointless.

Then he asked me what I was going to divorce Twatface for. Unreasonable behaviour was normal, he said; adultery with an unnamed third party was quite common, but people rarely wanted to shout about it. The other party, in cases such as this, rarely contested, unless you tried something bonkers like naming the other woman. 'Name her?' I asked. 'Can I name her?'

'Oh yes,' he said, smiling away. 'But it just causes acrimony, because the other party gets papers served on them, and they have to sign admitting their adultery as well as your spouse. It's really not wise.'

Ooh, this sounded good. I liked the idea of acrimony. I particularly liked it if it would drop him in it. I liked it because her family would go mental. In fact I couldn't think of anything I didn't like about it.

'I think it'll be adultery with a named third party then, Maurice,' I said.

'It may just antagonize your husband,' he said, with a near-grimace.

'Good,' I replied. 'I haven't the money to start things now, and there's some talking still to do, but I'll call you.' I left his office with a spring in my step for the first time in what felt like forever.

After that the week was dull – it's the time of year when everyone's on holiday, from MPs to coppers, criminals to celebrities, and it seems like every person in my contact book is out of reach. We call it Silly Season because for most of the summer there's nothing to write about but UFO sightings, tourist donkeys in need of rescue or large tabby cats being mistaken for escaped tigers on Bodmin Moor.

One night I trooped down for a drink at one of the pubs on the river. There we were, several bottles down and looking over the water dancing with bar lights: me, Fifi, Bridget, Porter, Princess, Buff and Nancy. Bish even came down and stood his round, gossip was spread and tall tales were told.

Towards the end of the evening, as the manager tried to collect his glasses and tot up his losses, and Fifi and Bridget were fighting over a £14 receipt they'd found on the ground and each wanted to use to claim back on expenses, I was drunkenly leaning over the railings when Buff came and leaned next to me.

We've always had an unspoken understanding, me and Buff. I know he's a dirty beggar who'd shag a warm loaf, and he knows I know it. We flirt and are friendly and it's all very pleasant. Just before I got married there were one or two occasions when I was aware his mind and eyes were turning towards the possibility of getting himself a no-strings, last-minute legover, and I was even half-tempted.

But he's not really my type, and besides, there's no point in a fling if you love your groom-to-be and never dream of being with anyone else.

Anyway, we leaned. We chatted, and he asked how I was doing. We flirted a bit, same as ever. Then he said, while we were talking about Twatface, that he'd suspected he was a bad boy. Sensing a line, I scoffed and said: 'Really?'

Buff was serious, and replied: 'Occasionally when I bumped into him around the place I would look at him, say hello, and I could just kind of sense something. And I used to think to myself, "I hope you're being a good boy." And it wasn't just because I'm friends with you, it was because I could see he had a glint in his eye.'

I was quite surprised, but frankly if anyone can spot a glint it's Buff. I told him about the stuff I'd found out, things that worried me before Twatface even met Fatty, and Buff said: 'In that case I reckon he was doing it before, too. You just didn't find out.'

I was coming to terms with this, and trying to work out who else Twatface might have been cheating on me with, when Buff touched my arm and said: 'Do you know, my girlfriend and I hardly have sex any more.'

Now, every girl worth her salt knows what that means. It is not a cri de coeur from a man desperate for the physical expression of love from his girlfriend. It could mean, 'It's got a bit boring,' or, 'It's a bit infrequent'– or anything at all. But it really translates as: 'I would like to have sex with you, if you will just react sympathetically to this blatantly obvious line, listen to me spin you some crap about how my girlfriend doesn't understand me, and then let me put my winky in you. Please.'

We were leaning close together, and I knew if I turned my head towards him he would kiss me. Everyone else was

69

inside, so I knew there'd be no gossip, but it still wasn't something I wanted to do. A no-strings shag with a dirty beggar might be just what the doctor ordered, but not when I knew he had another woman. I'm not certain of much, but I am a better woman than that. A better woman than Fatty.

So instead I kept my head facing out over the water, took a sip of my wine, said something jokey and inconsequential, and the moment passed. We finished our drinks, pecked on the cheek and went our separate ways.

Sat swaying drunkenly on the Docklands Light Railway as it swung through the apartment blocks back towards home, I offered up a prayer of silent thanks to whatever malevolent god might be taking an interest in my life, for reminding me that someone, somewhere still wanted to have sex with me, even if all it proved was that I didn't need a wash yet.

Whether Twatface had been putting it about all over town, whether I was pregnant or not, it really didn't matter. It was over now, and with each day there was more distance and less pain. In the words of the old country and western song he really had me going – but now I'm gone.

DAY TWENTY-EIGHT

TWATFACE texted last night: 'I miss you. I miss talking to you. I'm drinking alone and there's nothing to eat but nuts. Can I come and see you, talk things over?'

Oh, the joy. How did it get to the point where, when my husband says he misses me, my heart sinks into my shoes? I cried all night. Again.

I quite want to see him; I dream he'll say sorry, beg for forgiveness, ask to try again and that he loves me still. That instead of being the screwed-up tabloid newspaper exec he is, he'll go back to being the slightly alcoholic but fun tabloid newspaper reporter he was when I met him.

Maybe he wishes I was different, too?

I'm not how I was. I'm angrier, older, wiser. I was also a size ten when we married; after a while it was a twelve, with the arse bordering on a fourteen in the wrong shops. Considering he's run off with Fatty, he was probably feeding me up. Whatever, I'm about an eight these days. Looking in the mirror I can see the bum is definitely smaller, but inexplicably has more cellulite on it, and appears to sag alarmingly where it joins the back of my thighs. It looks all right in jeans, but I'm not sure anyone would like it in the flesh.

And Fatty is a better prospect than this. God, am I that unattractive? I feel like wearing a bag over my head.

Dragging my heels into the newsroom, I arrived my habitual ten minutes late, to be greeted by the lesser-spotted shriek of Bridget Jones.

'FOXYYYYYY,' she screamed down the office from her desk, where she was sitting with Fifi perched nearby. 'You won't BELIEVE what I did at the Glastonbury Festival!'

(Journalists, bless them, like to publish. Everything.)

'Morning, you,' I said. 'Tell me it wasn't another nineteen-year-old?'

Bridget laughed, plainly proud of her exploits and wanting to boast. 'Nah, mate, got that badge. Fifi here got me in on a press ticket because she was covering it. I met this guy in the dance tent, and I was quite drunk but not that bad, and he was a beautiful Arab man, like Omar Sharif. We talked for hours.'

'Oh yeah? What about?'

'No bloody idea! All I remember is waking up the next morning.' Her voice dropped to a conspiratorial whisper, and I leaned in. 'I cracked open my eyes and did that thing where you try to work out if you still have all your fingers and toes, and if you can remember what your name is. Counted my feet, found my hands. Then I caught sight of him at the entrance of the tent, lookin' out. Only in the morning he looked more like Mohammed from the kebab shop down Deptford High Street! I couldn't remember what had happened, so I peeked under the sleeping bag to check if my knickers were on or off.'

Eyes wide, I was gripped. 'And?'

'Worse!' said Bridge in mock horror, before starting to cackle like Sybil Fawlty. 'I had one leg in my jeans, and one leg out! Hahaha! Oh, the humanity! I said, "Did we have sex?" And he said, "No, you refused unless I could

72

get all your clothes off, and we couldn't get your other leg out." He went off to get some water, and while he was gone I bolted. I'd only got twenty feet 'fore he turned round, and saw me hoppin' between the tents still trying to put my jeans on. He called me back, but I kept hoppin'! Hahahahahahaha!'

Bridge, bless her, is an unending source of shameful shenanigans. She's secretly quite thoughtful and sweet, and everyone likes her, but she's perennially single, and I don't know why. She's pretty and clever and funny, but I think being a tabloid reporter scares men away – female reporters are by nature and environment tough, doing the kind of job not always easy to explain to a prospective mother-in-law. By dint of mathematics and working hours we're more likely to go out with a hack, but the male of our species is generally the kind who gets further with his wits than his looks. Hacks cross-breed all the time, although rarely with much success, as Twatface and I have just proved. I guess I'm about to have the same kind of problems as Bridget.

I joked, only half-heartedly: 'Come back, Twatface, all is forgiven.'

Bridget sobered up and exchanged a glance with Fifi. 'Oh yes. You know he was at Glasto too?'

'No. He said he was seeing family this weekend, asked to borrow my sleeping bag because his folks were going to be short of beds or something. He's never been to Glasto.'

Fifi grimaced. 'He was definitely there, luvly. With a girl so huge I presume she must be the Scarlet Fatso, izzeht.'

My heart, already low, plummeted to the Earth's core.

Fifi went on: 'He walked into the press tent with her. I don't know what he was thinken, I mean I was there,

73

Bridget, Tania Banks, loads of people you know – he must be bonkers thinken he can take her into a room full of your mates. Anyway he came up to say hello and we all blanked him. I gave him a mouthful and we all talked loudly about, "MY GOD, SHE'S 'UGE" and "HOW DER SHE", izzeht. Then they left.'

So that's what my sleeping bag was used for – him and Fatty. My eyes filled with hot water, and I stared at the floor while Fifi put her arm around me.

'Don't worry, babe, he's a twat. You're faberluss. You can do better.'

'He's 'sposed to be coming round this week to talk about things,' I sniffed.

Then Tania Banks walked in. She was with Evil Elliot, the deputy news editor, a man so paranoid and vicious he's not even in his own circle of trust. When he's bearing down on you, wielding his biro like a scalpel, you know you're about to be sent to sit on someone's pointless doorstep until three in the morning, for no reason other than that he's heard you had a night out planned and he likes to make people miserable.

He's like one of the dementors in *Harry Potter*; I could feel what little was left of my soul being sucked out through my ears at his approach. And Banks, oh, Banks I didn't want to see at all.

Elliot sneered as he peered at me over the rimless glasses perched on the end of his nose. He always sneers – it's his default face. 'Ah, it's you. When you've finished gossiping about your love life I'd like to discuss your latest expenses claim with you in the office. Perhaps you can explain why you think it's eighty-four miles to Peckham. Oh, and we're assessing all staff for the redundancies. I'm drawing up a *list*.'

He stalked off to what was affectionately known as the Bunker, which is technically Bish's office except he prefers to sit on the news desk, where he has the chance to chat to The Reader when they phone up. Elliot is a man more comfortable with clean white walls and a neat pen tidy, and tries to claim the Bunker as his own.

'I went via Harrow,' I told the girls defensively, as they raised eyebrows at me. 'Twice.'

Tania Banks stopped by me and crinkled her forehead. 'How are you?'

'Fine,' I said, wiping my eyes. 'You know.'

'Poor thing,' she said sympathetically. 'You should let me take you for a drink and a chat. I could tell from the Cheryl Tweedy stuff you filed you weren't your normal self; it wasn't quite you. I suggested to Elliot I give your copy a little polish, you know – I made it sing like it should. There's no need to thank me, it was just my way of helping out. You know I'm your friend, let's pop to the Slug later, yeah? Good, see you then.'

I looked at Bridget. She glanced back at me and shrugged. 'Maybe she's genuinely being nice?' she said, in a voice that suggested she didn't really believe it.

'Hmm,' I said.

Later, in the bar, a rude French barman had given us each a glass of Pinot Noir, and Banks had wittered on about some political story she'd been plaguing The Reader with. Then she said: 'Do you know what you did wrong? I mean, I know both of you, and love you equally, of course. You're a very bright and funny girl, great fun to be with, but you're *terribly* sensitive. It's very *draining*. It made things very hard for him, you know. And to be

75

honest, you can be a bit green, a bit immature. You've very high expectations of everyone around you and it's hard to measure up.'

I stared, hearing the words, agreeing with some of them, but stunned at the realization that while Twatface had been staying in Banks's flat he'd been telling her all this. He'd not said it to me. Did that make it a lie, to keep her onside, or was I the one being misled?

Banks could see I was struggling to understand, my defences down, and leaned across to squeeze my hand. She said kindly: 'I just want to see you both happy. You can lean on me, I won't tell a soul. Tell me what went wrong.'

So I spilled out my heart – my insecurities, my fears that maybe it was all my fault and I had pushed him into Fatty's bingo-wings. I told her things I had not even come to terms with myself, that I had not told anyone else. She listened, occasionally pointing out my mistakes.

Tears poured down my face throughout, as she picked over the barely-scabbed wound inside me and told me how I'd pushed him away but it could be fixed if I tried hard enough and made a real effort. I told her what my lawyer had advised, what I wanted and hoped for. When the bar closed Banks left me with a hug, and I felt I'd gained my friend back, someone to lean on. When I got home I was lower than I had been for days, convinced by her that I had somehow caused all this myself, questioning everything I'd learned, and mentally replaying recent history to see if I could have done things differently.

Then there was a text from Twatface: 'Are you seriously telling everyone I beat you?'

Banks must have rung him the moment she had left. Some friend.

DAY THIRTY-THREE

THE world's gone mad. Although the anniversary of Michael Jackson's death was a whole month ago, Bish has randomly decided we want a chat with his monkey.

'Be fookin' great read, that. And he's not a moonke, he's a nape. We could do "I WAS JACKO'S PLAYTHING" or maybe "BUBBLES' TROUBLES". I want a full sit-down chat, pictures, family album, the lot. A chimp's eye view o'the King of Pop. Go get 'im, don't let me down.'

I've been at it an hour so far, and to my certain knowledge there have been at least four Bubbles. Each and every charming chimp was replaced once he grew out of nappies and started masturbating indiscriminately – something which would, one might think, have endeared him to Jackson rather than caused offence.

It breaks down like this: first Bubbles is probably dead. Second Bubbles is in a sanctuary in Florida, and his owner refuses to expose him to 'media intrusion'. Third Bubbles is doing tricks in a circus somewhere in Europe that I can't track down, fourth Bubbles is living in an animal trainer's house in Texas, still masturbating indiscriminately, but the trainer is prepared to let us do a piece for a price.

Much is made, these days, of chequebook journalism and how the dreadful media offer vast sums for stories, contaminating our society with greed and propagating a fame-focused culture which sexualizes our children and blah blah blah. The truth is that, yes, the media can be accused of all those things, but a far worse culprit is *people*. A person you meet one to one is sensible, sane and entirely reasonable. People en masse are tribalist xenophobes out for what they can get. *People* buy Coldplay records, *people* voted for Hitler. People can't be trusted.

People, more often than not, are contaminated with greed long before we get to them. I spend more time telling them we're not paying than I do telling them we will, or at the very least that the story they've rung up with is only worth six pars and £75 rather than the thousands they were expecting. We all have budgets, you know.

Bubbles may be a notch down the evolutionary tree, but he has grasped the basic concept of media manipulation and has demanded £20,000, copy approval, his choice of headline, and is refusing to do any pictures.

I reread the email from his trainer, who among a long list of demands, said: 'Bubbles is very concerned about misrepresentation and would like his lawyer to suggest amendments to your contract in order to protect his image and professional reputation . . .'

Just then another missive dropped into my inbox with the annoying squeaky sound I thought was funny once, and now can't switch off.

It was Twatface, saying, 'I miss you. Can we talk?'

'About Glastonbury?' I asked him. He said 'she' had been expecting to go and he was sorry because he knew I wouldn't like it. 'Didn't go well, if it makes you feel better.'

I replied that it didn't, and asked what he thought he was playing at, taking my sleeping bag for the event. He insisted they still weren't having sex and bizarrely blamed it on the fact her dad was a vicar and furious with her.

Then he said, 'Are you around tonight? Maybe we could meet for a chat.'

Vicar? This was interesting news. I forgot about Bubbles and instead ferreted through the clergy lists and electoral roll to find her father's parish. Family stinking rich and much posher than Twatface's. So he's telling the truth about something, for once. I decided to ring and ask him over for dinner – it can't be too hard to be nice to each other, can it?

He was obviously on the office phone because his mobile clicked through to voicemail. And then, without thinking about it, I'd typed in his security code to listen to his messages. Yes, technically it's illegal and it's phone-hacking, but if it's your husband and he's maybe lying to you, you're allowed, right? Morally?

Let me be clear – I've never been asked by any editor to hack a phone, nor worked on a story where I thought it was the only option. It is not a practice as rife as polit-icians and other enemies of the tabloids would have you believe, and certainly not in the decade or so I've been in Fleet Street. There are thousands of journalists in my trade and only a handful of them will ever be linked to the practice. Celebrities knew about it twenty years ago and it should be easy enough to dodge if you want to – get a pay-as-you-go phone, change your PIN, delete your messages. Or alternatively you can keep your nose clean, and then it doesn't matter if a journalist hears your messages. I picked up how to do it not from Fleet Street colleagues but from the phone company, because when I was abroad I had to dial my own security code to get my voicemails, just like millions of their customers did.

There's no defence in law for phone-hacking, no pub-lic interest case to be made for it. Personally, I think it can be justified in some instances, along with a range of other minor crimes. Trespass, theft, speeding offences, impersonating people I shouldn't – I have done and will do any and all of these things, and a few more, if the story justifies it. I'd hack a phone, too, if I thought it was the only way to prove a truth that needed to be known.

I'm not doing anything so high and mighty here, though. This is just a cheating husband and a suspicious wife. But I don't believe, were anyone to present the evidence to a police officer, that he'd want to bother with the paperwork. I don't reckon a jury would think it so dreadful they had to convict, and if they did I'm reasonably sure the judge would not do much more than shrug. It's a crime and a betrayal of trust, but so is looking at a loved one's text messages and emails, and how many of us have done that?

How many, moreover, would *not* do it in my shoes? That very afternoon a person I only half know and who works in the same place as Fatty had sent me a text saying: 'Overheard a phone call this end – apparently she's buying SOMEONE steak and strawberries for dinner and eggs and bacon for breakfast.' I didn't much like being told, especially as the reason for telling me was presumably just to stir up trouble which I was going to feel the worst of. But on the other hand he was claiming they weren't having sex and asking to see me.

So there I was calling Twatface, and – he always had the same PIN code for everything, he knew mine and I knew his – when it clicked through to voicemail my fingers tapped in the code before I'd realized what I was doing – without thought, or plan or even temptation. My first instinct was to hang up but then I heard:

'You have three. Saved. Messages.'

Ooh.

There was one from her about dinner and breakfast, another telling him she loved him, and one from his mother asking if he was bringing me up to visit the outlaws this weekend.

My stunned fingers hit the wrong key, and a message in my ear told me I had successfully changed the security code. Bugger. Then another squeak, and more demands from Bubbles' publicist about syndication rights and an enquiry as to which Texas-based freelance I was going to send round to interview him – there are some, apparently, he does not like. I ignored it and emailed Fifi:

<From: Foxy, 12.35 p.m. To: Jones, Fifi
I've just listened to his messages. He's moved in with Fatty, but tells me he wants to come over and talk. What do I do?>

As I redialled Twatface to reset his code, she replied:

<From: Jones, Fifi, 12.37 p.m.
To: Foxy
Maybe he's lying to her more than to you?>

I pinged back:

<From: Foxy, 12.39 p.m.
To: Jones, Fifi
Is that seriously a best-case scenario? That my lying husband doesn't lie to me as much as he does to some tart?>

Then Twatface emailed me, demanding to know whether I'd been listening to his messages.

Then Fifi:

<From: Jones, Fifi 12.41 p.m.
To: Foxy
Did you realize you copied him on that first email?>

WHAAAAAAAT? I looked back through my emails . . .
shit, bollocks and balls!

To Twatface I typed: 'Ha ha JOKE. Get over yourself.'
And to Fifi: 'I'm pretending it was a joke. I'm so busted.'

A minute later Twatface sent me an email saying he'd
ring the police and get me two years in jail unless I agreed
to meet up and agree a divorce. He added he wasn't
threatening me but would advise having a quick glance at
section one of the Regulation of Investigatory Powers Act
2000.

'Well, that's something of a change of tone,' I thought.
Speechless, I forwarded it to Fifi.

<To: Foxy, 12.46 p.m.
From: Jones, Fifi
Pompous arse. Like it even registers against what he
did to you. You totally have the moral high ground!
Besides, aren't you having us round to drink his
booze next weekend? You can't let him ruin it!>

<To: Foxy, 12.46 p.m.
From: Bubbles
Bubbles is concerned about how he will appear to
his fans. He would like you to send him a list of
questions for approval or he will be forced to pull
out of the deal. In this instance he will accept a
£10,000 kill fee.>

Right, I've had it with this flipping monkey now. I told Twatface he could meet me for a chat on Wednesday and to Fifi I said: 'OK, drinks are on. After all, it's my thirtieth and that booze he left behind needs to be drunk.'

<From: Foxy 12.52 p.m.
To: Bubbles
We're not going to pay £20,000 to an ape with ideas above his station. We'll pay £2,000, and for that we will want a full chat with YOU, not the ape, pictures of you with the ape, and something interesting about Michael Jackson. And no wanking, or you can forget it.>

<From: Bubbles, 12.56 p.m
To: Foxy
£2,000 is fine. Send your reporter round tomorrow. Bubbles was addicted to methadone when they dropped him off. Sorry to mess you around.>

Now all I have to do is issue Twatface an ultimatum – Fatty or me, for ever. Easy.

DAY THIRTY-FIVE

THERE is one source of joy on the horizon, amid the spectres of divorce, emotional breakdown and redundancy – Tania Banks is in trouble.

She's been known as 'Teflon Tania' since she joined, because no matter how bad she is, trouble never sticks to her. She's one of those reporters who gives the rest of us a bad name.

She's so competitive she makes great white sharks look timid, makes up whole stories with casual disregard for the consequences, and is a blatant byline bandit – sticking her name on someone else's story after they've done all the work – to steal their glory when it's published. Last year she entered other people's tales into the industry awards under her own name.

There was a byline incident this week, after I'd spent days standing up a Beckham tip. I'd found it, checked it, and written it. Except Elliot had asked Banks, inexplicably, to go to the agent for a comment. Instead of filing it as an extra line, she picked up my story from the newsdesk 'basket' in the computer system, cut and pasted my words from 'FSFBeckham', and put it in a new file she called 'TBBeckham', sticking her byline on it. The only changes were a stock denial from the agent and Banks' name perched smugly on top. I didn't even get an 'additional reporting' credit.

Luckily someone saw she'd burgled my byline, and changed it back. But Banks was less than happy, and was seen stamping around the newsroom after the first edition dropped, demanding to know who was responsible for this 'discourtesy' on 'her story'.

This morning I had an email from her on the topic:

<From: Banks, Tania 9.47 a.m.
To: Foxy
Thanks for your help on my Beckham story. I just thought you should know that technically Victoria should be referred to as a fashion designer now, not ex-Spice-Girls singer. Pretty basic mistake, but luckily I spotted it before it got into the paper and embarrassed you.
Regards, Tania>

For the past week she's been in Cumbria trying – and failing – to buy up a swine-flu fatality. Apparently the family politely refused to do a story, then tearfully requested she leave, and ended up ringing the police. Banks kept going at them like the Black Knight until finally, locals threw up roadblocks and refused to let her into the village. The local chief inspector's been on the phone to The Editor, who told Bish to call her back.

'Fire up the broomstick and get yersel' 'ome,' he said abruptly to Banks down the phone. Then he banged down the receiver and announced to the world at large: 'Bluddy waste o'time that were n'all. All she did was piss off The Reader, and it's not like we've that many to spare.' Then he stamped out for a Woodbine and a fume.

Which just proves that journos like Tania are as disliked by their colleagues as they are by the public. Not that she seems to care – now that we're no longer friends I can see she has the moral code of a hyena, only without the sentimentality. She's far better suited to be friends with Twatface than me.

But being unpopular, when you're a hack, is water off a duck's back. It's like being the fat kid at school – you get used to being the last one picked for anyone's team, and the person who makes everyone else feel uncomfortable. We lead moral outrage against others, so it's only fair that when the finger of blame points at us we have to take our share of the flak. Tin hats on, heads down, and press on, as my granddad used to say.

After Princess Diana died I went to work with my heart in my mouth for a day or so, expecting to be lynched – not helped by the fact that the local newspaper I worked on at the time had its name emblazoned across our rusty old pool cars – but the righteous outrage at the paparazzi chasing her faded a bit when we all discovered the driver was drunk and the daft bint wasn't wearing a seatbelt.

That's not going to happen with the phone-hacking story. At first it was all about celebrities and politicians having their voicemails listened to by tabloid hacks, and everyone involved was thought so little of by the general public that it seemed to be of only passing interest. It was investigated by anti-terror police, who had more important things to do than check D-list celebrity phone bills from years ago. Most of us – journos and civilians – just shrugged at the idea of people who lived off public exposure complaining about press intrusion.

Then it was revealed that years ago a private detective employed by a newspaper had hacked the voicemails of a missing schoolgirl and some of the messages were deleted, giving her family false hope that she was still alive, when in fact she'd been snatched off the street by a paedophile, murdered and dumped in a wood. There can never be a reasonable explanation for listening to them – the morality of whoever decided to do that is so far off the scale it's not even in our solar system.

That killer went on to kill again, largely because of flaws in the police investigation, but the revelation that phone-hacking was involved in those early days of the schoolgirl's disappearance turned a gossipy Fleet Street scandal into a national disgrace. The private detective responsible for the eavesdropping – who earned six-figure sums for his work – wrote everything down in notebooks seized by a new police unit set up to investigate. The explosive contents sent the story around the world, wiped billions off share prices and led to the closure of that newspaper, summarily sacking hundreds of innocent staff and ancillary workers. The tale has spread out to take in the government, almost everyone in public life, and dozens of ordinary people who became newsworthy for a while and were targeted by a handful of bad hacks with bigger budgets than they had brain space.

Now (and forgive me if I rub my hands a little here) Tania Banks has got herself involved. There was a tale today in one of the snoresheets that when Banks used to work on another paper a few years ago one of her stories had been got through hacking.

Hacking, it must be said, of *my* voicemails.

What happened was this. A female soap star had a story for sale. Although she had been a staple of family viewing for years, she had a drink problem and an extremely colourful love life. Her lovers included politicians, famous businessmen, and a kinky children's television presenter. The actress had a taste for white wine before

87

noon, and had just been thrown out of her last home for missing the rent, so decided to make a bit of money.

She had gone first to a big newspaper with a huge budget. Tania Banks was working there at the time, and promised her a five-figure sum for the yarn. The soap star signed a contract, told Tania everything she could remember, dug out some photographs, and was surprised to find on deadline that the newspaper wanted to pay her only half of what Banks had agreed.

The actress had pulled out of the deal, torn up the contract, and taken her story to a smaller, poorer newspaper, where I had the task of babysitting her until we published the story for even less money. She was nice enough, but interesting to deal with after lunchtime. On the day we ran the story Banks' paper did the same, a trick known as a 'spoiler'. It had ruined our exclusive and caused a great stink, with an inquest headed by Bish about how our story could have leaked.

Up until now I had always assumed it was the soap star's fault. She was desperate for cash and might have earned something for giving Tania's paper a heads-up; and was, anyway, so unreliable that after her third bottle she could well have spoken to Tania just to taunt her about the story going elsewhere.

But now the actress had been told by the cops she may have been hacked, and had engaged lawyers to sue for as much money as she could get. She was, rather marvellously, quoted as saying: 'I am appalled that a tabloid newspaper has violated my privacy.'

Never mind that she'd sold that same privacy twice over. And never mind that I could now recall numerous times when she'd phoned me drunk and angry because I hadn't returned her messages, which means that if she was telling the truth then whoever was responsible was probably hacking my phone, too, and deleting them. Never mind that if you dance with the devil you're bound to get burned.

I was not about to go running to lawyers or trying to find out if someone had hacked my voicemail. To tell the truth, I'd be offended if they hadn't. There was no point taking Tania to task because by and large the reporters were unaware of hacking, which was outsourced to the private detective. I changed my PIN, deleted my messages – and shrugged it off. What had happened wasn't great, but I didn't care that much.

If you deal with newspapers, work for them, sell your story, or maybe pose for paparazzi pictures and cut a deal for some of the money when they flog them, then it's all part of the game, a step in the dance. Murder victims and innocents should be treated a little more kindly because they're involved only by misfortune, not choice. The average hack's moral compass may swing a little crazily some days, but so long as it points the right way 90 per cent of the time they're all right in my book, and no worse than most of humanity. A phone-hacker's not a Nazi.

But needless to say, if Tania Banks' reputation gets a little more tarnished then I won't complain. One day she's bound to embarrass the paper so badly that Bish will have to fire her – or at least, I hope she will.

Leaning back in his chair, surrounded by his expenses forms and those of 650-odd MPs, Porter greeted the news of her potential disgrace with glee.

'Marvellous,' he grinned. 'Maybe Teflon Tania's arrogant reign is coming to an end. Can't wait. And you'll LOVE it if a fatty got the bullet, wouldn't you? You're so fattist!'

I leaned against his desk, regarding the pile of paperwork. 'Of course. Wouldn't you be in my situation? Are you still doing MPs' second-home claims? Hasn't it all been done to death?'

Porter spluttered in mock-horror. 'My God, I'm not writing a story! Far too early in the day for that. I'm comparing my expenses claims with those of our politicians to see how I'm doing in the fraud stakes. So far Westminster is winning, the greedy, grasping, two-faced bastards! There's no way I can hope to match them for avarice or cunning, although I shall give it a good try. Anyway what's happening with your idiot husband? Come crawling back to you yet?'

I shook my head. 'Not really. He wants to talk but he's still seeing Fatty. He says he's not, and then one of my mates sees them at Glastonbury, or bumps into them in a pub. I don't know what to think. I've got to make a decision somehow, but there's nothing to base it on.'

Porter cleared a patch on his desk for me to sit on, shoving papers out of the way and binning an elderly banana skin. I plonked myself down and he put his feet up on a corner of the desk, leaning back in his chair and steepling his fingers like the Old Man of the Newsroom. There is nothing a political reporter enjoys more than telling other people what to do.

'You have plenty to base it on. Everything, in fact. How he's behaved, and what he's done since.'

'But I haven't – he never used to be like this,' I protested. 'We'd bought the house, and he had a new job, and it was really stressful. He just reacted badly. I know him, he wouldn't seek it out. He just let himself be led because he's weak.'

Porter looked at me over his fingertips. 'You've been through an horrific experience – and months of hell before that. You're strong, surrounded by friends, and you're pulling yourself out. He's weak, indecisive, and floundering in his own mess. It goes a long way to show you the mettle of the man. And it seems to me you don't have a lot in common with each other, if you can react in such different ways.'

His words echoed in my head as I left the office, echoing in time with my high heels on the concrete steps of the underground car park – 'the mettle of the man, the mettle of the man, the mettle of the man' – until I was back at my car, parked in its usual spot, and saw Twatface standing next to it. 'Hi,' he said, stubbing out a cigarette. 'You wanted to talk?'

We got in the car and I stared out of the windscreen at nothing much at all, thinking how acrid the lingering cigarette odour was. He always used to smell of soap.

'How are you?' he asked. 'I'm sorry I threatened you about all that phone-hacking stuff. I was just, you know, upset. I'd listen to your voice messages if I could. Anyway, sorry. I didn't mean it. I was just wondering, you know, if you'd seen a lawyer . . . ?'

I looked at him. 'Have you?'

'Yes, she was really good, actually, but bloody expensive. She said you should get one, and it'd make everything easier, and we can divorce in maybe six weeks or so.'

'Six weeks?' I was stunned he could be so certain, and so ruthless. 'Is that what you want?'

'What else can we do? I mean, that doesn't sound like I meant it to. What else could we do, do you think? I'd like to know how you feel. Might we be able to sort it out?'

91

'I think,' I said, picking my words carefully, 'that divorce is the easiest thing to do. If we tried to sort it out – if we said we wanted to try again, to fix things – that would be harder. It's not impossible, but it's a lot of hard work. Is it something you're prepared to do?'

'Define "hard".'

'Well, obviously we would have to go to counselling.'

'Right. Then could I move back in? Maybe this week?'

'NO! Bloody hell, no way! You're already living elsewhere; the best thing would be for you to carry on doing that, and for us to see each other once or twice a week to find out how things go, with a view to you moving back later.'

'Right. Well, that seems sensible. It's really expensive paying my share of the mortgage and renting a flat, though.'

'You could afford it fine if your wages didn't disappear every time you went to the pub,' I said. 'And you should have thought of that before you took your trousers down.'

I paused and thought, then spoke more slowly, feeling my way through the thoughts which had flooded my mind for the past few weeks.

'We need to learn to trust each other again if we're to have a functioning marriage, but more important is the fact that you did this to start with. I think you would have to figure out why that was, and fix it so it doesn't happen again.'

'Oh, so it's all my fault now, is it?'

'That's not what I said. But you can't argue with the fact that there have been problems, and now her . . . I accept my faults, I know I nagged you and worried and shouted all the time, but a lot of that was because I was scared of what you were doing. I was so worried about you that it never occurred to me that I was miserable. But I was.

Before we go to counselling to fix our marriage, I think you need to go to counselling to fix you.'

He looked blankly at me as I spoke, then immediately acted as if I hadn't. 'Right. I see. Well, I need to think about what you've said. Can I see you at the weekend?'

After weeks of being in limbo, unsure whether I was married, single, reconciling or divorcing, I decided I was fed up of dancing to his tune, waiting for him to try to mend the hurt. He was doing what he always did: following the path of least resistance and relying on me to make the decisions – which he would only stick to if they suited. I'd had enough. He had caused this problem, and he was going to have to decide what to do about it.

'No. You can't think about it. You either want to be married to me, or you don't. You either want to fix it, or you don't. How we do that is secondary. You only have to decide if you want to fix it.'

'Of course I want to fix it – my parents want me to, all our friends want me to – I just don't know if I can. If I do the counselling, do we definitely get back together?' he asked, as though haggling with a car salesman for a better deal.

'I'm not going to promise anything. You decide what you want, work at it for a bit, and then we'll see if it's working. But if we take the hard road, then we have to fight together. I'm not doing it on my own, not just putting up with everything and hoping it won't happen again. You need to prove you've learned from this as much as I do.'

He sighed, looking at his watch. 'I really do need to think about it, I can't decide this now.'

'You've had weeks,' I told him, my voice rising. 'Weeks in which you've had plenty of time to swan around town with her while I sit in misery wondering what's happening. You've had enough time. If you want me then you have to dump her, right now. The only way I'll believe it is if you ring her on speakerphone, while I listen, and tell her it's over. You can do it now, or get out of the car and we'll get divorced. Take the hard road or the easy road – but you have to take it right now. I'm not waiting any more.'

I had said it before my brain had noticed what I was doing. But once it was out I was relieved, glad to have reached a fork in the road. Then his phone rang and he looked at the number before hitting the red button to send it to voicemail. He told me: 'I need to think, I can't decide right now. I'm late for meeting a friend in Westminster. I have to go. I'll think about it, I promise.'

And with that he got out of the car and walked away, shoulders slumped. My heart in my boots, I watched him go with dry eyes and realized that no decision was still a decision – I was not something he was prepared to fight for. I drove home, then, knowing he would be on the Tube, I rang his number. It clicked straight through to voicemail and I keyed in his PIN code.

There she was, saying she was just leaving work, would see him in twenty minutes and had bought salmon for dinner. The 'I love you' at the end was particularly awful to hear.

But it was all I needed. Tears pouring down my cheeks, I rang the merry solicitor, Maurice, and booked an appointment to sign the paperwork and get things started. Somehow, even though I knew it was the easy path, it felt very hard indeed.

DAY THIRTY-NINE

IT all started so well.

My thirtieth birthday. A tiny, slinky frock. Vast quantities of soon-to-be-ex-husband's booze. What could possibly go dreadfully, humiliatingly, awfully wrong?

When I woke up this morning I lifted my head off the pillow and presumed someone had suspended a slab of granite six inches above the bed. It was the only explanation for the sudden pain rampaging around my skull. After some moments of extreme agony I decided life would be better with my head in the toilet, and dragged myself down the hall and into the bathroom.

Where I stopped in the doorway from shock, hangover completely forgotten.

The toilet seat was up.

Now, this hadn't happened for some time. Twatface, for all his faults, usually managed to put it down. In recent weeks everything in my house had been de-boyed: no more CDs of miserable music, no more socks on the floor. The house is a boy-free zone, and I love it like that.

But there was a boy in it now. A boy who had left the toilet seat up. And I was naked.

With a sense of foreboding, I turned around and crept quietly back to my bedroom. I peeked through the door. There, in the marital bed, was a head covered in short, curly blond locks. I don't know any blond men. Arse.

Back to the bathroom. Sat down for a bit on the toilet, resting my forehead on the cold porcelain of the sink next to it, waiting for the nausea to pass. One thing was clear – I had to get rid of this person. The thought of having a boy in the building was making my palms sweat. I was actually scared, and it wasn't just the hangover. Men are scary, men hurt you, men are stronger and you don't know if they might flip out and hit you. I certainly didn't know anything about this one. But how the hell was I going to get rid of him? I'd known Twatface since I was twenty-three, and hadn't been round the block much before that. I had zero experience of booting people out after one-night stands. What's the etiquette? Call them a cab? Cook them breakfast? Or, the way I was feeling, vomit on them and scream 'TOILET SEAT! OUT!'

I gathered my strength, wrapped myself in a dressing gown and crawled downstairs to make a cup of tea. Everything looks better with a cup of tea. I put my head around the living-room door. There were mini-sausage rolls and jelly all over the carpet, a set of still-flashing disco lights on one of the bookshelves, a pile of half-opened presents and a gunked-up chocolate fountain on a table – and a pair of tiny feet sticking out from under a duvet on the floor.

'Fifi?' I enquired of the heap. It groaned Welshly.

'Tea,' it said.

I made us both a mug and brought it in. A hand snaked out from under the duvet and took it back under the covers. I heard a slurp and another groan.

'Fi,' I whispered. 'There's a boy in my room.'

'Faberluss,' she rasped.

'How do I get rid of him?'

Cough. 'Tea. Cab. Ow.'

Right. I could manage that. I made another mug, took it upstairs and put it by the bed. 'There's some tea,' I said.

'Oh thanks,' he said, rolled over and looked at me with a smile. Oh, it's Tim from the sports desk. I remember now.

There was some chit-chat. We sipped our tea, not knowing quite what to say. Then there was a stamping sound like a herd of bison coming up the stairs, which stopped just outside the door. There was a tap and it swung open, to reveal tiny Fifi in a sequinned frock, false eyelashes awry and back-combed hair stood up like she'd been plugged into the mains.

'What am I doing on your floor, izzeht?'

I was at a loss, so Tim said: 'You fell asleep about four o'clock in the morning, and we put the duvet over you.'

'Oh. Right. Faberluss.' Then she took in the scene – me in bed with a boy. 'Did you just bring me some tea?'

'Yes. We had a conversation.'

'Don't remember. Oh, my head. Can you call me a cab, lovely? Sorry to intrude, izzeht.' And she stamped back downstairs again.

'For someone so small she walks very loudly,' said Tim.

'Hmm,' I said, dialling a cab firm. Ten minutes later it had pulled up and they were both dressed. Fifi, bless her, grabbed Tim and shoved him out of the door. I gave them both a peck on the cheek and then slumped, relieved. Unable to face the clean-up straight away – there was an unpleasant odour of spilt beer from every direction – I went to take a shower.

Pulling off the robe as I walked into the bathroom, I caught a glimpse of myself in the mirror over the sink and stopped dead for the second time that morning. The hair, the face, the eyes I would worry about later. But why

97

oh why were there two large, red Xs over both of my nipples? WHY?

As I stared, the memories came flooding back.

The party had a James Bond fancy dress theme. There had to be a theme, because the birthday year had a '0' in it. And while fancy dress is usually a pain in the arse, I reasoned, a Bond theme meant the boys could wear a DJ (yum) and girls could glam up. What's not to like?

Food was laid out in the living room, with fresh strawberries and a chocolate fountain. Twatface's booze had been pulled out of its hiding places – bottle after bottle of fine whites, tasty Bordeaux, and Italian Prosecco by the case. I bought some fruity pink pop and a few bottles of vodka, and a roulette wheel was set up on the kitchen table. All my friends and dozens of people from work were invited, and as far as I was concerned they could trash the place. The house was a wreck, anyway.

I went as Shirley Eaton, the girl painted in gold from *Goldfinger*. Despite the recent and rapid weight loss there was no way I was going to cover myself in gold paint and strut about wearing only a thong, so instead I covered myself in a slinky gold minidress and coated my extremities in fake tan and shimmery leg make-up.

The dress was backless so a bra was impossible; but to avoid embarrassing nippleness I carefully stuck two bits of tit tape in a cross over each boob to keep them in.

People turned up, looking glamorous as hell. The cricket lads arrived in dinner jackets, Nancy came as an Indian assassin from *Octopussy*, and Buff Arnold covered himself in green paint and told everyone he was legendary Bond producer 'Chubby Broccoli'. Bridget came in a long black frock, while Porter turned up in red braces and a set of fake teeth as Jaws. Tim from the sports desk was Blond Bond. I made a lot of pink pop and vodka drinks, and drank most of them.

The Prosecco bubbled, the chocolate fountain flowed, the music thumped. For the first time in almost six years, thanks to Twatface's absence, I was able to throw a party without someone constantly trying to switch my music off and put on Nick Cave instead. We got to enjoy musical legends like S Club 7, Abba and 5ive. When the opening bars of 'The One And Only' thundered out at about midnight, Bridget – by now more than a couple of sheets to the wind – screamed 'CHESNEEEEEEEYYYY!' and began whirling like a dervish. I loved it. It was freedom. It was my music, my party, my idea of fun. When my personal theme tune, 'Keep On Movin' came on, for once I didn't worry someone was going to turn it down or moan. Instead I turned it up and shouted the words as loud as I could.

My recall of what happened after that is patchy. Everyone left about 3 or 4 a.m. As the last people piled into a cab, Blond Bond turned to me in the hallway and asked if he could stay. We checked the living room, discovered Fifi curled up on a cushion, threw a cover over her and retired upstairs.

We lay in bed and talked for a bit, then kissed and . . . well. You know. Most of it's a drunken haze, but I remember thinking I had to keep the lights off, because I couldn't bear the thought of him seeing me naked, telling myself 'you've got to break your duck', and that being really, really drunk would probably help get over the born-again virgin hurdle. It didn't help with the keeping awake hurdle, and that was the problem occupying my mind as I lay back and gazed blurrily at the ceiling and Tim started kissing me all over.

'Just keep your eyes open and make encouraging noises,' I told myself. 'Falling asleep would appear rude.' Then he raised his head.

'Have you got something on your boobs?' he asked.

'Hmm? Oh . . .'

I was so drunk I'd forgotten all about the tape, and had merrily undressed without giving it a second's thought. Now tit tape is very thin and papery, and sticks to you with the same persistence as NASA's favourite superglue. After eight hours of body heat the stuff had bonded to my skin on a molecular level, and me trying to peel it off when absolutely spannered must have been like watching a blind dog chasing its own tail.

There was I, drunker than George Best on a late-night chat show, picking furiously at my own tits in pitch darkness at 5 a.m. with more vodka in my bloodstream than actual blood. And all the while trying to make small talk with someone I barely knew about how all of this was really funny and happens ALL the time, honest, every girl I know does the same thing . . .

I must have been at it for five solid minutes. Eventually I found the ends of the tape, ripped it off along with several unnoticed layers of epidermis, and Tim carried on with the business at hand.

And now here I was looking at this creature in the mirror, a sexually promiscuous woman approaching middle age, with bloodshot eyes and an ability to skin her own boobs.

Please God, let him have been so drunk too that he won't remember it. Please.

When I rang Fi, she stopped laughing long enough to say: 'That's faberluss. You've broken the seal, you're over Twatface. I love Tit-Tape Tim. You're only thirty once, izzeht?'

But then she doesn't have to see him in the office tomorrow.

:-(((((((((((

(But only because there isn't an emoticon for burying your head in your hands or hitting it against the wall.)

DAY FORTY-FOUR

WELL, work this week has been fun – running to the loo every hour to reapply Germolene to my wounded boobs while avoiding Tit-Tape Tim from the sports desk out of sheer embarrassment.

It would be a lot easier if I didn't bump into him everywhere I go. It's like he's homing. Go to the canteen for a cuppa – he's there. Go to the paper shop – he's there. I would think he was following me except he looks more embarrassed than I feel every time it happens, so I think it's just one of those horrible tricks of fate. We've worked together for years, and only chat at the Christmas bash, and now, suddenly, it's like the world keeps tilting to throw us in each another's path while we try to scramble pink-faced out of the way.

I got in the lift on Wednesday, late as usual, and just as the doors were closing he snuck in between them. We recognized each other, smiled politely, then said nothing for the slow grind up to our floor, staring at the blank metal doors in a hot blush, willing them to open so we could both scoot out in opposite directions and pretend we hadn't been ignoring someone we'd had drunken congress with only a few days previously.

Ick, I HATE this! I mean, I worked with Twatface when we got together, but that was love, and so it was nice to see each other all the time. This is hot and uncomfortable, and makes me cringe in shame and want to crawl under a rock. Maybe if I'd had more experience of these things I could be more nonchalant about it, or would it be just as bad?

It feels very weird to have slept with someone other than my husband. Adulterous. All right, he's doing the same, and we're separated, and probably going to get divorced, but yet it's odd. Strange to wake up next to one man when you know your husband is waking up somewhere else in the same city with another woman. It's not how it was supposed to be, and makes me feel disjointed, like I've put my shoes on the wrong feet. I doubt the Archbishop of Canterbury would have a problem with my having slept with Tim (although I'd be interested to hear his views on the tit-tape debacle), but there is still a low-level, niggling sense of wrongness that I cannot overcome.

And the bed, of course, the marital bed. It feels empty without Twatface there, so I just curl up in a corner of it, trying not to fall into the hole he left behind.

I had just had a run-in with Tim at the water cooler – 'Oh, hi', 'Morning', 'Scuse me', 'Of course' – and had got back to my desk where I was fanning myself with the *Wellygraph,* hoping the sexual humiliation would soon pass, when 'What a wanker!' rang out. I sent it to answerphone, telling myself I really ought to change the ringtone.

This was his message. Said in a thin, mopey, sad little voice.

'Hello, you. Um. How was your party? Err. Is it true you might be made redundant? I miss looking out of the train window and seeing the river on the way to work. Um. I miss the house. There was a story today, too, about Venice being flooded again; it made me think of our holiday there a couple of months ago. That was fun, wasn't it? Anyway. It would be nice to talk to you, you know, if you like. Um. Bye then.'

He sounded down, sad, lost. I felt sorry for him. Maybe he wants me back? At that very moment an email from him plopped into my inbox, in which he complained about falling down a Tube escalator, cutting himself with a razor, and wearing a stinky suit. He said he'd found a flat to move into in a few weeks' time but was tired of relying on friends and wanted to move back in to the house. 'See you there at 7?' he finished, rather peremptorily.

Wordlessly, I turned my screen round so Bridget could read it. Her advice was simple. 'Don't. He'd change the locks as soon as you were out. Or move his fat fancy-piece in.'

I emailed him back and told him to meet me in the Cutty Sark at 7 for a chat.

I spent the rest of the day brooding, turning it all over in my head. Not him moving in, that's not going to happen, but just him, his phone calls, the late-night texts, the worry. The constant drip-drip of 'Is he with her? What's he thinking, what's he doing? What would he think of what I'm doing?' which makes my mind turn like water on a prayer wheel, producing a never-ending stream of permutations. And the certain, rock-solid knowledge – thanks to more than enough stories I've written on this very topic – that if they cheat on you once, they'll cheat again. Plus if he's falling down the escalators he's been hitting the bottle, his habitual escape route from worry. It's all such a mess.

At the pub he was waiting for me in the garden, at the bottom of his first pint although I was only five minutes late. We said hello and he lit a cigarette, his hands shaking really badly. What on earth was that about? I wondered. Was he nervous?

We talked about boring stuff – the house insurance, council tax – and he complimented me on my dress. He said he needed to pick some stuff up. But he kept trembling, looking at his feet, fidgeting nervously, talking too fast. He asked about moving in, and I laughed, said there was no way. He smirked nervously and said he'd go to court. I told him to feel free, but considering there'd been violent rows no judge was going to order me to let him back in the house. Then he asked if I'd seen a lawyer yet to start the divorce, and I said I had, but needed to give the guy money up front so was waiting until I got paid.

Then he said: 'If you don't start the divorce, I will.'

Me: 'On what grounds, exactly?'

'Your unreasonable behaviour.'

I laughed so hard I nearly fell off my chair. Then he said it again, and I told him I'd fight it, and that seeing as he was earning £50,000 a year sat on his arse in the newsroom of a top newspaper he could more than afford a flat and let me have the house.

He said: 'The flat's quite cheap, but it's not very nice. It's in Walthamstow and four of the neighbours were arrested for running a bomb factory last week.'

'Ha,' I told him. 'Maybe they'll drop one. This would all be a lot easier if you died.'

He looked horrified.

'It's true,' I told him, 'although a horrid thing to think. When I walk in from the car park in the morning I reach for my phone to ring you, and have to remind myself I can't do that any more. The same thing happens at lunchtime, or when I'm on a doorstep, and when I go home. There's a big gap where you used to be, just like when someone dies. Except there isn't a death certificate, and mourning, and a funeral and a recognized way of going about things.

'Instead the corpse keeps jerking back to life, and is shagging a woman who is, shall we say, jolly. I feel like I've been bereaved: the pain and loss is the same, but instead of remembering someone with love there's just hurt and hatred and it feels like you're trying to drag me into the grave with you. Instead of mourning, I have to fight you. It would be much easier if you died. I could think nice things about you. All the suffering would be done with. Instead I'm in pain and I know there's only more to come.'

His face was white. He took a drag of his third cigarette; he was smoking much more than he had done when we were together. 'I suppose you're right,' he said. 'I hadn't thought how it felt for you. If it's any easier, I have to stop myself ringing you, too.'

'You've never thought for a second how I feel about anything, or you would never have behaved like you did.' With that, I gathered my things and left the pub. He followed me in silence. Outside he stopped and turned to me.

'I do miss you, you know,' he said. 'Do you miss me?'

'Miss you?' I thought about it. 'I don't miss *you*, no. I miss having a husband. I miss talking about what we'd call our children, and where we'll go on holiday next year. I miss having someone to run my bath when I've had a long day, sit on the toilet and talk to me. I miss cuddling on the sofa and watching the telly, I miss having someone to cook for, or shave my legs for. I miss having someone to put their hands on my tummy when I have period pains, or let me warm my feet up on them when I'm cold. I miss having a companion, planning your birthday, having an extended family. I miss the dreams we had. But no, I don't miss you. I don't miss talking to your answerphone, I don't miss wondering what time you'll come home, I don't miss apologizing to my friends when you're drunk, I don't miss checking up on you, and I don't miss worrying what you'll do if I make you angry. I don't miss *you* at all.'

Tears had poured silently down my face as I spoke. He stood and stared, shocked.

'I'm sorry,' he said quietly.

I turned and walked away, and didn't look back. The tears kept falling as I walked home, and I decided it was time to cut off contact. It was too painful, and it didn't get us anywhere. No more emails, no texts, nothing. From now on it would be through lawyers, because I was simply not strong enough to do it on my own. I decided to make an appointment with the solicitor and start things moving.

It was time to move into the centre of the bed.

DAY FIFTY-ONE

THERE are days when you despair, when everything in the world seems not just to be against you, but actively out to get you. And you start to wonder whether killing all of humanity might not be a bad idea.

Evil Elliot has been spectacularly insane this week. He's one of those bosses that's quiet but deadly, an unpleasant little playground bully in his treatment of staff but still, somehow, incredibly polite to them – which only makes it worse.

A typical phone call from him to a reporter on the road will start off with, 'It's Elliot. Can you talk?' before his clipped, public-school tones slice you carefully into delicate little pieces. 'Where are you? What are you doing? Have you found his sister? Why haven't you rung in to tell us what you're doing? Are you aware that the *London Evening Post* have already spoken to him on page thirty-four of their late edition? Why haven't you seen the *London Evening Post*? I don't care if you are in Shropshire. Find one. Go back and knock the door again. Rewrite the copy, it's dreadful. And when you've done that I want you to get to Norfolk before first edition. It shouldn't take even you that long, it's only an inch away on the map. Don't come back until you make it work.'

I have, in the past, had to file five different versions of a two-thousand-word spread for Elliot before he was satisfied. He is just as hateful to everyone, and a terrible brown-nose to The Editor. He's got family on the company board, so is secure yet chippy in his job, safe but resentful as Bish's deputy. He never drinks, never has a girlfriend or boyfriend, and is stretched tighter than a drum. On Tuesday he made a trainee cry, on Wednesday the news desk secretary retreated to the loos traumatized and refused to come out, and on Thursday Bish rang me at my desk.

'Come t'Bunker, lass,' he said.

The Bunker – where Bish's twenty-year collection of old newspapers are piled up to the ceiling – stinks because it's the last place in the building anyone can smoke. Elliot, who shares the office, has so far failed to separate Bish from his beloved Woodbines. On one wall is a pinboard which is a schizophrenic mix of newspaper cuttings Bish thought were funny – 'ASBO FOR YOUTH WHO MOLESTED DOG', 'SEX PEST UNZIPPED IN FRONT OF NUN' – and his favourite Page Three girls, as well as Elliot's charts showing how many stories each reporter has brought in, with black dots next to those at the bottom of the league table. When he finds a suspicious expenses claim Elliot pins it up until the reporter, broke and after phone calls from the bank manager, finally plucks up the courage to enter the Bunker, asking why their expenses haven't been signed off and paid into their account. Elliot will question the poor sap about why they said it was 120 miles return to Hastings, and why they went via the M25 if it was only a hundred if they'd gone another way, until finally, desperate for cash so they can eat and pay the bills, the reporter will agree to have the

109

claim sliced. Elliot wields his red pen, knocks £4 off, and struts around like he's king of the moral high ground.

Elliot is a pain in everyone's neck.

Bish was sat in his chair, scowling like normal. 'Shut t'door,' he said grumpily. 'Right. Some little toad's rung up wanting to flog a sex tape. Says it's got somebody important in it. You're to meet 'im and get it off 'im.'

'Fine,' I said, wondering why he was so moody. 'Who's in it?'

'Dunno,' replied Bish with a scowl. 'Just get it in here, right? Promise him whatever he wants. No mentioning it outside of this office, and no official paperwork.'

I left, confused – why was Bish interested if he didn't know who was in it? – and headed to an address in Mayfair. It was a flat in a good block, and a woman buzzed me up.

At the door of the flat she greeted me and introduced herself as Martha. I guessed immediately she was a hooker. High class, but easy to spot nonetheless. The nails, hair and make-up were perfect, but the heels a bit too high and the eyes a bit too dead. Her breath smelled of wine, and it wasn't quite noon. As Martha walked me into the living room, which was spacious and clean, I caught glimpses of a dirty kitchen with dishes piled in the sink, and a bedroom with the curtains still drawn and pill bottles by the bed.

In the living room a suave man in a dark suit got up from a sofa to shake my hand. He wore an expensive watch, but had too much oil in his dark hair and his eyes constantly flicked from side to side, like a snake's. Meet Martha's pimp, Danny.

Danny said he had a video and was sure it was worth a lot to the newspapers. I explained that I could tell him a rough figure, once I'd seen the video and worked out what we could do with it, but my boss would need to see it, too, before we could offer a firm sum. Danny smirked and said he was happy to show me. He gestured towards a huge flat screen on one wall, flicked a remote control, then lounged back on the sofa.

It was grainy CCTV footage of a bedroom, presumably at night-time. Martha walked in, leading a man by the hand, and they were joined by a second girl. The two women put on a show of taking off their clothes, watched by the man, who had his back to the camera. There was music playing in the background, and you could hear the women giggling while the man made appreciative noises.

So far, so usual. The kind of thing I see regularly, before having to tell somcone that the person they thought was David Beckham is, in fact, just some scrote, and it's not worth anything to us. I looked at Danny and raised my eyebrows; he gestured to keep watching, and smirked again.

I looked back at the screen. Martha had beckoned the man on to the bed and was kissing him. Then he turned his attentions to the second woman, and I saw his face for the first time.

HOLY HELL! I couldn't believe what I was seeing. It was like catching the Queen and Terry Wogan *in flagrante*, or hearing Bish was boffing Cheryl Tweedy. It was astonishing.

It was Elliot.

Tight, prissy, sanctimonious Elliot. With two hookers. I could feel Danny smirking again, but refused to look at him. The video wound on and I saw bits of Elliot I never want to see again. He had sex with both girls in a variety of ways with a range of props, then the action began to flag. 'Thank God,' I thought, hoping I could stop watching. Then Martha reached into the bedside unit and pulled out a small bag of white powder, which Elliot snatched off her excitedly. He positioned both girls on their hands and knees on the bed in front of him, and carefully shook the bag until he had four rough, fat lines laid out on each of their bum cheeks. He knelt down, put a finger against one nostril, and snorted each line up with every apparent sign of glee.

Then he leaned back on his haunches, wiped his nose and said, loudly and distinctly: 'Don't worry about the cost, girls – I'll be able to put all this through on expenses!'

I put a hand over my eyes. 'OK, I've seen enough,' I told Danny. 'You can turn it off. What do you want?'

'Forty k,' he said with a reptilian grin.

'FORTY K? We don't pay that for a splash!' I exclaimed.

'Won't look good for your newspaper, though, will it? I could take it to one of your rivals, they might publish it. Or the BBC, they don't like the tabloids much. It looks bad when you think about how many stories your paper has done about other people's misbehaviour.'

Outraged at being put in the same category as politicians and celebrities, I nevertheless realized he was right. The *Groaner* would never pay £40,000 but they hate us and would make a meal out of Elliot and our whole newspaper, as would the Beeb in revenge for the kickings it regularly gets over what it does with the licence fee. I remembered Bish's orders – get the video at all costs, but nothing official – bit my morals back, and told Danny he'd 'probably' get the money but I needed the DVD to show my boss first. He gave me a copy and said he was keeping the original, and I took it back to the office.

I handed it to Bish, and he put it straight into his bottom desk drawer, dropping it like it was hot. 'Is it worth the money?' he asked abruptly.

'Depends,' I said. 'Be cheaper to sack him.'

Bish gave me a look. 'Can't do that, lass. His auntie's a major shareholder. But we're not going to pay for his troubles, he can pay the man off 'isself. I'm not going to watch this. Was it . . . y'know, normal?'

'Only a bit kinky,' I said. 'Two girls, some lesbian stuff, a little light spanking. It was when he snorted coke off their arses and told them he'd get it on expenses that he really dug himself a hole.'

'Fook,' said Bish with a sigh. 'Oh well, at least it weren't kiddies. Thanks – and oh, not a word now. Not one, d'you hear me?'

Walking past Elliot back to my desk, I felt him glaring at me, and wondered if being busted would change him. Five minutes later he went into the Bunker. I could see him and Bish through the glass wall, talking. Elliot went white, began gesticulating, then fell silent as Bish carried on, staring at his desk and fiddling with paperclips. Elliot looked up for a moment, and stared right at me. Bish carried on at him, and then Elliot left and hurried straight out of the office. No doubt to his bank, and then Mayfair. I heard he got it for £20,000 in the end.

Rather than having the stuffing knocked out of his sails, Elliot has gone on behaving the same as always. He seemed to delight in getting me to rewrite a three-par picture caption eight times, and sending another reporter on a six-hour round-trip to Cornwall for a pointless story just as they were about to leave the office at 8 p.m. He obviously has no remorse, no self-doubt, no sense even of 'that was a close one'. Meanwhile I can now see Elliot's bad moods are the result of drug paranoia – and what he does in his private life impacts on dozens of people every day.

But that's the way of it now. Selfishness has become socially acceptable, along with nebulous 'rights', hypocritical demands for privacy from celebrities whose only income is from hawking photographs of themselves, and a refusal, at the highest levels, to take any kind of responsibility.

MPs blame 'accounting errors' and 'oversights' rather than admit they are frauds; Kate Moss can be pictured snorting lines of white powder but is never prosecuted; bankers who brought the world's economy to the brink of collapse get bonuses; celebrities caught at orgies criticize others' prudishness. No one puts their hands up to say 'I'm sorry, I did that, it was my fault.'

And the average cokehead in the street thinks their little habit affects only them, so they can do what they like. They think it's *their* choice, *their* fun, or *their* pain. And they think it's not a problem.

Not everyone who uses becomes an addict, but many are more dependent than they realize. Worse, you don't know in advance how you will react to a drug – you might just have a giggle, or you might go home and argue with your wife. You might get hooked.

Take the Suffolk Strangler killings of 2006. Each of the five murdered women was a prostitute who sold herself on the street to get her next fix. One was from a poor and troubled family, another from a balanced middle-class home with tennis lessons and ponies. A third was pretty, a fourth was not, yet another had fallen in with a

114

violent man who forced her on to the streets. They all ended up dumped in a ditch.

The one thing they had in common was that with one hit, they were hooked. One girl started on glue, another skunk, a third on speed. They simply had the kind of brain chemistry which made them susceptible, and by the time they realized that, it was too late. I've got plenty of friends who indulge appetites for one thing or another, and most of them are fine with it. They'll have a bit of this or that on a night out and see it as nothing, more or less, and I daresay Elliot is the same. Twatface went out partying with him a few times – friends in common, that sort of thing, although Elliot always used to look down on him – and while it didn't use to bother me now I'm left to wonder what they might have got up to together. Elliot is paranoid and mad with me at work, and Twatface would be angry and mad with me at home.

Everyone who develops a problem with drugs has loved ones who are equally abused and damaged by the addiction. When I think back to the year things were really bad with Twatface all I can really remember is a constant sense of low-grade fear – a vague worry that the next phone call would bring me dire news of some kind or another.

Even recreational users are paying money to nasty people who murder, rape, beat and intimidate on a global scale in order to maintain their grasp on a criminal network that does zero good for anyone, anywhere.

Of course, it's impossible to make every pound you spend a clean one – for some part of it not to go to a country or company that does things which you don't like, even if you're buying only broccoli. But there are not many ways I can think of to make that pound as dirty as you do by giving it to drug lords.

How many of the estimated one million people in the UK who regularly take cocaine think, before putting it up their nose, how it got there? Or wonder how everyone else manages to have fun without it?

And it's all to feel like slightly less of a prat for a few minutes. For the sense of imperfection, of ugliness or stupidity or pain – or the bad memories that we all have – to recede for a while, so that we can pretend they were never there at all.

I have lost count of the numbers of rapes I have covered; but most were allegedly carried out when the girl could barely uncross her eyes, much less her legs, and most of the men walked free. I have heard in inquests how one spliff led to another and another, then eventually to mental illness, years of agony, and suicide. I have sat through hundreds of trials for sex assaults, violence, murders and mistakes, fuelled by too much booze and too many drugs. I have knocked on the doors of dozens of families whose children have died or been damaged by too much of something.

Each of those people has pointed the finger – at their son's bad friend who sold him the dope, at someone taking advantage of their daughter, at society for allowing cheap booze to be peddled to children, at the government, at schools, at the system. They don't point the finger at themselves. Or ask: 'What did I do?'

No one takes responsibility, and the same story is told so often it is no longer shocking. The Reader just rolls their eyes and turns the page.

There is no fault or blame to be accepted for anything. No one is punished, no one is held to account, and the

116

finger always points elsewhere. Questions are asked, but usually of the wrong damn people.

Well, I question why no one holds their hand up to anything, says they were wrong, and publicly atones for it. That happened publicly in 1982, when Lord Carrington resigned as foreign secretary because he had not foreseen that the Argies were going to invade the Falklands. He said his department had screwed up, and as their boss he took the blame. But nowadays a politician will hang on for as long as he can, pointing the finger at someone else, say sorry while never feeling it, without a thought for old-fashioned public honour. A celebrity will only admit their behaviour was a bit off if they're caught on video smoking crack, or kill some children while drink-driving. The rest of the time they cry 'intrusion' or threaten to sue; they blame the Press for catching them out rather than wonder if they should have been doing it in the first place. When a parent raises a child badly, they say: 'What can I do?' and shrug their shoulders. Children are no longer naughty – instead they are diagnosed with Oppositional Defiant Disorder, and we are told to make allowances.

And when you get divorced, it is officially no one's fault. Whatever the reason for your split, legally it does not change the financial settlement or any rights over children. That may be fine for some couples who just decided it was for the best, but what about the woman who for thirty years had every bone in her body broken by an abusive husband, and who, when she finally gets the strength to leave him, has to split the proceeds of the sale of their marital home 50-50? That's not right. What about a husband whose wife cuckolded him for years, who made him think her children by other men were his? What

117

about someone whose partner one day just ups and goes, without any reason, breaks their heart and leaves them railing at the world? Not right. Not right at all.

It's not right that Twatface can get a divorce, sign a form admitting adultery, and no one seems to think any the worse of him for it. I want him in the stocks for a day, to have rotten tomatoes thrown at him, to hear him admit he bears the blame for breaking my heart.

It's not right that no one tells Elliot his bullying is wrong, not to mention the hookers and drugs. If Elliot had been a Royal, we would have run the video, caused a scandal, and he would have apologized publicly and been sent off to rehab. Instead it's swept under the carpet and we all pretend it's normal.

Well, fuck that shit. We are not islands, to do as we will and sod the rest of the world. Humans are a network, and everything we do has an impact on other people. You cheat on your wife and hurt her, and you also hurt your children, your parents, her parents, and all your friends. You fail with your kids, and they will go down the pan taking other people with them. If you take drugs then you fund a network of really bad people who do more bad things with your money in a cycle of horribleness.

And you're not cool – you're just selfish.

It's enough to make you want to switch the world off at the socket, reboot and start again. This time without people.

DAY SIXTY

BEING cheated on is bad for your brain. Aside from anything else, you get so used to claiming the moral high ground that you become a monster. You rewrite your own moral code at will, certain you can do no wrong because you are In The Right. Stalin had much the same problem.

It's perfectly explicable; your friends are on your side, so tell you how wrong he is and how right you are. The lawyers tell you how wrong he is and how much he should pay you. The central drama of your break-up occupies all your waking moments and conversations to the extent that you believe everyone else feels it as painfully as you do, and that karma, Buddha and the Force are all going to gang up and kick your husband in the nads.

This is normal human behaviour I suppose – we'd soon go mad if we realized just how small a minority our peccadilloes put us in. For example, there was one national newspaper where I had been working for only a few weeks before I was taken aside and had it kindly pointed out that if I wanted to get on I should not wear trousers to work.

This is the kind of suggestion that would send most women rampaging straight to human resources and the sort of 'ism' which would, in any other situation, make me willingly hurl myself under the winner of the four-thirty at Epsom in protest. But journalists are a practical breed and prefer to go under the radar whenever possible, so I took no offence, and switched to skirts and heels even on cold and rainy night shifts. It didn't make an awful lot of difference – a few more stories and the occasional ogle by the scary editor, and I soon left anyway. But as far as I was concerned the misogyny was a trap for them, not me – something that constrained and ordained their behaviour, whereas I had the freedom to change how they thought of me simply by switching my clothes and shoes, the poor muppets. If any of those bosses had seen themselves as I did they would have crumbled to dust.

In the case of divorce, especially when you are the wronged party, there is so much leeway given by friends and family that it would take a saint not to fall into a petulant psychosis. Polarized by the legal process, and emboldened by a sense of ethical certainty so strong you could bend horseshoes around it, you stride on defiantly, unable to see any of the pitfalls until suddenly you're at the bottom of one and the light's gone out. Or, in my case, you start arguing over the most minor things. There were holiday photographs (I went through the albums, took out every picture of him and his family, and gave them to him. 'Can I have some of you?' he asked. 'Why?' I said. 'I'd like something to remember you by,' he replied. 'Drop dead,' I told him). There were CDs ('Is this my White Album or your White Album?' he asked. 'Mine's the one without coffee stains,' I said, and he didn't believe me, so we argued viciously about it for an hour or so). It got so petty I was genuinely worried he'd claim the fridge magnets too.

In my defence they are a damn fine set of magnets. An ironic, nerdy collection of mementoes gathered from around the globe. There is one from the set of a TV soap, which I bought after two weeks' work on a highly successful attempt to catch the soap's barmaid shagging the soap's Romeo. Then there is the one from Indonesia, which I grabbed at the airport after three weeks covering the tsunami, up to my arse in rotting corpses and rat curry. There is even one of the Portuguese church in Praia da Luz, where Madeleine McCann went missing and most of Fleet Street spent what felt like ten years of our lives trying to find either her or a good line on the story – we failed at both.

I would bring these magnets home from my globe-trotting, whack them on the fridge and tell Twatface my travellers' tales while he cooked me my first decent meal in weeks and listened, admiring and a little jealous because he was no longer an on-the-road reporter but chained to a news desk in an open-plan office with pretend daylight and internal politics.

As the divorce rows got more silly he sent, via his lawyer and mine, petty little lists of worthless bits and bobs he insisted were his. He claimed one of a pair of chairs, a bookcase that wasn't straight, a bare lampstand. On one visit I had caught him in front of the fridge with the Praia da Luz church in his hand and a stupid smile on his face, and it took all my control not to claw his face off but simply grab it back, and tell him to not even think about it. We argued about every little unimportant thing.

Then one day and without telling me Twatface cancelled the mortgage payment. The bank insisted we use only one account to pay off the loan, so we had set it up that I paid my half to him a few days before the payment was due, and then he would pay the bank for both of us. It had been that way the entire time we lived together, and after we split it carried on. Every month I paid him £600 and he paid the bank £1,200.

One afternoon at work, a week or so after my £600 had gone out of my account, I suddenly had a call from the bank's debt collectors saying we were £1,200 in arrears. I had to pay both our shares then and there, was left £1,800 adrift and when I phoned him to ask what the hell had happened he said it wasn't his problem, he wasn't giving the money back until he could pick up the last of his furniture, and how dare I accuse him of theft.

Everyone in the newsroom stopped what they were doing as I screamed four-letter words down the phone at him, slammed the receiver on to the cradle and then shouted a bit about what a petulant, pointless little twat I'd married. Apoplectic with rage I stalked to the end of the office to punch the wall (luckily, this is not unusual behaviour in a newsroom). He was holding my money ransom for a bunch of crappy furniture not worth a tenth of it.

Back at my desk, I decided I'd had enough of constant argy-bargy and £1,800 was something which merited getting the lawyer involved for. What followed was a petty war of words via two dozen legal letters. It was £75 for my lawyer to write to him, and about £125 for his to write to me. Plus VAT. It would have been cheaper to forget it, but I had right on my side and pettiness in my brain. It was a war I could not afford to lose.

God only knows what fools our lawyers thought we were. But after several weeks and an extra £2,000 on my bill alone, Twatface promised to return the money he had no earthly reason to keep, and a date he could get the very last of his belongings. More importantly, I had victory and it seemed like we were one painful step closer to sorting things out.

On Wednesday I had the girls over for one of our frequent attempts to drink all the wine before Twatface turned up. I served up bowls full of king prawns with garlic, regaled them with blow-by-blow accounts of our exchanges, and was confident of their continuing, unquestioning support.

We were six bottles down, and I was mid-rant, when Fifi Jenkins, thinking I was looking elsewhere, rolled her eyes. I stopped and said: 'I'm sorry, is my agony boring you?'

Nancy chipped in and said: 'Don't be silly – it's just, you know. We understand how awful it is, but you need to let it go. You're a bit bitter.'

I was astonished. 'BITTER? I'm not bitter. Bitter means you wish you were still with him. There's not a fibre of my being that wants to be with that toad. What I am is angry. Very. Bloody. Angry. There is a difference, you know.'

I glared at my wine glass. Silence fell, feet were shuffled, and we talked of other things. My sense of rightness faded not in the least.

When I told my mum – who I genuinely think is more upset than me at Twatface – he was paying me back and picking up his stuff she insisted I find a way to sabotage everything so he could never use it.

So I unscrewed the lamp base, cut some wires, and screwed it back together. I couldn't do much with the bookcase which was already knackered, but I carefully tore one page out of each of his books – a pointless exercise because he never reads them. The chair was an IKEA thing, a canvas cover stretched over a metal frame with a couple of legs screwed on to the sides.

'Take it apart and shove something stinky in the frame,' said Mum. 'What right has he got to enjoy sitting down?'

At this stage even I thought she was taking things a bit far; but she encouraged me, y'honour. So I took the chair apart and washed the canvas. I unscrewed the frame. I picked all the king prawn shells out of the bin and shoved them, one at a time, into the hollow metal tube which formed the main structure of the chair. I left a couple of screws out so there were air holes for the stink, ironed the canvas cover and put it all back together. I quite enjoyed it, and snickered happily to myself throughout. Then I put all of his things on the pavement outside the house and went out for a couple of hours.

When I got back most of it had gone. The bookcase he had demanded was on the pavement, with a note he had written saying 'FREE TO A GOOD HOME'. My elderly neighbour, Valerie, who spends all her time sat at her front window watching the street, was watering her flower tubs so I wandered over to find out what she'd seen.

'Did you see anyone take the stuff?' I asked, after some chit-chat about her knees.

'Ooh yes, dear, your husband came and took it. He was driving a flash little sports car, but it was belching out black smoke, bit of an old banger. He was on his own, dear, and he couldn't fit it all in, so he left the bookshelf, as you can see.'

'And, er, did you see a canvas chair? Did he take that?' Please God, let him have taken it. Aha ha ha!

'Oh no, dear, he couldn't fit that in, either. He left it outside your house. I expect someone walking past saw it and took it for themselves.'

Aaaaaaaah, shiiit! All that for nothing. I was disappointed, but then began to worry. Who had the chair?

One of my neighbours? What would they do when it started to smell? Would they bring it back? They would demand to know what I was playing at, leaving a nice chair on the street for someone to take and then stuffing it full of decaying shcllfish. They would think I was insane, accuse me of being petty and – almost certainly – bitter. I realized that I had not stopped to think how I was behaving, simply rampaged on and acted like just as much of a twat as him in the race for cheap divorce points.

So if you ever read this, Twatface – and if you get this far before reaching for the phone to call a lawyer – I'm sorry. Sorry that I crammed a chair full of rotting prawns just to earn some kind of meaningless victory. To be honest, if you'd taken it I would have been highly delighted and had not the tiniest twinge of conscience. The only reason I regret it now is because you didn't, and there is an innocent third party somewhere who thinks I'm a basket case. It was only seeing how my behaviour would look to strangers that made me realize that although it was funny it also plumbed new depths of pettiness, was motivated purely by vengeance, and made not the slightest difference to the end of our marriage. It was just that I wanted to hurt you, a little bit, like you'd hurt me. So as much as it sticks in my craw to apologize to you for anything – I am sorry. I'm sorry I wasn't the wife you wanted, too.

She's still fat, though.

DAY SEVENTY-THREE

SOME things never change, no matter how hard you try. The sun rises, the tides turn, and I am always ten minutes late for work. If I get up half an hour early, the universe conspires to block the road or provide an annoying phone call just as I'm going out the door. If I oversleep by half an hour I still, somehow, manage to be at my desk at ten past. I have ceased to question or fight it, and have come to accept it as a force of nature, along with the fact that chutzpah beats skill in almost every situation and that I will always laugh at things that really aren't funny.

Evil Elliot, however, still rails. Bish occasionally mutters a sarcastic, 'Afternoon' at me as he stomps past the desk, but Elliot takes the 10.10 a.m. start of my day as a personal thorn in his side to be niggled at until the thorn gives up and goes away.

Last Friday I was hoping to slip under his radar and get to my desk without being seen, juggling several bags, a pair of stilettoes and the previous night's hangover. But I had barely slumped into my seat, perspiring gently, before he silently appeared beside me.

'I see that investigation I asked you to handle into holiday rip-offs has surfaced in our rival paper,' he hissed, slapping the offending organ on to my keyboard. 'Any thoughts?'

This is Elliot's most sadistic pleasure. Asking bafflingly

open-ended questions that are impossible to reply to, and which are designed simply to give him a good reason to slice you off at the knees with a vicious scythe of his tongue. He will say, 'Your copy's dreadful – any thoughts?' Or, 'It's been a while since you had a splash. Your thoughts?' while you writhe at his feet, scrabbling for something sensible to say.

The best method of dealing with this is head-on. You should state boldly, 'I'm glad you asked me that . . .' and deliver a strong line of bullshit too bombastic for him to get a word in edgeways. Chutzpah, you see. I rarely manage it, though, and certainly not when caught in a bit of a flurry with a hangover of 6.2 on my personal Richter scale. So instead I looked at him, mouth agape, while my brain went, 'click, brrrrrrrrrrrr . . .' like a phone line that had gone dead.

It lasted only a couple of seconds, but that was all the time he needed to skewer me. 'No excuses? How unlike you,' he oozed.

I gathered myself and fought a valiant rearguard action, explaining that yes, I had come up with some stuff, and had mentioned it to Bish, but he'd been completely lukewarm on the idea, so it'd rather gone off the boil. In desperation I made a lame joke about staycations being much more the thing these days. Elliot merely raised his eyebrows and said: 'Oh, so now you're blaming the news editor for your failings? You should have sold it to him, insisted we spend some time on it. In the *current climate*, and with your personal problems, I would have thought you'd try a little bit harder to hold on to your job and cease acting the clown.'

With that, he turned on his heel and stalked off to terrorize some other poor soul, and I slumped in front of my computer despondently. Chutzpah is not always the same as funny, I told myself. Two desks away, Tania Banks smirked at her screen. Next to me, Bridget was on the phone and crinkled her forehead in sympathy. She was dealing with a ring-in – a caller who reckons they've got a good story, and needs to be squeezed for all the info before we can take it to Bish and see what he thinks. I listened to the conversation as I dolefully turned my computer on.

'. . . and was he still fingering her at this point, or having sex? Having sex. And was she on top? And what was she doing? Well, of course, you'd want to see what was going on. Were there any pictures taken? I see . . .'

Two minutes later she hung up. 'Jeez, the things you see when you're an air stewardess,' she said, shaking her head. 'Remind me never to get on the same plane as a bad boy of rock. Afternoon you. Elliot's in a bad mood, by the way.'

I laughed. 'Spotted it, thanks. Any thoughts?'

'Ha, I'm glad you asked me that . . . no, seriously! Have you seen the email about Greece from the travel editor? She says there's a space going on a break next week if anyone wants it and can knock up five hundred words for the holiday supplement afterwards. You've got a week off, haven't you?'

'Yeah.' I sighed. 'Twatface and I were going to his cousin's wedding in the States. There's no way now, and I think he's going with Fatty. He even asked me to arrange their bloody flights for them.'

'He's a twat,' said Bridge. 'You need a break. Take this Greece thing.'

I looked through my emails and found it . . . and my mood sunk even further. A singles holiday at a villa on

Rhodes. Oh, God, had it come to this? I emailed the travel editor with a heavy heart, saying I'd take the offer, and on Sunday found myself alone on a Sleazyjet flight from Gatwick, surrounded by stag parties and A-level students.

Three hours of booze and hell later, I walked out of the arrivals hall and saw a rep holding a big card with my name spelled wrong.

'You must be for us!' The rep beamed, a friendly woman called Marla. 'Great! This is Simon and this is Kate, and there's just the three of you on this flight, so off we go!'

Kate was a petite woman in her fifties and Simon looked about twenty-five, a giant of a man. On the bus to the villa I discovered Kate had recently lost her husband and Simon had recently lost ten stone. The road wound through the mountains to a hillside just outside Faliraki, where Villa Minerva perched. Why they named it after a woman with snakes for hair is anyone's guess, but there was a pool and a bar with about a dozen people lazing about, who welcomed us as three interesting new specimens.

Over dinner we all sat and shared the tales of romantic woe that had led us to a singles holiday. Widow Kate had been married since she was seventeen, and had never done anything on her own. Fat-fighter Simon proudly retold his battle of the bulge and showed us that while he had lost a lot of weight he still had all the skin. Then there was Jilted John, whose bride had dumped him at the altar, and who was supposed to be on his honeymoon right now, a couple of fat ladies, and Slightly Mad Melissa, who was a thirty-five-year-old librarian with a lot of cats and a succession of bad boyfriends. Lastly there was an

Irishman called Rory, who made a big point of spelling his name for us – Ruairi, I think – and had been single since the love of his life, Eleanor, had dumped him nineteen years previously. Even Marla had her own story, having found out that her husband was gay only when she walked in on him shagging the pool boy at their Cretan holiday home. I regaled them with my own story of adultery and arrest, laughing loudly throughout, and was probably labelled by each of them as some kind of loon.

'So,' I thought as I lay in my cheap slatted bed, listening to the bar next door play a crap pop song for the fourth time over a heavy drum 'n' bass track. 'This is, quite literally, Heartbreak Hotel.'

It was only a four-day break, but at the end of it I would have to write a review for the travel supplement. So I lounged by the pool in the afternoons, and in the mornings signed up to all the activities I could find – waterskiing classes, bungee jumping, pony-trekking – so as not to be brooding on the lesbian wedding, and how Fatty was getting on with all the people who a few months ago were my family.

And I had fun. I was on holiday with a bunch of rejects who made Heather Mills look emotionally healthy, but it was funny. I have been known to laugh at funerals – and not at the bits you're supposed to. So when the bungee man asked me in broken English, 'I buy you beer, you be my wife for week?' he looked on blankly as I snickered uncontrollably for five whole minutes. When a fat little pony I was riding bolted down the mountainside with me clinging to the saddle, I was so busy screaming and laughing at the same time that I slipped sideways around its barrel-like belly until I was at right angles to the ground and nearly choked to death. Held in place by one leg, I was only saved when the beast became so confused by the noises I was making that it stopped to look at me in amazement.

It was all stuff that would never have happened if Twatface had still been around. He could never bungee jump – the man could barely cope with going up a stepladder – so I embraced it, and insisted my fellow refugees from romance did the same. I dragged Widow Kate waterskiing, and the Two Fat Ladies pony-trekking (their horses couldn't bolt), and found myself unofficial court jester, pulling the others along in the hunt for something new to laugh at.

On the last night our Lonely Hearts Club trooped down to the town for dinner and a bar crawl. Ruairi made a point of sitting next to me and pressing his knee to mine, and as I got drunker I mulled over the idea of a holiday quickie. He was a bit short, not much taller than me, and a good twenty years older. He had spent the entire week lying on a lilo in the hotel pool, baking his skin until he looked like a sultana. I didn't really fancy him, but after a few cocktails I was starting to think his Irish lilt was quite sexy.

Suddenly I was tapped on the shoulder by a fat sweaty Mancunian from another table. 'Your go,' he said, shoving a microphone in my hand.

Arsebuckets! I had foolishly put my name on the karaoke list an hour or two earlier, for the sole reason that Twatface would never have let me do such a thing for fear of embarrassing him, and because the others were all too shy. I'd never done karaoke before in my life. Now I was three sheets to the wind, the bar was quietly expectant, and Jilted John and Fat-fighter Simon were lifting me on to the table we were sitting at. Arse, balls and buggery!

I hadn't even picked a song. Heavy piano chords started to thump out, and I recognized Elton John's song for surviving singletons. Oh, marvellous!

'Well, my girl,' I thought to myself. 'There's only one way to deal with this. Chutzpah.'

I started to sing. The first few words were strangled and nervous as my eyes sought out a point on the back wall to stare at, but after the first verse something magical happened. Somehow, as though we were in a movie, the song moved everybody in the same way, in a perfect storm of mood and alcohol. First the Lonely Hearts Club joined in, and then the whole bar followed. It was like being the novelty act on *The X Factor*, where the judges roll their eyes but the audience still cheer. I even managed to hit some of the notes as I danced on top of the table, doing an admirable impression of Elton John in Slightly Mad Melissa's huge red sunglasses while the Lonely Hearts Club thumped their hands on the table and their feet on the floor.

The Two Fat Ladies jumped up on to their chairs to do backing singing for the chorus, and when the guitar solo kicked in, Fat-fighter Simon clambered on to the bar and rocked the air guitar, while Jilted John played the drums on some upturned pint glasses, and Ruairi and Kate danced rock 'n' roll in the middle of the floor. It was one of those times where everything just seems to come together, and when the song finished the whole bar cheered as I collapsed back in my seat. Ruairi sat back next to me and said admiringly: 'Why, you're da white Aretha Franklin!'

I refrained from pointing out that I was nowhere near that fat, and took pleasure in the fact that all the lonely hearts had big smiles on their faces. During the course of the evening Simon and Melissa snuck off and got it on, Kate made plans for Christmas with the Two Fat Ladies, and Ruairi made it plain he fancied me, but by that point I was too drunk to pay much notice. Next morning the raging hangover didn't seem so bad, even on the flight back home with yet more stags drowning in Strongbow.

Back in the office, tanned and relaxed and for once un-aggravated by Twatface, I spent a happy half-day writing about all the things I'd seen and done. It was five hundred words, with the intro chirping happily about bungees and how, as someone who was suddenly single, jumping off a bridge was quite a lot of fun. I hadn't mentioned Twatface by name or made any other reference to him, but I knew he would hate it. And, I reasoned, why not ruin his holiday with Fatty while I'm at it? So I texted him. 'A two-page spread about our divorce is going in this weekend,' I lied, cackling to myself as I imagined the horror spreading across his face and what he would tell Fatty.

I'd filed the piece and forgotten it when, two hours later, the phone on my desk rang. It was the paper's lawyer, Nick 'The' Crow, a man who always looks like he's on his way to a funeral and has the mood to match. In a classic case of your name determining your job, he spends his days hunched over a keyboard pecking over the corpses of stories. It's his task to bat away lawsuits, advise reporters not to do it like that, and check the paper for legal bear-traps before we publish them and have to apologize. Or worse, pay out. Reporters often grumble the lawyers make us play it safe, but without him we'd get in even more trouble than we already do.

'Your husband's just been on the phone,' said The Crow. 'He's threatening to sue us.'

Click, brrrrrrrrrrrr . . .

DAY SEVENTY-EIGHT

THE problem with jumping off a cliff is that you are so convinced that it is better to live without regret that, by the time reason reasserts itself, it is too late.

The initial excitement, adrenalin and fear combined to propel you over the edge and it is only when you feel a yawning chasm beneath your feet that you stop, and just as a sense of your own fallibility begins to dawn you're grabbed by gravity and pulled towards the rocks.

Divorce is much the same, I find. Anger shields and guides you, blinkers you from noticing that you are behaving like a sociopath, until one day you're left with a niggling sense of having overstepped the mark, vis-à-vis the shellfish you stuffed in his favourite chair. Actually that might just be me. As far as temper tantrums go I'm a slam-and-storm kind of girl, and always have been. I slam a door, and storm off until I calm down. Often my rage propels my legs to stalk in a random direction for a good half hour, until I come to my senses in a less than salubrious spot, suddenly aware I no longer have my fury to protect me from rapists, murderers or vengeful fatties all keen on pointing out the consequences of my actions. I should be used to it. I should realize what is going to happen, learn my lesson, and stop before I go too far. But of course I don't. Dogs return to their vomit, and the fool's hand always goes wandering back to the fire.

There is a theory I read somewhere that, with every decision you make, a perfect copy of the world peels off from this one and an extra reality is born where everyone continues down the path you didn't take. So there is a world where Hitler decided invading Poland was a bit grandiose, one where your parents never met, one where I am still married to Twatface, and maybe even one where he isn't a twat, although that seems far-fetched if you ask me. If the theory is true, there are a lot of angry little planets spinning through space, and the more bewildered ones are almost definitely my fault. But it means you don't need to have regrets, you see, because on one of them you did all the things you didn't do here.

For better or worse, however, I was in this world, which was the one where The Crow was on the phone saying Twatface was threatening legal action against me, the newspaper and my editor because I had, quite correctly, pointed out that jumping off a bridge was more fun than he was.

I wasn't surprised, if I'm honest. I was kind of astonished Twatface was living up to his nickname so magnificently, but resigned to the fact I'd done something stupid. 'Funny' and 'defamatory' are rarely a wise combination, while 'redundant' and 'mortgage' likewise do not make the best of bedfellows.

'He was ranting and raving for a good half an hour,' said The Crow in his sternest, Christopher-Lee-in-a-graveyard tone. 'He said that it was invasion of privacy, defamation of character, and breached articles one through eight of the Press Complaints Commission code of conduct.'

'Really?' I asked in a strangled voice. 'Hang on, isn't article six about not interviewing children?'

'It is, and well done for remembering,' said The Crow,

laughing – although he still sounded like Christopher Lee, only this time while stabbing someone. 'Ha. Ha. But then he did sound a lot like my two-year-old throwing a paddy. He's such a twat, why'd you marry him?'

I rolled my eyes, having become accustomed to this question over the past few months from everyone, starting with my mum and going all the way down to the postman, to whom I had to explain that I was forwarding Twatface's letters on to his squalid flat in Walthamstow because he couldn't be bothered to pay for a redirection.

'Anyway,' said The Crow. 'He can't be a very good journalist, otherwise he'd know that phoning up threatening to sue means only one thing.'

'A kneecapping?' I asked hopefully. Please God, don't let it be 'the sack'.

'No, I have to tell The Editor. Which means your piece will now be subjected to an extremely thorough rewrite, and if I know The Editor Twatface is going to come out of it a lot worse than he went in.'

And so it came to pass. The Editor emailed me, demanding my copy. So I pinged it back, all twenty or so words in which I said bungee jumping was more fun than being married, and another 480 words about a holiday in Greece. Barely a mention of Twatface, but then again, he wasn't to know that.

<From: Editor, The, 12.15 p.m.
To: Foxy; Crow, Nick
Not hard enough. What else can we say about him?>

<From: Foxy, 12.17 p.m.
To: Editor, The; Crow, Nick
Um, well I did toy with another couple of pars that seemed a bit strong to go in . . .>

<From: Editor, The, 12.18 p.m.
To: Foxy; Crow, Nick
Show me.>

<From: Foxy, 12.20 p.m.
To: Editor, The; Crow, Nick
Right. Well, he used to puke in the sink rather than the toilet, which doesn't sound so bad except it means the vom fountains up the wall – never nice and especially not with red wine and chips – and leave me to clean it up in the morning. Er. Or there's his pants. His favourite ones were these leopard-print boxers I got him as a joke once. He used to do a little roar when he put them on. He wore them so often the gusset rotted away, and he insisted on full funeral rites and a minute's silence when we finally consigned them to the dustbin.>

<From: Editor, The, 12.26 p.m.
To: Foxy; Crow, Nick
File on the pants.>

<From: Crow, Nick, 12.30 p.m.
To: Editor, The; Foxy
Just how cold is this dish being served?>

<From: Foxy, 12.31 p.m.
To: Editor, The; Crow, Nick
12.31 p.m.
40 below.>

Unbeknown to an enraged Twatface, by the end of the day he and his pants had been snickered over by two dozen sub-editors, ten reporters, two photographers who wandered into the office, the news desk (although Elliot merely sniffed), the sports editor, a work-experience kid, and a man fixing the photocopier. Then my editor phoned his editor, so his news desk got a chance to snicker at it, too. And when it was published, several million more all had the opportunity to say to themselves: 'What a twat. Why'd she marry him?'

Which is a thought that occurred to Twatface when he returned home a few days later to read a travel supplement that didn't mention him by name but had been noted, carefully, by everyone he worked with, all his friends, and all of Fatty's friends, too. Regrets? What are they?

He emailed me today, apologizing for being such a twat and saying he didn't stop to think. 'How are you?' he asked, like I cared that he was pretending to care.

I replied safe in the knowledge that for once the consequences of my actions had been glee and moral victory.

<From: Foxy, 10.43 a.m.
To: Twatface
Cock off. How was the holiday with MY in-laws that you went on with YOUR Fatty?>

It turned out he'd lost his passport, they'd missed a flight, had to sleep in the car for two nights and my former in-laws had spent the whole trip asking about me and telling him off for having an affair. Ha ha.

I turned to Nancy, who had just walked in, and launched into a long diatribe about how, if people were going to behave a certain way, they had to accept the results of their behaviour.

'It's no good sprinkling cannabis on your feral children's food and then complaining that social services have let you down, or flashing your skanky pants at snappers and moaning they've invaded your privacy,' I raved. 'And if you *act* like a twat you will get *treated* like a twat. For Pete's *sake*,' I muttered, finally subsiding back into my chair as Nance wiped the spittle off her keyboard and moved my mug out of harm's way. 'Why can't people accept the consequences of their actions? Why do they have to blame someone else?'

'Hi,' she said. 'Twatface been in touch, then?'

'Hmpf,' I replied grumpily, just as Princess Flashy Knickers tottered in and plonked herself in the chair opposite.

Now, Princess is a Yorkshire lass whose dad is a self-made millionaire in an industry of some sort, and she's so privileged she sees nothing unusual in £500 handbags, holidays four times a year, and living in a stately pile with a different pony for each day of the week. Heaven knows what she's doing in a newsroom earning a measly £35,000 writing up interviews and picture spreads, but feature writers live in a different world to the rest of us. And she is so completely without class – in every sense – that she can make friends with rich and poor alike. While wearing a lot of gold jewellery, or perhaps because of it.

Only now she was wearing a bandage. On her face. Specifically, it was wrapped under her chin and over the top of her head. Nance and I stared and blinked.

'So, you've been away for a couple of weeks . . .' Nancy began gently.

'Have you had a facelift?' I demanded.

Princess rolled her eyes. 'No, I have not. It's medical.'

We continued to stare. 'You've had a facelift,' I insisted. 'You're only thirty-two.'

140

'I've not. I wish I had, though.' Princess dumped her latest Mulberry and sighed. 'I've been at home waiting for this to go down.'

'Facelift,' I said to Nance. 'Definitely.'

Princess sighed again and told us the full, horrifying story. I have made reference above to living with the consequences of one's actions, and once you have got to the end of this, Dear Reader, I hope you will think twice before doing anything. And I mean anything at all.

'I went home for a couple of days, and met up with some of the girls. We went out for the night in Sheffield, got absolutely twatted. I wasn't too bad, actually, but the others were. Anyway I got talking to this lad called Pete. If I'm honest he wasn't that good-looking, but he was keen, and, well, to be frank, it had been a while. So when the club shut I took him home.

'Anyway, nothing unusual to report. He wasn't all that great, but it was a relief to know I hadn't forgotten how to do it. The only thing was that he had some very sharp stubble, and the next morning there were, like, grazes all over my chin. So, whatever. I walked him down to the station in the morning . . .'

I butted in: 'You mean you had him escorted off the estate?'

'No, I walked with him all the way down the drive to the village,' she said, affronted. 'And I noticed that everyone we passed was better looking than he was. I mean, I walked past two of the gardeners who were hotter than he was. And the newsagent and the grocer – who doesn't have any teeth – were both better looking, too. I began to regret it but then thought, "No, it's fine, the twenty-first century, stuff the *Daily Wail*." Anyway, I put him on the train and drove back to London. It was Sunday night

141

and I felt like going for a swim, and went down to the council pool near my flat.'

Nancy and I both pulled a face. 'Last time I went there, there were flies in the changing rooms,' said Nance. 'And I'm sure there was sperm in the water.'

Princess went on: 'The next day my chin began to itch. Really itch. Soon it was unbearable. I scratched it. Blisters started to pop up all around my mouth. By lunchtime I'd started oozing green pus, I kid you bloody not.'

She stopped to look disgustedly at the two of us while we spluttered into our hands and tried not to laugh.

'Green pus on my FACE. Oh. My. God! So I put a bag over my head and went to the doctor, who said I'd got impetigo from the pool in my stubble rash.'

'*IMPETIGO*?' screeched Nancy and I in unison, from our positions writhing on the floor in merriment and disgust.

'Impetigo. I got green pus, and a children's skin disease, from snogging a bloke I didn't much fancy anyway. I'd rather my fanny was sealed shut and covered in cobwebs.'

We continued to cackle, and I had just crawled back into my chair when Princess delivered the coup de grâce.

'The doctor says it will keep flaring up, so actually I have a recurring skin disease from, like, a totally minging shag. Could you two not laugh quite so loudly?'

I laid my head on the desk while Nancy wiped her eyes. 'We're sorry, Princess, but you should have known if you were going to tell us a story like that we'd find it funny. Impetigo, hee hee . . .'

Hauling myself upright and back to my keyboard, I said: 'Jesus, Princess. That'll learn you. No more having a

142

shag just for the sake of it! I mean there are times that it's completely understandable—'

'Er, Tit-tape Tim?' she pointed out.

'. . . because you have to get over someone, BUT if it leads to a recurring skin condition I'm not sure it's worth it. Although you will be able to dine out on that little tale for several years. He will be known, henceforth, as Pustulent Pete. He beats Tit-tape Tim hands down.'

'Well,' said Princess in a martyred tone. 'The doctor gave me antibiotics, so I'll just have to live with it, I suppose. There's no point in crying over spilt spunk.'

And there you have it, folks, our lesson for today summed up in one succinct phrase. Every failed relationship, every argument, and pretty much every war in the history of humankind can be encapsulated with those eight words. By using them, emotions like anger, betrayal or fear fade away, to be replaced with a feeling of, 'Oh, eeeuw, clean it up, and no, NOT LIKE THAT!'

If only politicians and social workers and teenaged mums all had that phrase stuck to their computers, tattooed on their hand or framed in a cross-stitch sampler and nailed to their walls, I genuinely believe the world would be a more relaxed place. Perhaps there is a world where those cross-stitch samplers actually exist. Next time Twatface pisses me off I shall repeat those words like a mantra and realize how ridiculous, pointless and stupid it all is – and maybe for once I won't slam-and-storm in my normal fashion.

But if I do – and I'm not saying I will – I won't beat myself up too much. No. I'll just tell myself: 'There's no point in crying over spilt spunk.' Genius.

DAY EIGHTY-EIGHT

YOU don't have to be casually racist to work in a news-room, but it helps. It's also useful if you can be sexist, ageist, heightist, fattist, classist, nationalist and, if you work in features, unable to see a picture of any female without spotting some cellulite and zipping off two thou-sand words on the subject.

It's not that journalists start out that way; but after long years of contact with mankind at its most extreme and emotional – death, lust, birth, Kerry Katona – you become so inured to the human condition that mockery is inevitable. There's something strangely fitting about the fact that cabbies all hate driving, doctors can't stand illness and journalists dislike people.

Well, all right, we don't *dislike* them so much. Journalists are usually empathetic to a fault, whatever you see on the telly – we couldn't do our jobs if we were unable to understand how other people felt, even if we do bend it to our advantage. It's just that, after a while, it becomes apparent that there are perhaps only a handful of real stories in the world, retold over and over again. The corrupt politician, the cheating spouse, the sick baby, Cinderella and Dick Whittington. Open any newspaper and you see a version of the same fairy tale played out with different names and dates, but each one is like a screw that follows the same thread. Barack Obama's road to the White House, for example, is pure Dick. Most female celebrities indulge in a bit of warped Cinderella mythology. The economic crisis is just one big hunt to find a villain to pin it on.

I don't know whether there are really only a few basic stories in the world, or if human brains just prefer to put things in simple categories to help them understand. Most journalists think they can persuade others to do almost anything, as though people are machines for which you simply need to figure out the switches, a vanity which leads to a sense of wearisome predictability. You know those newspaper labels people get – 'Troubled Glamour Girl', 'Disgraced Children's TV Presenter', or maybe 'Dog-eared Cage Fighter'? Well, when you're a journo you often find yourself giving labels to everyone you meet. I tend to think of Mum as 'Gardening Guru', while Dad is 'Mr Fixit'; the lady in the shop at the end of the road, who talks all the time and has a voice like a dustbin being dragged over cobbles, is 'Gravelly Shop Girl'; and elderly Valerie over the road, who's actually very sweet and rings to make sure I'm all right if my curtains are still drawn at 10 a.m., is 'Street Snoop'.

I suppose that once you learn shorthand a need for brevity seeps into every part of your life. All I know is there comes a point where you could swear you've written it all before but with different names, and that's why it was so easy to catch out Twatface after a mere two weeks of adultery.

Journalists don't start out cynical. In fact pretty much everyone I've ever worked with started out well-intentioned and with a burning passion to change the world and write the pages of history. I remember watching the news about the Berlin Wall coming down in 1989,

Germans from east and west attacking the barrier with garden tools and kitchen utensils and bare hands while Kate Adie stood there telling us about it in her pearl earrings, and I turned to Mum and said that was what I wanted to do.

'What, be on the telly with a spoon?' she asked.

'No,' I replied, for this was in the days before 'being on the telly' was a job. 'Telling everybody all the important things they need to know.'

And now here I am, a shilling-a-line hack on a tabloid, who spends her days stalking people and writing about their love lives while her own is in the toilet. Oh, the fairy tale!

Anyway the point I was trying to make is that most reporters are pretty decent sorts. Honest. It's just that the line between comedy and offences-that-would-get-you-sacked-anywhere-else is a lot finer in a newsroom, perhaps because we're so busy flouting social niceties for work we can't see the point of sticking to them in our leisure time.

For example, I'm sitting at my desk drinking my first cup of tea of the day – only there's no plastic spoons, so I'll have to use my biro to fish the bag out again, honestly the stuff I put up with – and Porter's walking the length of the office talking loudly to a contact on his phone.

'But he's SUCH a bell-end! Honestly, a great, big, gaping, raped-raw bell-end! Why doesn't he just give up, the big, gay ARSE?'

I think he's talking about the Prime Minister. Or it could be the Chancellor. Neither, as far as I am aware, is actually gay, it's just how journos speak. But it's the kind of talk which my friends who work in banks – and even those on magazines – say would get them shown the door while their biro was still spinning in the cup. Elliot,

146

taking me to task over a story which had slipped through my fingers, once told me: 'You've been raped over this story. *Raped!*'

As far as the racism goes it doesn't involve any of the Bad Words or seriously attacking another race. It goes something like Bish's phone call the other day to a press officer at the Ministry of Defence.

'. . . yer fookin' right we're sending a girl to Afghanistan with yer boys. We're an equal opportunities employer, yer know. An'the fookin' ragheads should have the same opportunity to get the shit scared out of 'em as us. I tell yer what, I wouldn't like to meet her on a dark night . . .'

'OH MY GOD!' I thought, barely noticing the isms. 'AT LAST! I'M BEING SENT TO WAR! Brilliant! Will I get a gun?'

Bish banged the phone down, grabbed the office flak jacket from his bottom drawer, and strode down the newsroom, buttons popping as his chest puffed out with pride. I trembled. He stood over the reporters' desk, legs braced like Lord Nelson bestriding the poop deck and surveying his victorious but raggedy fleet. Every reporter, from showbiz to politics, stiffened their spine and prayed their call had finally come.

'Banks! Get yerself to RAF Lyneham, there's a Hercules waiting for yer, and don't come back until you've found a British boy in a terror training camp.'

Teflon Tania smirked her way out of the office while the rest of us subsided, disappointed, back in our seats.

'Shit me,' bitched Bridge.

'Christ, is he serious?' asked Princess.

'At least she won't need armour plating,' griped Fifi.

147

Then Porter butted in: 'On the plus side, we'll finally defeat al-Qaeda. I mean, she'll either make it up or they'll all throw in the towel. I can see it now, a final video with someone tearfully saying – [please imagine a dreadful Arabic accent here] – "Fine, all right, we give up, cursed infidels. We will come out of our cave. Just for Allah's sake, get this Banks woman out of here!"'

But, to be honest, Banks is probably the best person to go, in that she is bulletproof, empathy-wise. The trick to a good newsroom is having one person suited to each type of story, a many-headed Brothers Grimm. So you have someone like Princess Flashy Knickers to talk to rich people, Fifi to schmooze PRs and hang out with models and celebrities, public-school Porter to backstab with the politicians, Banks to send trundling out like a tank when you don't want any prisoners or witnesses. Me, well, I get the stuff no one else wants: the jokey stories and the puns.

For example: Elliot slapped a story down on my desk about how some academic had done a study on illnesses in the works of Shakespeare. 'You've got the kind of stupid brain that's good at this,' he said through gritted teeth. 'I want ten puns, and make them *sing*.' I didn't write the story, but did come up with 'Much Achoo About Nothing', 'Romeo and Fluliet', 'The Temperature', 'Chlamydioanus' (that one didn't go in) and 'How Do I Infect Thee? Let Me Count the STIs'.

Journalism: giving good jobs to silly people. Well, it keeps us off the streets.

Reporters also dress like those they deal with, and become a little like them, too. So Bridge looks like a lady DCI, in a Jaeger suit which makes her seem severe; Fifi wears designer knock-offs and survives on champagne, canapés and nicotine; and Porter wears an old-school tie

148

and lives in wine bars. Cubby the health reporter is a naturally-messy hypochondriac with drifts of vitamin supplements on his desk. Because I knock on doors and loiter around car parks I wear stuff smart enough that a policeman wouldn't notice me and casual enough that I don't look like a social worker. People don't open doors to social workers.

Then we've stories about lap dancers, drug dealers and criminals, and for someone like that you need Bruce Willis on an angry day. We don't have him, but we do have Buff Arnold, a shaven-headed, tattooed, West Ham-loving chap who despite having a face like a cobbler's thumb can be really quite charming, simply by opening his blue eyes as wide as he can.

Buff is just shabby, the kind of person who looks like he's tumbled out of a strip-joint and needs a wipe with a dishcloth, but gifted with a charming manner that makes people open up because they think he understands.

One day he went out on a story about a TV actor who was shagging someone significantly older than him. It turned out that the mistress was a granny, his real missus was a granny, and they were both widows called Doris. Buff got the chat off Doris Two, confronted the shagger and was punched in the face, then had to call an ambulance when he went to see Doris One and found her keeled over with a heart attack. The following Tuesday Buff went round to the family home to see how she was doing, on the off-chance she might talk.

He wandered into the office looking pleased with himself. 'You look smarter than usual, did you wash this morning?' asked Porter.

'You won't believe it,' said Buff. 'I knocked on the door and the bloke answered. He nearly hit me again, but I

149

talked him round. Poor bastard. Turns out she died over the weekend and today was the funeral.'

'Shit!' we all said in unison – every reporter has been in the unpleasant position of knocking on a door at really the wrong time – 'What did you do?'

Buff shrugged. 'I asked him if he wanted to talk about it. He sat down and told me everything, said how his heart was broken but he was torn between Dorises. He went on at length about his love for older women with blue rinses. He gave me the photo album and then dropped the bombshell – her kids wouldn't let him go to the funeral. He had a new suit and everything.'

A sense of where this story was going, and the reason for Buff's wide grin, began to dawn. He went on: 'Then he looked me up and down, said we were probably about the same size, and asked if I wanted his suit. Whaddya think? It's Boateng.'

Unbelievable. We spent the afternoon calling him Buffy the Granny Slayer, but the TV guy is now his best friend and has already given him three stories this week – all because, for some reason, he felt Buff was on his side.

It is the ability to empathize which divides the world into the haves and have-nots. The person who cheats, steals or smashes stuff up lacks it, otherwise they'd never do that in the first place. The person who hugs you even though you're a stranger, because you're outside on your lunch break and crying on a bench while on the phone to your divorce lawyer, has it in spades – and will get their reward in heaven if I have any say in the matter. Buff has more than his fair share, Elliot doesn't have any, nor does Banks, and Twatface probably can't even spell it. Putting yourself in someone else's shoes is something wired in so deep that if you don't have it there's no way to get it. And

150

if you can't care about a stranger, what hope is there for the people who love you?

Perhaps if Twatface had more empathy in general he'd have cared more about me, and we'd still be together. But then how many people really have a happily ever after? Maybe we just force the events in our lives into a fairy-tale format so that we can pretend we know how it works and fool ourselves: he's a villain, she's a hero, and here's your happy ending.

But then it's a journalistic conceit that we hacks think we know everything, when actually we only know a little about a lot of things. For example I could storm Mastermind on questions about Big Brother contestants or the illnesses of Shakespearean England, because I've written about those. But anything I haven't written about or experienced – happy marriages, childbirth, why Katie Price is a nice person underneath – is a mystery to me. Perhaps I'm the one who lacks empathy, and has to package other people neatly as stock characters to make sense of them. Maybe Twatface is sitting somewhere right now, wondering why I dislike him so.

But that doesn't stop me feeling I've written this story before, and already know there's no such thing as a happy ending.

DAY NINETY-FOUR

HINDSIGHT is not only a beautiful thing, it's a bloody annoying one. Just like being in love: you don't notice it until you need it, and by then it's too late to do anything about it.

There are some things you realize only when it is too late – such as there are some differences between couples which are too fundamental for marriage to overcome. Smokers and non-smokers, for example; tea-lovers and coffee-drinkers, people who argue and people who simmer silently. Those who like dogs, and sociopaths who like cats. If you pair up with someone who is on the other side to you it will simply never work out. At the time you're in love, and it feels like anything is possible, but then hindsight sidles up, taps you on the shoulder and rather unkindly points out that smokers smell, coffee stains your teeth, and cat-lovers have a problem with giving and receiving affection.

But then being in love is very different to being without it. Once upon a time I needed only to see Twatface's name pop up on my phone or inbox to feel warm and happy. These days it provokes despair, rage or pity and an angry puzzlement at how he can have changed so much from the person I remember.

He only wants to know if I've had the latest directive from his lawyer, or how I dare try to name Fatty as the third party – or if I've seen his favourite red silk tie anywhere. He swings from angry, to pathetic, then to maudlin reminiscence – 'Today's the three-month anniversary of our separation. It makes me so sad, my darling' – and I'm left wondering what on earth happened to the person I married, because this idiot's a stranger.

Where once there were cuddles and closeness and farting-in-bed competitions – the romance faded after a while, I must admit – there is now just a monster rampaging around and stamping on my poor battered heart. It's already broken, can't you leave it alone?

Did he keep his true self from me for years, or was I an idiot? I can't believe he was capable of the huge, elaborate and consistently clever deceit that this would have required, which leaves me with the unpleasant possibility that I'm a fool. Heck, let's be honest and call it a high probability. Have I really spent all this time crying for no one?

These thoughts send me trawling back through old love letters and photographs in an effort to piece together the truth, trying to work out what was real and where I was misled. It's a painful business and not much fun, although I did find an old picture of Twatface under a Swiss road sign in a town called Cunter, which cheered me up for a bit.

It brought up long-forgotten memories of things half-said, plans we made and the first time we met each others' parents. His never argued, whereas mine do it all the time, and he couldn't get his head around how to do it in a healthy, clearing-the-air way. He used to say I was like a volcano, that I'd be fine for long periods and then suddenly go KABOOM, and afterwards subside, and it'd

153

be like nothing had happened. He said he quite liked that, because I didn't simmer about things, but then that was before the whole getting arrested episode and my trip to the nick.

And I used to like the fact that he didn't know how to argue – it meant I usually won. But now I can see that what actually happened was that he'd avoid the issue until I quietened down and forgot about it, and then go and do whatever it was anyway and just hope I wouldn't find out. Which, when you're married to a tabloid journo, is like jumping off a tall building and praying gravity doesn't notice.

The oldest mementos remind me how much he loved me and the promises he made, but as I hunt through the albums towards the present day the lies creep in, and the recollections that all was not as well as I'd thought at the time.

Exhibit A is this email that I sent in May, after our trip to Venice, and just a few weeks before the end. I'd been to the wedding of Harry Porter, who was sensibly marrying a non-journalist, in the shape of his Swedish girlfriend Godrun, who worked in a law firm in the City, like normal people do. I sent the email to my then-friend Tania Banks, who couldn't make it, with a blow-by-blow account of everything she'd missed.

<From: Foxy, 10.40 a.m.
To: Banks, Tania
Subject: wedding of the century.
1. I decide to wear tight red dress. Due to season, pack bright red leg warmers in expectation of church-based coldness during service. No one will see in a church, right?

2. Husband has night shift the day before. I boot him out of house early and we belt down to Sussex, arriving at church mere moments before the bride. Don leg warmers immediately.

3. Nancy and her husband and new twins, who had got ready at nice hotel, turn up and hop on pew with me and husband. We gurn at Porter at front of church. Porter resignedly waves and gesticulates.

4. I have £10 bet with Nancy's husband that bride will blub. Bride turns up and there is definite moistening. Loser of bet insists she was not crying. Argument ensues about who owes who £10.

5. During ceremony husband embarrasses everyone nearby and fascinates rest of church with his baritone, which is so low it loosens an old lady's bowels. Nance simply stares aghast at him.

6. After ceremony totter across fields to hotel for reception. Pull leg warmers up to knees due to total freezingness, then turn into hotel gateway only to find all guests have been gathered on steps for joint photo. I am last one there, due to pain of high heels, and after much 'excuse me's' and 'so sorry's' ram self in at back so no one can see bright red woolliness of legs. Husband disappears.

7. Mulled wine is served. This is good. Have three glasses.

8. Hacks are informed they are needed for photo with bride and groom, plus partners. However husband cannot be found despite searching for quarter of an hour. This means hacks have photo taken and all partners are banned from shot as bride says it 'won't look right'. Husband turns up, claiming to

have been on phone outside, and bride tells him he has ruined her picture. More wine.

9. Lunch. Gathered hacks are on table of shame in corner along with friends of bride's parents, all of whom seem to be Essex-based self-made scrap-metal millionaires, or highwaymen if you listen to husband. I am plonked next to one who won't shut up, and find him utterly delightful fun. Husband looks down nose.

10. Bride's father makes nice speech. Porter's is slushy and pathetic, with lots of references to 'my wife'. He has a bit of a blub, and Nancy's bloke starts the £10 row again. Best man is OK, quite funny.

11. Gets to 6 p.m. and husband, who has been scathing about scrap-metal millionaires throughout meal, is pissed. Me tired. Everyone decides to go to rooms for little snooze. Husband has fingers prised off bar only after I convince him a sleep will help him drink more later.

12. Reception starts at 7.30 p.m. but husband and I turn up around nine, due to laziness and start of hangover. Hacks have also surfaced, gangsters have been drinking all the way through, and new arrivals include legendary drinker and feature writer Valentine Lush, Buff Arnold, Evil Elliot, Bish, Bridget Jones, Fifi Jenkins, and Princess Flashy Knickers. Much drinking ensues.

13. Husband forces me to dance, despite fact he can't dance. I kick off shoes and start wolfing canapés. Lush says he is praying for redundancy announcements this year, as he has been at paper for 463 years and could sell the occasional paragraph to the *Daily Glimmer*.

14. As evening progresses I discover Bridget is not wearing knickers, as would show VPL. Bridge confesses same to one or two others.

15. One of bride's mates, a Mancunian known as Gavin the Gas Fitter, pants after Bridge all night.

16. Me, Nance and others dance drunkenly with gangsters, who liken party to one thrown by the Krays in 1962. Bish dances like a demented David Brent. Everyone too drunk to work camera phones to capture the moment.

17. At 1 a.m. band gives up, exhausted, and hard core of hacks head to bar. Princess and I watch as Gavin the Gas Fitter challenges Bridge to a game of strip Connect 4, no doubt confident he needs only to win one game before she loses her single item of clothing and is bare-arse naked. Bridget loses but refuses to strip, small fight ensues. Memories of night now bit of a blur . . .

18. Fifi forces Princess and Bridge into cab back to their B & B nearby. Gavin the Gas Fitter goes to bed alone, disappointed and with black eye. At 1.30 a.m. Nancy and I head to rooms with husbands. Husband says he is getting drink of water, and won't be long. At 3 a.m. I awake, go to bar in jim-jams, drag husband to bed. Valentine offered cab to his own hotel, but drunkenly refuses and reels into the night, looking for a rural lock-in.

19. Awake at 9 a.m., ignore husband, breakfast in sunglasses. Husband turns up and says sorry. On way out bump into Nance, who is packing car with babies and had row with husband in corridor at 4 a.m., which the manager had to break up. I tell how husband is in doghouse due to whole pyjama-bar

157

debacle. At this point both meet a fresh-faced and happily smiling Porter and bride, whose nuptial bliss is spiked by the tales of marital disharmony. We reassure bride marriage is great, it's just being married to a man which ruins it. Porter rolls eyes.

20. Fifi rings from nearby hotel. Hacks were asked on way to breakfast if they knew the tramp asleep face down on floor in reception. Did their best to look innocent. Valentine later strolls in and distributes hugs, but stinks like he's been weed on by a herd of cows. Explains staggered back to hotel across fields, fell over a lot, then could not figure out how to open door to room, so slept on nearest soft surface, which happened to be lobby carpet.

21. Gavin the Gas Fitter stalks Bridget for several days, demanding date. She ignores him. He keeps ringing and eventually, employing the canny trick of withholding his number and catching her when she is hungover, gets her to answer, 'Ooh, I'm just really busy, no, I'm not ignoring you at all, yes I'll ring you straight back.' That was three days ago. Eventually, after is pointed out she is acting like worst kind of bloke and asked how she would like it, Bridget texts Gavin to say not interested. He is most hurt and replies, 'You should have been honest.'

22. Think Nance has taken husband back. Mine still drunk. Not really seen him since.>

Instead of simply seeing this email as an account of debauched rowdy fun, I noticed for the first time that I'd spent the whole day arguing with Twatface, who had in turn spent it behaving as rudely as he could. And while everyone gets boozed at a wedding, his attitude to the free bar suddenly seemed close to alcoholic.

I had thought he changed from loving husband to monstrous bastard overnight when we split. It seemed so sudden and unexpected; I was stunned. But in reality the process was such a slow and steady one that days like this simply didn't register as anything out of the ordinary. His benders, my worries, our problems became the norm and I got used to them. Just as I also became accustomed to overlooking his frequent absences 'to make a phone call' or the way he was rude to my friends or embarrassed me. And in my turn I became the kind of wife who didn't want to dance with him any more, and spent the day bending his ear about whatever he was doing wrong. When the end came it wasn't out of the blue, but I had my head stuck so far in the sand that the only way he could get my attention was to give me a kick up the bum. And by that point it was too late to do anything but fight.

He asked to see me yesterday, to talk things over yet again. I asked sarcastically if Fatty was away, and he said she was in Spain. I said we could talk, but not about any of the legal stuff. He wanted to go to a bar, but I insisted on a coffee shop in the hope that he might be sober. I was waiting for him when he arrived; he kissed me on the cheek and said I looked amazing. We sat there for an hour and he asked four times if we could go to a pub, while I ranted at him that he had no moral fibre, backbone, idea, clue, parenting skills or anything else worth mentioning.

He said he hadn't thought over what had happened between us; that no one would talk to him about this stuff; and that he always used to rely on me to give him advice, and now he couldn't. I calmed down a bit and stopped haranguing him. I said, more calmly, that he should find someone to talk to, a psychiatrist, anyone, just sort himself out so this didn't happen again with the next woman. That he couldn't spend his life avoiding things, and that if he just faced them head-on a little more often – and I faced them head-on a little less – then maybe we'd both be better off. Then he said that he missed me. He kept saying sorry.

Last night, late, he texted me: 'I'm so, so sorry. I fear I'll end up like Valentine Lush one day, face down on a manky carpet. I've mistreated you so badly, and all you've been in return is strong, loving, tough, fair. I'm not the man you deserve. I can't be the first to say this, but you can and will find better. I'm so sorry I screwed up and wasted your time like this. I'm an idiot, chump, fool, git.'

If I'd known at the start that this was how it would end – when I walked into his newsroom all those years ago and wondered who the smiley chap was – and that it would bring me one day to a sorrowful little message like that, would I still have done it all? Yeah, probably.

But I'd have done things differently, too. I'd have kicked him out a lot sooner, and I wouldn't have thought twice about it.

DAY ONE HUNDRED AND THREE

THE ideal interview, from the journalist's point of view, starts with flirtation, leads to seduction, and results in betrayal. In my case it's more usual to flirt, fall over and fuck it up, which I suppose is why I don't get asked to do the big chats very often.

It goes wrong almost every time. I was asked to interview an author I much admired when he was on a book-signing tour years ago, passing through the town where the local paper I worked on at the time was based. My news editor came over and asked me to do it, because he knew I was a fan. Naturally, like anyone going to meet a hero, I was excited. I rehearsed some questions, and tried to think of things that made me sound clever and witty, while at the same time covering all the bases expected by a local newspaper interview, which had to include, 'What do you think of our town?' and 'Do you back a bypass?'

I got myself down to the bookshop, spoke to some of the fans in the queue, then was shown up to the manager's poky office, where I met the great man and was disappointed to find he was a bit short, in both stature and manner. He sat one side of the manager's desk and I the other, I chatted, flirted, smiled, complimented him, joked about his fans. After a few questions he seemed to warm up a bit, so I went for the big seduction, revealing

I was his number-one fan. He was slightly nonplussed but remained polite. By the end I felt the whole thing had gone quite well, and had even managed to get his thoughts on our town – 'Lovely place, lovely, where are we today, again?'

I stood up to shake his hand across the desk. Then, as I tried to make a final witty comment which was so good I can't remember it any more, I drew my hand back from his and swept the entire contents of the manager's desk – pen tidy, stack of coins, piles of paperbacks, two cups of tepid tea and a plate of biscuits – on to the floor with an enormous crash. The author and I gazed speechlessly at the mess. The manager and the book agent, who had been sitting in, stared, too. Then all three turned to look at me in silence. I blushed hotly and knelt under their continuing gazes to pick all the bits up, put them back on the desk, wiped some tea off the wall with my sleeve, wittered brightly: 'Well, thank you SO much!' and backed out of the door as fast as my feet could carry me.

Then there was the time I had to interview a *Big Brother* contestant after she left the show and was zipping all over London between photo-shoots. We were accompanied by a documentary crew, who filmed the two of us in the back of a black cab, me trying to ask her questions while we bounced over road humps and I tried not to think about the unblinking eye of the camera lens – which was making me so nervous I couldn't think of anything sensible to ask. When the programme aired I featured briefly as 'tabloids bought her story but only wanted to know if she'd really slept with that footballer'.

My strained expression in the cab led to a text from a friend, who said: 'You were looking at her with utter disdain on your face. It was like you *loathed* her. It was HYSTERICAL.'

Now, on the rare occasion anyone is stupid enough to ask me to do a big interview, I explain kindly and gently that it's just a silly idea. Flirtation and seduction aren't really me.

But then lots of things that are said in journalism don't translate into real life. 'Fancy a drink?' is one. It usually means eight pints, some Jack Daniels, an Amaretto and a cab home if you can still remember your address. 'I have a morally-sound reason for lurking in this person's rose bushes, officer,' is another. And then there are terms that are used in the pages of newspapers but never anywhere else.

Take fracas, for example. Ever seen one? No, because if you did you'd call it a fight. If you saw two they would be 'fights'; in newspapers they become 'running battles'. (Which I've always thought sounded like marathon runners slapping each other. I don't know what the plural of fracas is. Fricassee?) How about a spat or a rumpus? Has anybody, in the history of mankind, ever really romped? Presumably it requires a lot of oxygen, because it only ever appears to happen in mid-air or open-air. And what the hell's a tryst when it's at home?

Technically, breaking up with Twatface led to a street fracas and a bit of a rumpus. I'm reasonably certain that I have romped a couple of times, although I'm not sure if the back of a Citroën really counts as open-air. I have never slated anyone, seen a tot, tragic or otherwise, nor described anyone as a sex fiend in everyday conversation. 'What happened with that guy you were dating?' 'Oh, he was a sex fiend.' See? Never happens.

'No one talks like that,' I declaimed loudly from one of the triangular stools at the bar in the Bell on Fleet Street. 'It's a strange, archaic branch of language that survives only in tabloid newspapers. Like Gaelic in some tiny village that won't join the twenty-first century because they're still busy ignoring the twentieth.'

Porter, who was leaning across the bar next to me, snorted over the top of his eighth pint and tried to focus, blinking slowly. 'Ha, like bizarre collective nouns. Like, like a parliament of owls, or a murder of crows. Why do we have them? They're ridiculous.'

Bridget wheeled in from outside, where she'd been having a smoke. 'Most of them are bollocks anyway,' she slurred, one claw reaching out for her warm wine. 'Shurely it should be a hoot of owls?'

'What would a collective noun for journalists be?' I asked, turning to survey the pub where the finest of Fleet Street had gathered. 'A gossip? A meddle? A slander?'

'Nah,' said Bridge, burping. 'Should be a scandal of journalists.'

Before we knew it we had collective nouns for everyone. A cretin of Elliots. A cackle of Bridgets. A bluster of Bishes, a prickle of Porters. A knobbing of Princesses. (Porter came up with that one, with a leer.) A vomit of WAGS, a bell-end of footballers, a smear of politicians.

But a scandal of journalists is something that I think should stick. The reason we were all in the pub and quite drunk, even though it was only two in the afternoon, was a funeral. It was for Thomas Tudor, a legend in the street, who had worked on almost every paper over forty years or more, as well as at the BBC, where he had honed his baritone into the kind of beautiful speaking voice which could have made whole armies put down their guns and,

164

had he been ungentlemanly enough to try it, any woman drop her drawers.

Having been around the block a few times and being into his sixties, he would man the news desk some nights, and when young reporters rang in from some god-forsaken spot on the road, desperate for a hotel, a wash or human contact, his was the most welcome voice in the world. It was like listening to warm treacle, and it helped, too, that he had a big white beard and looked like Father Christmas. Maybe the door had been slammed in your face, maybe you'd been threatened or arrested or told there was no room at the inn, but a couple of minutes on the phone to Tom while he said, 'Oh, poor you,' made it all seem better.

Unfortunately Tom was no longer with us, and his memorial had brought out the staff of six newspapers or more. There was us lot, a squad from the *Daily Glimmer*, a smattering of retired male hacks who'd moved out of the city to the districts years ago to avoid creditors or alcoholism, some radio twats in corduroy, and various former staff members who'd gone on to other papers. Executives, hacks, snappers, trainees – the full glut of what was left of British journalism – had turned out to remember one of their own. It wasn't just a Fleet Street piss-up; we all genuinely cared for Tom and he was our friend. His family were with us in the pub. But the fact remained that our turnout was also partly a duty, to give a brother the send-off he deserved. We were like vultures putting a mangy wing around one another in comfort, an unusual trade union of professional carrion-eaters gathered to mark the passing of a comrade.

Black jackets dusted off, we'd all packed into St Bride's, the journalists' church just off Fleet Street, for the service. I don't know how much of hell froze over that morning, but it must have been a sizable chunk, judging by the shamefaced loitering as long as possible on the pavement outside, the shuffling of feet, the shiver down the spine as each of us crossed the threshold. Journalists hate the thought that they might be caught out by anyone – that's our job, after all – and going to church is a bit like stepping into The Editor's office. It happens rarely, and usually only after something bad which we might get the blame for. Religion for its own sake is something most of us neither understand nor need. Not unless the beer runs out.

The trouble was that we'd met in the pub first for a heart-starter – well, waited there for everyone else to turn up – then staggered into the pews. The vicar, who was used to our sort, greeted us warmly to possibly the only church in the land where we are actually welcome. I've sat in churches for funerals I've had to cover, sometimes invited and sometimes masquerading as a mourner, making surreptitious notes, trying to ignore but internally writhing under the baleful glares of the genuinely grief-stricken. Even if the family ask you in, someone always mutters about 'vultures' and talks about Princess Di.

Anyway, the vicar at St Bride's is the only one I've ever met who looks down from his pulpit in the certain knowledge that most of his congregation can be categorized under the heading 'utter bastards', and doesn't seem to mind.

And this service was quite good fun. Journos who hadn't seen each other for years waved across the aisle, clapped one another on the back over the pews, and blundered their way through the singing until they hit a chorus they knew and could pound it out with all their

166

strength – 'All things BRIGHT AND BEAUTIFUL . . .' – while holding a church-wide sweepstake on which mobile would be the first to go off.

As we filed out afterwards, the hacks all loitered in the entranceway, and Valentine Lush, who'd been 'waiting' in the pub slightly longer than the rest of us, scooped me up in his arms and twirled me round while copping a happy feel at the same time. 'Val!' I stage-whispered. 'We're still in the church! And that's my ARSE!'

'And a lovely one it is, too!' he cackled, reeling off into the Bell with Sickly from the *Sunday Scandal*, a health reporter whose constitution has been so weakened by booze that he once had a 'seizure' which involved repeatedly ramming another reporter's head into the hand-towel dispenser in the gentlemen's toilets at the Old Bailey. He later claimed latent epilepsy was to blame, and apologized to his victim by taking him out for a drink.

Tom would have loved his memorial. He would have been in the middle of his old muckers, telling tall stories from back in the day about how he had been the first to enter Port Stanley in the Falklands War, bugger what Max Hastings says on the subject, and how another time he had caught Prince Philip's secret girlfriend, but was told to lay off because The Proprietor was angling for a knighthood and tea with the Queen.

We reminisced about Tom's career, including how he was once seen, in blazer and kerchief, grooming his beard in the backdraft of an aid plane's engine while covering the Ethiopian famine. Another story was about how Tom was trapped in his hotel in Baghdad as the Americans were dropping bombs during the first Gulf War. He was filing copy over a satellite phone, a descriptive piece known as 'colour', dramatically telling how bombs were dropping and people were fleeing. But the Republican Guard didn't want the news to get out, and tried to confiscate all the sat phones. Armed guards were going room to room. Tom barricaded the hotel-room door, locked himself on the balcony, and filed stream-of-consciousness copy throughout the bombardment.

'Beautiful words, and grammatically perfect, too,' remembered one rheumy-eyed colleague. 'Tear-jerking stuff and not a comma out of place.'

By dinner-time Porter had thrown Guinness all over me by accident, Nancy had pulled a sports writer and snuck off down an alley for a snog, and I had persuaded the landlord to take the paper-towel dispenser out of the men's loos for safety's sake.

At one point I found myself at the bar with one of Tom's brothers, who shared his dulcet tones and avuncular style. He thanked me for coming, and said how much it meant to the family to see so many of us there. In my cups, I muttered something about how we were all bastards in most people's eyes.

I told him: 'It was this lot, you know, these same misfits who would be thrown out of a pigsty for their manners, that stood by me and refused to gossip when everyone wanted to know about my husband cheating on me and my getting arrested for trying to kill this fat bird he was seeing. And d'you know, that's the nicest thing anyone's ever done for me?'

'I know what you're saying,' said the brother. 'It somehow means more when bastards are nice.'

'Yeah,' I slurred, slipping off my stool on the way to the ladies. 'It's very moving, the solidarity of scum.'

I barely registered his guffaw because, halfway to the loo, I walked straight into Twatface.

'Hello,' he said. 'H-h-h-how are you?'

'F"ckov,' I burped, continuing on my way to the loos. He was still there when I came back, grinning nervously. Although I walked past him with my nose in the air, he followed me to the bar and explained he'd come with his boss, who'd once worked with Tom, and didn't mean to make me feel bad.

'I don't feel bad,' I lied, looking him up and down. He was fatter than I'd ever seen him before. 'Good to see you've kept the weight off.'

He laughed and patted his expanding tummy. 'Yes, well, there's more of me than there used to be.'

'Huh,' I sniffed. 'Must be beer. Can't believe Fatty's letting you near her food.'

He said something inane about how nice it was to see me, and how were Mum and Dad? And I replied as rudely as I could that it was none of his damned business. We circled each other like two dogs fighting over their vomit, until he said 'I miss you, you know', and I sighed.

'How did we get here?' I asked him. 'I did everything I thought you wanted, got on with your family, showed you how much I cared. Maybe it wasn't enough, but you got everything I had to give.' I sighed again. 'I don't think you appreciated that. You didn't think I was worth doing the same for, nothing worth looking after or trying not to hurt.' He said sorry again, quietly, and left the pub, leaving me hollow upon my bar stool. A bit later Bish wandered up to me, drunk and therefore able to talk about personal stuff for once.

'Eh, lass, jus' bumped into your worse half outside while I was having a Woodbine,' he said, as Buff Arnold

169

and Val came to blows behind us over whose mobile phone had rung first in the church, since the sweepstake pot had now reached £250.

'Oh, yeah? Whatever,' I said, waving my empty glass at the barman, who was apparently considering abandoning his post to cower in a back room.

'Aye,' said Bish, swaying on the spot. 'He stopped to talk to us an' all. He asked how you were and that, and said you'd been bollockin' 'im. Then he said, and this is a quote, like, "God, I love her."'

'What?'

'Yeah. He said "God, I love her. I mean, I'm glad I'm not married to her any more, but isn't she great?" Then he wandered off. I didn't know yer divorce had come through, lass.' He drained his glass.

'It hasn't. We're still married,' I said flatly.

'He's such a twat, lass, why'd you marry him?' said Bish, before wandering off to find a cab.

DAY ONE HUNDRED AND FOUR

THE next day my liver was in near-total collapse. When I dragged myself to my desk I found the Fleet Street grapevine alive with the news that Val had a black eye, Buff had somehow landed a bar bill for £300 after losing a poker game, and Sickly of the *Scandal* had spent his hangover ringing around the gossip columns begging them not to print a rumour about him battering the landlord into a towel dispenser. 'It was months ago, and it was a reporter!' he was heard to howl. 'I would never harm a landlord!'

I snickered into my cup of tea, took a bite out of my emergency bacon sandwich and brown sauce, and sorted through the post that had been dropped on my keyboard. There, under the press releases and tickets to things I'd never go to, was a formal-looking envelope in thick white paper, lurking like a shameful cigarette end at the bottom of a beer glass.

It was from the lawyer, and was my decree nisi. Which I hadn't known was coming, and Twatface obviously had. Our marriage had been officially declared dead and I'd barely got my head around the fact that it was even unwell.

So there it was, gurning up at me from my desk like a gargoyle in paper form, daring me to get upset, get angry or get arrested again. But the strange fact is that the decree nisi leaves me feeling absolutely nothing – nothing at all.

I'm not making it up, not just saying it as part of the whole brave-face thing. It doesn't even leave me cold or numb, it's just an envelope of big, empty nothingness. In the strictest sense, of course, it's simply a piece of paper with some words on it, but so is a wedding certificate, and that means a lot. Weddings come with happy memories. (Or in my case, recollections of the groom spilling beer on my frock and a drunken aunt bitching about my dress.)

Marriage certificates have a coat of arms on them, and writing in proper fountain pen, and cost thousands of pounds and a year to organize, and require mothers to be kept happy, and lots and lots of shopping trips, and a photo album that makes you feel all warm, and an anniversary which later turns out to be the only time all year you have sex. Decree nisis, on the other hand, are matter-of-fact forms run off by the court on an inkjet printer, which tell you that all that is over, and was such a waste of time and money that you'd have been better off digging a hole in the ground, covering yourself with a duvet and hibernating for the whole five years of the relationship.

The sex would probably have been better, too.

But nevertheless there's a piece of paper sitting on my desk now that says my marriage is dead. Oh, all right, I admit it's been rather gasping for breath since Fatty had me dragged off in cuffs, and frankly had not much chance of recovery thanks to Twatface's buggering about, and had in fact been limping for quite a while before that, with hindsight. But now a judge has signed it off there's no arguing the point any more. It's over: the

172

dreams, the plans, and the babies' names we decided on together, which now I can't use if I have a baby with someone else, in case the child is hexed.

The fact that I still have my wedding dress, never dry-cleaned it, and couldn't even wear it again in case it somehow used up its magical properties, is no longer touching. It doesn't remind me of a happy day any more, either. Now it's just a bit of silk that smells of beer and makes me sigh, like an old pair of lucky pants when the elastic's gone.

And despite this piece of paper I'm still married. I still have a husband, and I wish like hell I didn't. I still use the phrase 'my husband', only it's no longer said with a sense of togetherness. We still have a house and a mortgage and lots of crappy things to argue about, yet at the same time we're supposed to be starting our lives anew. It's like trying to climb a ladder with someone on your back, with the added problem that they're trying to prise your fingers off the rungs and drag you down into an abyss of self-loathing with them. If I found someone new, technically I'd be an adulterer, too, and indeed I already am. I cannot move on as I should. My feet are glued to the floor because I'm still legally and psychologically tied to someone who is the direct opposite of the smiley, sweet man I fell in love with, someone who is being such a bully about the divorce I literally hate him. There have been moments – hell, whole weeks – when I felt like killing him, simply to make the world a slightly less twatty place.

But there is an unwritten code about these things: that even, and *especially* if, you were the wronged party, you will continue to bear the other party's behaviour with nothing more than a grimace and a quiet bitch to your mates over a glass of wine. I'm not supposed to send the boys

173

round, despite the many offers my fellow hacks have made. (Buff Arnold wanted to do the deed himself, but most suggestions were more along the lines of 'I know someone who . . .'). I'm not allowed to haul Twatface into the town square and invite the world to throw rotten eggs at him. And maybe because most of my friends have yet to get married, there comes a point where they turn to me and say, 'Isn't it time you moved on?' And yes, it is, and I'd love to – but *we're still married*. It slows you down, like a ten-ton weight.

I rang Maurice the smiling lawyer to find out what was going on and he explained, in his jolly, isn't-all-this-a-lark? and that'll-be-another-£150-thanks way that the decree nisi was, 'Just a formality really, a recognition that you both agree the situation is irretrievable. You signed the forms last time you came in, don't you remember?'

Well, no, Maurice, because mainly I just remember the big cheque I signed at the same time. It left an indelible stain upon my memory. By the time you pressed some other documents into my hand and asked me to daub a mark on them my brain had spun off into a horrible world of massive debt and government bail-outs, so I wasn't really thinking clearly. But while it's a surprise it's nevertheless welcome, I suppose, like when the end comes for a terminal cancer patient; as much as you wish they didn't have cancer you're kind of glad when death finally arrives.

If the decree nisi is the formal recognition of a marriage's demise, the certificate stating baldly that the cause of death is 'adultery', then there's only one thing which ends it for good and proper, and turns 'my husband' into an ex. The decree absolute, the final closure, the end. The funeral, as I am swiftly learning to think of it.

But that, Dear Reader, is nowhere in sight.

Maurice giggled. 'Ooh no, you have the nisi to formally recognize the whole thing's over, but we haven't agreed a financial settlement yet, which can take years in some cases. Some parties never apply for the absolute, they're happy to just have the nisi.' (Who are these nutters? Are they allowed to drive?) 'Although, in your case, without children, I shouldn't think it will take more than a few months to hammer everything out.'

'Months, Maurice? How many months?'

'Oh, who can tell with these things? Unfortunately your husband's lawyer doesn't see things the same way as us.'

The main thing Twatface's legal eagle doesn't see is why he owes me any money, because we don't have children. We do, however, have a house, bought with the help of a small inheritance from my granddad, which, as Maurice gleefully pointed out, once I had put into the marital home became, technically, half Twatface's.

And Twatface wants it back. Well not back, because it was never his, but he wants five figures in lieu, or for us to sell the house and split the proceeds. Which if he was dirt poor I could understand, but a couple of months before we split he had an inheritance himself, and that one was about ten times the size of mine. It was destined for the mortgage and me getting pregnant, but because it was in his bank account and not our house it's all his, apparently. So now he's shacked up with Fatty, whose family reek of money, and he's sitting on a big stinking pile of cash, and yet he wants to chase me for a few pennies more and make me homeless into the bargain. He's even threatened to have my car off me. What a nice man.

Well, I'm not having it. NO. FLAMING. WAY. I hit back with a succession of estate-agent valuations, each of which valued the house as the same or slightly less than when we bought it, and which therefore technically means he has to buy his way out of the deposit. Bless the recession! I would tell you that legal letters have been flying, but they've not. They've been limping, slowly, between solicitors, with zero result apart from making me worry what'll happen next. It's like water torture: days waiting for a letter to drop on the doormat and slice another few pounds off my bank balance and years off my mental health. So far it's cost more than getting hitched in the first place, only without the nice frock. Why did I get married? If we'd just lived together one of us could have chucked the other out, and this would all be over.

But then it seemed like the right thing to do at the time; we were in love, once, and while you might think holding on to that thought is a bad idea, it actually helps to remember that things weren't always like this. And while it might have been a mistake, it was something I can't wish away or regret. And I don't – I know that one day the hate and upset and anxiety will pass.

Twatface and everything he did will never leave me, for better or worse. It's up to me to make that a lesson to be learned from rather than a scab to be picked over. In the meantime the corpse of my marriage is laid out in the living room, waiting for a decent burial and starting to stink.

Just as that thought trundled its way across my frontal lobe and I was toying with the thick vellum of the lawyer's envelope, there was a whoosh and a thunk as Bish dropped a bundle of paper on to my keyboard.

'It's that time o'year, lass. Appraisals. Come t'Bunker in five.'

Thanking the fairies that at least it wasn't with Elliot, I

leafed through the bureaucratic, asinine nightmare which is a personnel review spreadsheet thingamabob.

Such things are rare in newsrooms, where assessments are usually carried out on the hoof and on deadline, and normally involve being bawled out by the boss if you've screwed something up or, if you've landed a world-beating splash and saved the day, you might get a, 'Not bad, you can come back tomorrow.' Last week Bridget managed to rile Bish by getting in a fluster and not filing her copy quick enough. After calling down the newsroom to her three times to, ''urry the fook up', he eventually went purple, leapt to his feet and bellowed, 'YOU ONLY COME IN HERE FOR THE HEAT AND LIGHT, DON'T YER? We haven't been this late off-stone since the old king died, NOW PULL YER BLUDDY FINGER OUT, you useless heap o'shite!'

Elliot, in his more furious moments, has been known to sidle up to a trembling hack whose splash has just collapsed, and quietly whisper in their ear: 'If you can't find something for the front in the next five minutes I'm going to kick your cunt off.'

And of course if you do well and they like you, like Tania Banks, you get gifted the stories that come in to the news desk: the sure-fire splashes and two-page spreads which get you a good show in the paper and a slap on the back from The Editor. If I didn't know better I'd say Banks was sleeping with someone important, the way the good stories get neatly packaged up with a little pink bow, laid on a silver salver and then carried to her desk by a strutting Elliot, looking like he should be wearing tails and a pair of white gloves, while she simpers delightedly.

In the cut and thrust of newsrooms the assessments go both ways. The last editor was a shouty old bastard, and one day he pulled a two-thousand-word spread by Valentine Lush, who had lavished love on it and spent a hellish ten hours dealing with constant rewrites and meddling. Told his prose had been 'sent to spike', Val decided he was going to make a stand. Stiffening his spine with a couple of slugs from the hip flask he kept in his drawer, he stalked up to the back bench where the editor was laying out the paper, tapped him on the shoulder, and when he turned round laid him out cold with a technically perfect right hook. Val flicked a resignation letter on to his boss's unconscious form with a flourish, said, 'Fuck you, you old bastard,' and swept off to the pub to a round of applause. That editor left shortly after, and his replacement rehired Val on day one of the new regime.

Anyway, the paperwork and form-filling of the corporate world has wound its tendrils even into the shenanigans of journalists. My review asks the kind of non-quantifiable questions that simply don't apply to reporters, but get asked anyway in an effort to make our work a series of boxes to be scored out of ten, which can be presented as a profit-and-loss table in the annual meeting for shareholders. Rather than 'gets splashes' or 'writes well' or 'has shorthand and knows their law', it's all multi-media arse-wipery which has little to do with how you actually do the job.

For example:

* Is the resource [seriously, we're a resource] good with multimedia?
Translation: Can she nick pictures off Faceache?
* Is the resource aware of the issues surrounding journalism?
Translation: Does she mind being despised?

* Is the resource aware of how a journalist should
behave ethically and professionally?
*Translation: Does she stand her round and share her
Berocca?*

And that's about it, along with the normal guff about
whether you've hit your targets from the last review
(drink less, earn more), and where you see yourself in
five years' time (please Lord, a book deal and a column).
Oh, and it runs to about twenty pages. Shame there isn't
a similar thing for divorces, really, or marriages, come to
that.

Anyway it now sat between Bish and me on his clut-
tered desk in the Bunker, along with a smouldering
Woodbine in his overflowing ashtray and twenty-years'
worth of newspaper cuttings. His most recent favourite's
from the *Scum*: 'YOU CAN'T SLURRY LOVE', about a
pervert caught pleasuring himself in a muck-spreader.

'Well, lass, how's it been?' he asked, flicking through
the bundle of papers and 'the resource's' attempts at writing a load of old bollo about multimedia buggery.

I wittered something about wanting to do more writing
jobs.

He shook his head at me. 'No lass, not the bluddy job.
At 'ome. What's happening with that bluddy twat yer
married?'

Surprised he was asking, I stumbled through a brief
explanation of how things were moving on, just the financial agreement to go; that I really wanted to keep the
house but didn't know how I'd afford it on one salary,
and that it was a bit of a worry with redundancies in the
air. Bish nodded and mmm-hmmed, trying to ignore his
phone ringing. With a glare through his glass wall at the

179

newsroom, he said: 'Am I the only bugger answers the phones round here? Bluddy Kelvin used to, yer know, it was a chance to talk to The Reader. 'Ang on lass. Yes, what? Who? No, we don't do pizzas. Piss off, caller.'

He hung up, took a drag on his dog-end and said: 'Look, I've talked to The Editor and we've agreed to recommend yer for a small pay rise. Won't be a lot, but we want to help all we can. Me first wife were a right cow, and we were only married a year and a half. I know how it feels, lass. Anyhow, to get it past the board we've got to pretend you're God's gift to reporting, so leave this form with me, I'll make up some shite and fill it in for yer. They're a load o'claptrap any road.'

Lost for words, I stammered some thanks. Bish waved a hand and told me to bugger off, not to tell anyone else or they'd all want some, and to send the next one in.

Back at my desk, I realized I'd somehow managed to swing a pay increase in the middle of a recession. A whole extra peanut.

But it made me think. If there was a review of how this divorce was going, what would it say?

'Has the resource made peace with her spouse?'
No.
'Have both parties come to an amicable understanding?'
No.
'Has the resource let go of her marriage?'
Not by any means.

Well, that's all a load of old bollo, too, if you ask me. I'd far rather it asked:

180

'Who's winning?', 'Who's happiest?', 'Who's better off without the other one?'
Me, me, me.

I'm prepared to admit it has to get boxed off and buried one day. I'll have to wait for the decree absolute, but when it comes I think I'll throw another party. Like the poem says, the end of love should be a big event. I'll have to do something about the wedding dress, too. If it stays in my wardrobe I'll inevitably get drunk and a bit Miss Havisham one night and decide to see if I can still fit in it, which even as a mental image freaks me out. The last thing I need to see is a weepy, drunk, badger-eyed woman in the mirror in a beer-stained frock which probably won't fit me any more.

Celebrity ex-wives seem to be a lot better at this sort of thing than me. They get a big house or a place on *Strictly Come Dancing*, while their lizardy exes make public fools of themselves. I did read once that Jo Wood had a coffin-shaped box for her wedding ring, although rather than burying it she keeps it on the mantelpiece, which seems rather daft to me. Talk about leaving the body on ice.

But if I did that, where would I bury it? I'd have to wrap the dress round my rings. Maybe I could tie it all round a rock and throw it in the Thames? But, just like a funeral, would it mean a damn thing? The whole affair's just as dead as it was before, it's simply more hygienic to get rid of the body. It's a case of getting your head around it, I suppose. And to be honest a burial's a bit undramatic, and therefore not really me. Do you say some words over it afterwards? 'Ashes to ashes, dust to dust, naff off Twatface, now where's the pub'?

No, I know what would be fitting. I'll build a little raft, tie the dress and the rings to it, set it on fire and let it drift down the river. A Viking funeral at sea. I'll probably end up with the river police on my back, but what the hell, this wound needs to be cauterized if I'm to recover properly.

Start as you mean to go on – in flames, if necessary.

DAY ONE HUNDRED AND FOURTEEN

THE one blissful thing about being suddenly single –
hell, one of the many blissful things – is that you can
make decisions on your own. No longer do I have to seek
permission, keep someone informed of my whereabouts,
or find a way to dovetail two social lives into one. If
there's something I want to do, there's no need to avoid
a row by engaging in a six-week campaign to make someone else think it was all their idea in the first place.

Wear my hair up or down? Paint the bedroom red or
blue? If I get an invitation, I don't have to defer to someone else in case 'we' had other plans. If I'm asked what
I'd like to drink, there is no need to glance at someone
to see how much he's had and whether I've ended up the
designated driver again. I can sleep on whatever side of
the bed I fancy.

It feels a bit like a dictatorship just after a revolution:
the despot has gone, democracy has arrived and suddenly
I'm being given a say in things.

But as any Iraqi will tell you, despots at least give you a
sense of certainty, whereas unlimited freedom leaves you
facing the tyranny of choice. Not only is there now a
choice, but you *have* to make one: there is no middle
option. Do you want to stay in or go out? Do you want a
super-tall skinny latte with chocolate sprinkles or a full-fat
decaf mocha chococino?

'Hurry up, my lovely,' complained Fifi next to me in the queue at the coffee shop on Monday morning. 'We're late as it ez, and I need a coffee, izzeht.'

Sighing, I gave up and ordered the Earl Grey like I always did, waited while she got her frappa-whatsit and then we sauntered into the office next door, trotting to catch one of the clanking, ratchety lifts just as the doors closed.

'So 'ow was your weekend7, then?' Fi asked me.

'Ah, not too bad. I spent most of Sunday in B&Q unable to pick a wallpaper for the bedroom.'

'Are you decorating, then? I thought you'd have to sell up?'

I laughed. 'Ha, no. Well, I thought the same, but the bank said I can take on the mortgage, so long as I don't mind living on cold baked beans for the next twenty-five years.'

'Faberluss!' gushed Fi as the lift paused for breath between floors. She stabbed at the buttons and it sighed, then continued to wheeze its way upwards. 'Damn thing. That's amazing! You totally deserve the house, and once you've done it up it'll be worth a bomb, izzeht. You'd have been gutted if you had to hand it back after all you've ben through. What if you'd 'ad to sell it to Twatface an' Fatty, can you imaaagine?'

We stepped out of the lift, which did its daily jerk-of-death as we straddled the doorway, forcing us to snatch our limbs out hurriedly before it plummeted back down the shaft with a leg still in it.

'God, don't get me started. I've become quite obsessed about the house,' I said, holding open the newsroom door for her. 'It's like my castle or something; I go home and shut the gate and lock the door, and feel totally safe.

184

I've got so many plans and dreams for it, and I don't see why I should lose everything.'

Plonking my bag down, and slurping my tea, I thumbed through the papers on my desk. 'There's no way I could have sold it, to Twatface or anyone. If they sent the bailiffs round they'd find I'd cemented my feet into the patio, or my fingernails on to the front step. I'd never give it up, it would be like admitting defeat.'

Fifi grinned over the top of her computer. 'Then we should celebrate, don'you thenk? Porky from the cricket club's avin' a birthday party on Wednesday, do you want to come?'

She turned her screen around so I could see her email inbox.

'Of course I want to come, there's boys and beer . . . hang on, TWENTY-FIRST BIRTHDAY? Are you mad?'

Fifi laughed. 'There'll be a whole cricket team, though! And reserves, izzeht!'

'Yes, reserves of children. Get knotted, Fi.'

So Wednesday dawned and set, and after work there I was, tottering over the hill to Blackheath in my tightest jeans and a tit top, clutching a bottle of white in one hand, texting Twatface with the other about his latest legal inanity, and telling myself this was a ridiculous idea. I'd not eaten all day in order to fit into the jeans, and was so set on my target of A Night Out that when Fifi told me she couldn't make it and had to go to a showbiz party in town for work it hardly put me off my stride. She rang as I dodged the traffic on the A2 and headed down to Porky's flat in Blackheath Village.

'Have a faberluss time, ring me and let me know how it goes!' she said.

'You're not coming? But I don't know any of them, apart from that one who snogged me once! And I didn't even have time to eat some emergency cheese. I'm bound to get smashed.'

'Ah, you'll be fine, my lovely, and anyway Spacker's not going. Talk later, byeeeee!'

Oh, marvellous. A thirty-year-old separated singleton wearing clothing she'd be too old for in another couple of years, knocking on the door of a twenty-one-year-old cricketer she saw once across a bar before snogging his mate, who was called Spacker. 'The joyride which is my life,' I thought, lifting the knocker.

Porky – whippet-thin and barely old enough to shave, by the look of him – opened the door.

'Er, yes?'

'Happy birthday!' I cried with false jollity, thrusting the wine at him. 'Remember me? Fi couldn't make it!'

'Oh, right, yes,' he said, the look of confusion on his youthful face lifting slightly as he failed to remember me at all. He was clearly thinking that if I was a friend of Fifi's then we must have met while he was drunk. 'Come in.'

I continued to burble small talk at him as I followed him down a narrow corridor to a kitchen, where his girl-friend, a few others, and a massive collection of alcohol was gathered, and I said hello to some faces I vaguely recalled. For some inexplicable reason Porky had decided to celebrate his birthday with a barbecue in the rain, and after opening the bottle of wine I'd brought with me and filling a pint glass with most of it (there weren't any other glasses, he *was* a twenty-one-year-old), I went out into the garden. The boys were huddled around the

186

barbecue, which had been put under a tree to keep it from being rained on. They were stood about in traditional male fashion, each with a pint of something in one hand, the other in a pocket, jostling to tell the funniest or dirtiest joke while avoiding eye contact by staring fixedly at the flames, which were failing to turn some sausages brown.

I pitched up into the middle of them, and was immediately welcomed. Fifi's brother Beamy took me under his wing yet again. Bazzo, the big blond one, remembered me from last time, as did Raffles and Slappim – whose wandering hands never forgot something he'd yet to grope.

Bazzo, as the tallest and loudest, was holding forth on the topic of his job in the immigration service, and said: 'Hey, you're a reporter, you'll like this . . .'

I sighed – people who think they've got a story for journalists rarely do – took a big gulp of my wine and said, with a sense of rising boredom: 'Really?'

Oh, how wrong I was. Bazzo was working in Dover that week. He and his fellow immigration officers delighted in searching the bags of girls they fancied, purely so they could chat them up while rifling through their knickers.

'. . . And the other day, right, this big coach came off a ferry, full of fackin' nuns who'd been on a pilgrimage to Romania or somewhere,' said Bazzo in his native south London patois, waving a can of Stella. 'So me and my mate thought we'd have some fun, and ordered searches on the whole lot of them, and the priest that was with 'em. The priest went fackin' batshit, but we told 'im: "Oi, no arguing, penguin boy!" Ha ha.

'Only it turns out, right, two of the nuns were wearing G-strings and a third one was six months pregnant! We couldn't fackin' believe it! We were just havin' a bit of fun, and really it was a scam, with these fackin' illegals dressing up as priests and bringing half their village in! How's that for a story then, eh? Nuns on the run! Ha ha!'

I was taken aback. 'Bloody hell, Bazz, you're right. That might actually be a story. Here, give us your number . . .'

Thrown into a good mood by the testosterone and alcohol, and with a vitally-important news contact under my belt, I continued to pay full attention to the wine until someone – Slappim, I think, and presumably as a way of distracting me while his hands were wandering towards my arse – said something like, 'Haven't you just split up with someone?'

Laughing – because I find that seeing the funny side takes the sting out of things – I regaled him with the story of my arrest and incarceration, which I've now told so many times it has become a well-rehearsed routine with sound effects, set pieces and timed pauses for canned laughter. I can't really remember much about my performance, except that at one point there I was, stood under the tree out of the drizzle, surrounded by a semicircle of men who barely knew me, and whom I had yet to either rule in or out romantically, regaling them with, 'But she's FAT,' and doing a Charlie Chaplin impression as I re-enacted pacing my cell in shoes too big for my feet. I distinctly remember the sensation of being effectively on stage, and thinking to myself that it was rather an odd way of dealing with heartbreak.

Then the little voice in the back of my head – the one you hear when you're drinking, that tells you when it's time to stop – said to me: 'You have the undivided attention of a dozen boys. Try to do something that makes you seem *attractive*, which is *not this*.' I remember hearing those logical words, and I remember completely ignoring them.

The boys had fascination on their faces, and fired questions at me about how big Fatty's arse was, how many times I'd kicked Twatface in the bollocks, and what had happened since. They refilled my pint glass, plied me with barely-cooked chicken wings, and pointed out they were heading off to a club later which was renowned as a meat market, and, 'You're bound to get a seeing-to there, girl!'

After a while I began to feel the worse for wear, and wandered into the toilet. I'm quite good at vomiting, in that I always know when it's coming and have time to prepare the scene. There was no way I was kneeling on Porky's floor because it was covered in pee, but I leant over the bowl, held my hair out of the way, counted to three and hurled raw chicken meat with wine. For once my aim was off, though, and it covered most of the toilet seat and a bit of the floor.

As a nicely-brought up girl I couldn't leave it like that. The trouble was, being a twenty-one-year-old's flat with thirty people in it, the toilet paper had run out. I looked about me for anything I could use to mop things up – there was a bath and a sink, but no cloth, no spare bog roll, no nothing. The only absorbent material in the whole room was a towel hanging next to the sink.

In my inebriated condition, I felt there was no choice. I had to clean up, and the towel was all I had. So I smeared it around the toilet seat, mopped up the floor, and tried to rinse the resulting goop off in the sink. It didn't really work, partly because I was too trashed to operate a tap, and partly because my drunken brain didn't want to get the towel wet.

Then, to cover up my antics and compound my shame, I thought it best to make sure the towel dried as quickly as possible. So I hung it on the radiator, with flecks of semi-digested meat dangling limply from the damp threads, and turned the heat up to ten.

I was just shutting the bathroom door behind me, congratulating myself on such a clever and hygienic method of covering my tracks, when Porky's girlfriend Louisa presented herself as though she'd been waiting for me to come out. 'Crikey,' I thought. 'Can't have that, towel won't be dry yet. Keep her busy.'

Instead, Louisa said loudly: 'You all right? We've called you a cab.'

'What? A cab? Why'd I want a cab?'

Bazzo came up behind her and steered me down the corridor and through the front door. 'It's all right, we thought it'd be better than you walking home,' he said, opening the car door and putting me in. Louisa thrust a plastic bag into my hands, telling me to use it if I felt sick, and told the driver my address. As he bounced me over the speed bumps I thought I had done quite well to have already emptied my stomach, and decided to text Twatface and tell him he was a cocksucker, and text Fifi to tell her that I was very popular indeed.

Just after the cab dropped me at home, Twatface rang. He stayed on the phone as I fumbled with the front-door lock, started undressing in the hallway and made my way upstairs. As I brushed my teeth I told him about the boys, and how tall they all were, and how one had given me a story, and hauled myself to bed. As I hit the pillow he said he was sorry not to have been there, and I told him he sounded like he was drinking. He laughed and said he was having a bottle of wine, yes, and was in his flat alone. I ranted at him for a bit about what a twat he was, then he sighed and said: 'You're too drunk for this conversation.' And he hung up on me.

Outraged, I rang him straight back in the highest of dudgeons. 'I may be drunk,' I told him. 'But at least *I* have been drinking with boys at a twenty-one-year-old's birthday party, whereas *you* are drinking alone. LOSER!' On which witty rejoinder, I hung up on him, and then rang Fifi and left a tearful message about how she was a terrible friend because she hadn't come, and if she had I wouldn't have rung Twatface.

The next morning, having scraped myself off the mattress and into the shower, and then staggered into work, Nancy silently put a cup of tea in front of me and said: 'How are we?'

'Nggh,' I replied from my position face down on the keyboard.

'Fifi says you've upset her,' said Nance, disapprovingly. 'Something about a phone call?'

I cracked an eye open and gazed blearily at her. I took a slurp of tea, and found the power to pull my phone out of the bag and flick through it. Presumably I had rung Fi too late at night. I checked the calls, and then with a growing sense of doom the sent messages.

'Oh no,' I said.

The first text I had sent to Twatface as I walked over the heath was at 7.29 p.m. The last one, in the cab back home, calling him a 'cockpuales', was sent at 8.43 p.m.

Seventy-four minutes. *Seventy-four.* From a standing, upright, stone-cold sober start, to falling-down, flat on my face drunk, in less than an hour and a quarter.

Eyes wide, I lifted my head, rubbed my cheek, where the word 'yuiophjkl' was imprinted, and told Nancy, who shook her head in disbelief.

'Jesus. What were you drinking, rocket fuel? You're a danger with that phone when you're pissed. When you're drunk even your texts are slurred. What time did you call Fi?'

'Twenty past nine. She can't be mad at that. Hang on, she tried to ring me back at 2.10 a.m. I remember now, she rang me all worried or something, and I didn't know what she was talking about.'

'She says you told her to fuck off, and were really rude,' said Nancy. 'I think you need to say sorry.'

Fifi refused to speak to me, take my calls or respond to my emails. I put my head on the desk and tried to get through the day as quietly as possible. I began to really worry that I'd lost one of my best friends.

The next night she finally called me back. 'Look you, ez bang out of order. It's teken me this long to calm down enough to tell you how mad I am. You tol' me to piss off, when I'd only rung to make sure you was OK. I came out of the party and got thez message from you in total tears about Twatface. I rang you straight away, and just got abuse. Is that all I'm good for?'

'I'm really sorry, Fi,' I said with remorse. 'I had far too much to drink, I'd been asleep – well, unconscious – for about five hours when you rang, and I just didn't know what you were on about.'

'Tha's no excuse,' she said sternly. 'You don' treat people like that. I was relly worried about you. And if no one else has told you yet, I well – you're drinking too much. You're startin' to act like your ex.'

192

She grudgingly accepted my apology and rang off. After the call ended I sat, staring into the fire in the freezing cold house where I couldn't afford to turn the heating on, and thought about what she'd said.

It was true, I had been too drunk. In fact I'd never been as drunk as that in my life. Seventy-four minutes? And no one else has ever had to put me in a cab home. I used to have to do that for Twatface. But now that he's gone there's no reason for me to stop drinking, no one in a worse state who makes me disgusted and stops my fun, no one to look after. There's just me, and I've been spanking the booze. I must have got through two bottles that night, on no dinner and a couple of manky chicken wings. And all I'd achieved was to embarrass myself in front of a bunch of strangers and – the shame of it – be told by Twatface I was too drunk to talk. It was like the Queen telling someone they were too posh. The thought that I had behaved like him made me shudder.

But, worse than that, I had upset a friend. If the past few months have taught me anything it is that the people I thought were acquaintances and colleagues, drinking partners or pals, are in fact some of the finest, strongest friends I've ever known or could have wished for. They stood by me in my darkest hour, cried with me, picked me up and helped me laugh again, and to each of them I owe a massive debt I hope they never need me to repay. They deserve more than I can ever give them, and telling Fifi, 'Sorry', after all she had done, was not enough to erase the dreadful thoughtlessness I had showed her.

It's fair enough to lean on your friends, fair enough to seek solace at the bottom of a glass, fair enough to ask a lot and rail at the world for a while, when your heart's been broken and your life shattered. But there comes a point where you have to decide that it's time to stand by yourself again, be responsible for your actions, and stop demanding that solace.

So I choose to be better than Twatface. I choose not to wallow, I choose to learn and to stand up straight. I choose to put my friends before myself, I choose to try to be better than I am. And bugger it, I'll paint the bedroom blue.

DAY ONE HUNDRED AND TWENTY-SIX

YEA, though I walk through the valley of the shadow of divorce, I will fear no evil; for if there's one thing I'm certain of it's that the worst is past. The second thing, which I find just as comforting, is that I no longer have any arguments. With anybody. I can't remember the last time someone annoyed me so much I raised my voice, the simple reason being that when Twatface left all the aggro in my life went with him.

There is no longer a fight to get £20 towards the groceries; there are no tensions over a visit to one or other set of outlaws; there's no rolling of eyes, crashing of pans or slamming of doors when someone blindly insists their view is right and yours is wrong. I remember once, soon after we moved into the house, that we were having an argument in the kitchen about something or other in which he resolutely stuck to his own pig-headed opinion and failed to listen to or consider mine. I felt like a fly battering itself against a window pane, so mindlessly frustrated at not being listened to that the only way I could see of getting him to pay attention to me for a second was to smash the ceramic bowl I was holding on to the concrete floor with all my strength. The shatter had not even died away when he declared I was 'mad', turned on his heel and walked off like he'd won the war.

In one respect he had. If you're compelled to smash the crockery in order to be heard you have already lost the battle, a fact I realized only while furiously picking up the bits of china, although at the time I was angrier still about the fact that he'd called me 'mad'. It's one of those words only ever used by men about women, and is just a way of dismissing indignation as a form of hysteria rather than something which might have a logical cause, i.e. the behaviour of the men in question. I used to say, 'Don't call me mad, call me angry,' because it denigrated my opinion to that of some consumptive Victorian heroine in a swoon. He never did that, of course: he just thought I was mad.

Smashing stuff was almost my only option – arguing with him was like attempting to nail fog to the wall. I would try logically to analyse the problem, and he would just insist black was white until I gave up trying to reason with him. The only alternative would have been for me to have ignored him completely and lived a totally separate life on my own terms except for the occasional conjugal, which is a situation I daresay he would have preferred immensely. One fact was constant: his insistent tones were all I could hear, even when he wasn't there, and I felt drowned out, squashed, in a world where someone else kept changing the rules.

But in the past few months there's been not one row, not one cause for my pulse or voice to be raised. Even though I had that upset with Fifi, there was no argument – one party was offended, the other said sorry, and that was that. If my mum annoys me I just roll my eyes; if the boss is a bully I shrug it off. I get enraged at Twatface still, but it's due to emails or legal letters which raise the blood pressure. I'm fine once I've punched the wall a couple of times. Although without someone to bounce off the house is frighteningly quiet and I end up having the radio on all the time, just for the company.

In the quiet moments I get to sit and think. I can hear my own thoughts for the first time in years, and I've discovered that I'm not, naturally, as mad as he said I was. I'm pretty calm, largely sunny-natured, and prone to laugh at everything. Maybe it's because there's no one to shout at, or perhaps we just rubbed one another up the wrong way, but the thought of smashing a bowl to make a point would now never cross my mind. It seems, well – mad. I read something once about a baseball player, who said, 'Watch the ball and do your thing,' that life is short and you only get one swing at it, but we didn't notice we'd dropped the ball. It's difficult to believe that, while we were so busy locking horns with each other, we never realized the spiral we were in. Looking at my marriage from here is like considering a maelstrom, or a distant whirlwind – very interesting, but a good thing not to be in.

The peace also gives me a sense of moral certainty. Not that I'm always right – Fifi taught me that – but that I know where I stand, where the edges and limits are, and what I can and can't put up with. Nancy took me out for a drink on Monday for a moan about her own divorce. I sympathized and said I was sure that children must make the whole thing more complicated and awful, but she waved her wine glass at me and told me I was wrong.

'Having the twins made the whole thing easier,' she insisted. 'We were arguing a lot, I thought maybe we could stick it out a bit longer but would probably break up eventually, and that it was better if it happened while the kids were too young to remember, rather than in five years' time.'

197

'Oh, well I always thought that I could get divorced because I didn't have children. That, you know, they kind of compel you to stay together.'

Nancy put her glass down and looked at me very seriously. 'Don't get me wrong; the twins are the best thing I've ever done. I'd never regret having them with him. But the love you have for your children is unconditional. They could do anything – murder someone, grow up and turn into paedophiles – and I'd always love them. But your love for your partner is completely conditional: it's dependent on their good behaviour, and on them sticking to certain rules. As soon as I realized Knobhead couldn't keep his side of the bargain, I let him go.'

And that, I suppose, is one of the things Twatface taught me – I realized what my deal-breakers were, for the first time. I used to think I could forgive cheating if it was just the once, but when it happened it turned me inside out with a pain too consuming to overlook. There were some things so bad I would have once thought they would make me walk immediately, but instead I stayed, believing his excuses. Desperate to keep him happy, find a compromise, understand why he was doing what he did, I listened only to his voice and mine never got a look in. Occasionally it screamed in frustration, and a bowl got smashed.

I heard someone say once that marriage is like a stick, and you each have to hold an end. Sometimes the stick is short and you're close together, and other times it's really long and you're so far apart you can't see each other any more; you just have to hope the other person's still holding their end of the stick. I am strong enough to go through life holding the stick on my own, but once it was clear Twatface had dropped his end and wandered off I didn't see why I should. The deal was that it was us against the world. It was a condition I didn't know I had, and realizing that felt like having a blindfold taken off, blinking like a hostage finally released from the cellar. If 'us' isn't happening, then 'me' is what's left, and that's something I can make work.

As a result I actually feel better for getting divorced; stronger somehow, like a diamond that's been cut or a warrior who's been blooded, but also much more like my old self. I am exactly the same, but imperceptibly better for the experience. Or at least, less inclined to put up with any crap.

For example, after more than ten years as a reporter – having doors slammed in my face, being sworn at, chased by men waving sticks, and on one memorable occasion being shot at – I have reached the end of my patience with the general public.

People, generally, are in my experience well-meaning and just doing their best in the only way they know how. But for some reason I can't put my finger on, the population's twat quotient seems to have rocketed of late.

Bridget knocked on a woman's door this week, asking her to talk to us about her ex. The woman said she'd think about it, and could Bridget come back later? Bridge duly returned that evening and knocked on the door a second time. It opened and the woman's boyfriend ran through it, picked Bridget up by the throat, and pinned her to the bonnet of her own car while screaming abuse.

Bridget is busty and blonde. She's been walking around with a bruised throat all week, coughing. The woman's boyfriend told the police, inexplicably, that he'd had no idea Bridget was a girl, and no further action was taken because the woman said Bridget had been harassing her.

If the victim had been anyone other than a journalist the boyfriend would have been charged with assault. How can it be harassment when they invited Bridget back?

Bridget and I were just complaining about this injustice in the pub when Tania Banks wandered in and joined us. Now, she's far from my best friend, for reasons already explained, but the work pub is neutral ground. She'd just come back from a job which left her so shaken she could barely hold a gin and tonic. The story she told even made me feel sorry for her.

She was on a door-knock in darkest Wiltshire. It was dark, and she was trying to find a farm which was the family home of a charity worker blown to pieces in Afghanistan. She eventually found a gateway with the right name on it, and a rutted track, but her car – like all reporters' vehicles a cheap and nondescript three-door thing – got stuck in the mud.

Abandoning it, she grabbed her bag and picked her way over the ruts, repeatedly turning her cankles in the pitch darkness as she made her way towards the lights of the farmhouse. Banks knocked on the door, shivering in the cold and the quietness of the countryside.

Her hands were still shaking as she told us: 'The door opened, and it was a young guy, the brother or something. Of course I was as nice as could be, said how terribly sorry I was to bother them at such a difficult time, but would they like to pay tribute to him? He said he would ask his family, and wandered off. After a few minutes the dad appeared and waved me inside.

'He took me through the kitchen into the back parlour. I thought it was a bit odd, because he was only wearing a dressing gown, and had this mad hair all standing up on his head, and he made a point of closing the door and then putting a chair in front of it. So I did my spiel again, and he just stared at me. Then he started ranting and raving, spitting about how he was going to keep me there because I was a journalist, and he was going to trap me like I entrapped others. I tried to calm him down, but it didn't work, so then I told him he couldn't keep me there, it was kidnap, and asking a question isn't entrapment, and if he didn't want to play that was fine, I'd leave and not bother him any more.'

Banks took a gulp of gin, a shaky breath, then carried on. 'He opened the door and walked out, but before I could follow him he closed it behind him and locked it. I banged on it, then tried to call the office, but it was real bandit country down there, so no signal. I was thinking, "Poot, I'm in real trouble here." It was all quiet, then this guy came back, this time with a shotgun. He started waving it around, saying he was going to shoot me like his boy was shot, and I was bricking it. I was in the middle of nowhere, no photographer with me, and I was about to get flipping *shot*!'

'What did you do?' asked Bridget, gripped. I was studying the spirits shelf and pretending to ignore the whole thing, lest I lose my carefully-cultivated air of disdain for Banks and all her ilk, who pretend that not swearing like the rest of us makes them nicer people. People who say 'Poot,' are just pretending to be nice, and that's the worst kind of nice to be.

'I was scared, and then I got angry. I thought, "How dare he treat me like this?" So I told him he was completely out of order, and that he had to let me go immediately, and asked him if he had a licence for his gun. And when he carried on shouting, I lost it. I tried to shove him out of the way of the door, I shouted for his

201

family to come and help, which of course they didn't, and then I just started hitting him over the head with my notebook.'

At this point I spluttered into my Pinot, and she glared at me for a second before carrying on.

'After a bit he got out of the way, and I managed to unlock the door and get out. I went back through the kitchen, and there was his entire family, sat around the table having a cup of tea, and listening to the whole thing as calm as you please. They hadn't lifted a finger while he was going mental with a gun. Honestly, it defies belief,' said Banks, shaking her head.

'Christ, lucky escape!' said Bridge in her Aussie drawl. 'What's wrong with people?'

The same thought crossed my mind next day as I was driving across town on a doorstep of my own. Waiting behind an old Nissan on a roundabout, I wondered why the driver wouldn't pull out. I honked the horn once, and when the Nissan still didn't move backed up and went around it. As I passed the car, I looked in the window and saw the driver was a grey-haired old lady of seventy or more, and she flipped me her arthritic middle finger with a sneer and something I lip-read as a 'Fuck you!'

'Jeez,' I thought, completely unsettled. 'That's someone's granny!'

When I got to the address it was a large suburban four-bedroomed house in a Surrey suburb. The guy I was looking for was the former husband of a woman who was shagging a married television celebrity, and while she was divorced we still wanted to see if her ex – as they often do in these cases – had an opinion about it. 'She's a dreadful slag and did the same to me', is always what you hope they will say, or at least a confirmation that yes, the ex was aware the famous so-and-so was her new boyfriend so we could run it.

Anyway, I walked up the front path through the neat garden, past the tidy flower beds, and knocked on the door, feeling a little deflated. It was all nice and middle class, and the middle classes never talk to the papers. They're too worried what people might think. The posh and the poor do because they just think it's funny. Anyway, the door opened and stood there was a little girl, no older than eight or nine. 'Damn,' I thought. 'He's got the kids. Well, can't have her hearing this.'

Out loud, I said: 'Is your daddy in?' She nodded and walked off to the back of the house to get him.

A nice-looking, sensible chap in a clean shirt and jeans came to the door with an enquiring smile. I looked past him to make sure the little girl was nowhere to be seen and couldn't hear me. Quite reasonably and quietly, I told him why I was there, and politely asked if it was something he might be able, even off the record, to confirm or add to in some way.

He exploded in rage. 'How *dare* you come to my house and terrify my children? How *dare* you tell them this sort of thing about their mother? Is this how you get your kicks, you sick, disgusting *freak*? I'd be ashamed to show my face in your shoes, what an appalling, disgraceful human being you are! Is your mother proud? Is she? IS SHE?'

It was all shouted at the top of his voice, carrying around the house and up and down the street, and with a sneer writ large across his formerly-reasonable face as I backed away before his fury.

Normally I would have apologized and legged it before a piece of wood or a sawn-off made an appearance, while ringing the desk to tell them this one was a no. But something in me snapped and had, finally, had enough. Twatface, Banks, the nasty granny; I was fed up of the world being mean to me when it didn't have to be. A reporter's never going to get a story by bollocking someone, but I was not going to take it any more.

'Don't you DARE speak to me like that!' I said, wagging a finger in his face like I was my own mother. 'Look, I appreciate that having a reporter knock on your door can come as a surprise, but I have been *nothing* but polite to you, and there is absolutely no reason for you to be so appallingly rude! For your information I made every effort to ensure that your daughter did not hear what I had to say, but your bellowing has made sure that she and most of your neighbours now know about it in great detail. So if anybody's acted like a rude idiot here, it's you. Well done, and goodbye.'

And with that I turned on my heel and walked back up his path in high dudgeon. I was still shaking with anger when I was back in the car, and my brain had barely stopped humming with the phrase, 'What a twat!' on a loop when I pulled up, twenty minutes later, outside the woman's parents' house.

Now, they were much posher: gates, gravel, two Mercedes on the driveway. Feeling extremely negative about the whole pointless story, I knocked on the door and explained in a grumpy tone to the snooty-looking gent who answered that we were doing a story about his daughter.

He sniffed, looked down his nose and said to me:

'One does not sell one's own family down the river for tuppence.'

'Fine,' I said, turning away. 'Sorry to bother you.'

He called out to my retreating back: 'Of course, it would entirely depend on how much you were prepared to pay.'

I turned back, smiled at him, and said: 'Oh, I think we can come to some agreement.' Then he invited me in for a cup of tea and a chat.

It was the kind of story Twatface would have loved to hear. And when I got back home that night, to a quiet, chilly house where no one had lit a fire, put any dinner on, or noticed the milk had turned to cheese, I heaved a big sigh that it would have to wait until I saw the girls in the bar or at the office, by which time most of it would probably have slipped my mind.

Thinking about it to myself just isn't the same; I'd far rather say it out loud and chew the fat with someone. But out here in the desert of singledom, the purgatory of the separated-and-yet-to-get-divorced, there's only one person to speak to now, and it's me. On the plus side I don't tell myself I'm mad – well, not often – and occasionally I give myself a pat on the head when my friends or my employers forget to.

Along with my voice, for the first time I have a sense of solid ground underneath my feet. I've got my balance back, and can see roughly what direction I'm going in. I know that my cup's going to run over with twats before I'm finished, but the test is not how many of them there are – just how I deal with them.

So long as you follow what you think is right, and steer clear of what you know is wrong – and don't let anyone mess with your swing.

DAY ONE HUNDRED AND THIRTY-FIVE

BENEATH the fun of being single again there lurks a darkness which I have no idea how to face: a complete lack of self-worth.

Almost every other task before me seems possible to overcome, apart from that. According to the crazy bankers I can take on a mortgage nearly six times my salary. I can get a raise for not being any better at my job than I was last year. I can chop logs for the fire, pay the bills, have my life shattered by a wrecking ball and somehow put the pieces together again. But as Humpty Dumpty and count-less tea mugs will bear witness, while you can glue the pieces back where they used to be as neatly and nicely as you please, nothing will ever fix the fact that it was broken in the first place. The cracks remain.

The walk from bathroom to bedroom is all of ten feet, but I can't stand to do it naked. I used to; I never had a problem with my figure, or what others thought of it. I was confident in myself and the love Twatface had for me. But now after my shower I get dressed every morning in the bathroom, where there is only a tiny mirror over the sink, rather than walk back to the bedroom where there's a full-length one. I simply can't stand to look at my own body; it's the same as it always was, a few pounds lighter, even, but it disgusts me because I gaze at it wondering what Twatface found so wrong that another woman was better.

The one time I went to bed with someone else I had to have the lights off and more vodka in my bloodstream than actual blood, and still found it terrifying. In quiet moments memories return of how often Twatface turned me down, how little he seemed to fancy me. It may have had more to do with him but I would be less than human – and less than a female, sadly – if I didn't wonder whether it was all somehow my fault.

I remember making a special effort at one point, when it seemed like we hadn't had sex in forever. We'd been out shopping, and I'd got some new underwear he'd helped pick. That night, I dolled myself up and waited, reclining on the covers, for him to join me. When he wandered to bed an hour later he didn't even look my way before getting into bed and turning his back. I lay in the dark feeling tawdry, wondering what I'd done, and eventually asked him quietly if there was something . . . wrong . . . with me. Y'know, compared to other girls. Something he didn't like, maybe? He sighed, said no, he was just tired, gave me a little squeeze and rolled back over. Maybe he was exhausted, but now I'm just not sure.

Then there is the distant prospect of meeting someone who might find me attractive enough to have sex with, and which might not involve being drunk and scared. How do I take my clothes off in front of him? Will I be able to not obsessively check his phone or emails? What if the next guy says 'I'd never do that to you,' and all I can hear is Twatface saying the same words? The worry alone would send any man screaming from my arms. And even though I changed the locks, even though the last time I was scared was months ago, even though a bit of me still believes what he said and that it *was* all my fault, what happens when I am behind closed doors with a man? Can I put myself at someone's mercy again?

And don't get me started on fat women. My eyes narrow at each one I see; this week I even caught myself hissing at one on the Tube, and then had to give myself a strong talking-to for being so unreasonable.

I was talking to a divorcee this week for a story about their parent being left to starve in hospital. My normal method of interviewing is to find something in common with the person I'm talking to, and tell them I've had a similar experience. It's not lying, there is usually something I can relate to, and it helps the interviewee to loosen up.

The divorcee's marriage was not linked to the story, but she mentioned it in passing. It turned out she'd been cheated on too, for years. Anyway, the interview ended with me virtually in tears on this poor woman's shoulder, and her patting me on the back, looking at me sadly and saying: 'You're right to be sad, you know.'

'What?' I sniffed. 'I thought you would tell me everything would be better one day.'

She shook her head and sighed. 'You will never trust anyone completely again. You can learn to love again, and of course you will, pretty thing like you, but next time you will always hold a little bit of yourself back; it's only natural. Your heart will be harder, next time.'

I mentioned this to one of the monkeys, Jock Beckett, while we were sitting outside the house of a Tory MP's mistress, waiting for the shagger to turn up so we could get a snatch pic in the street.

'Monkeys' is a highly derogatory term used by reporters to describe photographers, a reference to their habit of gathering in groups, skanking fags off each another and gibbering about the length of their lenses – while avoiding soap and anyone who uses long words. In return they call us 'blunts', which is a dig at the state of our pencils, and rhyming slang for what they really think of us. Both terms are intended to be unkind; but I didn't realize that when I first got to Fleet Street, and by the time it had been explained to me that I shouldn't be using it, and it wasn't funny, the word 'monkeys' had stuck in my brain.

In the newsroom there is rivalry and mutual distrust between words and pictures, but down here at street level we are bound together by shared experiences, comradeship and the threat of mutual destruction. I've crossed continents with snappers, braved elephant charges and near-starvation, interrogation, snipers, dysenteric hangovers and rotting corpses – and as a result monkeys are among my best friends.

You can spend three weeks with one, twenty-four hours a day, and not see him again for a year, but get so close on an intense but very shallow level, that you feel you know him better than his wife. If the two of you don't get along, or one of you is trying to grandstand and stitch the other up, you'll have a hell of a time. When the desk are on the phone screaming, when his missus wants to know where he is and neither of you are sober enough to get home, you need a wingman, not a colleague. You always cover each other's backs: monkey and blunt together against the world, that's the rule. If the snappers like you then you're all right; if they take against you your days are numbered.

Some snappers – the smellier ones – I would cross the road to avoid, but others I've shared some scrapes with are dear to me, like grown-up hairy children, and they don't seem to mind too much when I call them monkeys.

There's Nick the Wop, a don among snappers, who can swear in almost every language on earth; Ladders, who's so tiny he carries a set of steps everywhere; Dan the Van, who spends long days trapped in the back of a white transit with blacked-out windows, a bottle to piss in and a ziplock bag to crap in; Mike the Bike, who risks life and limb to do high-speed pursuits on his Kawasaki; and then there's Jock.

Whenever he sees me he says, 'Allrae, wee blunty?' and ruffles my hair like a mad Glaswegian uncle. When everything blew up with Twatface he offered to, 'Sor'i'oo'fer ye,' which if I had understood what he was saying I might have taken him up on. So with hours to kill sitting in a car on a doorstep, I filled him in on the news that from now on I was apparently going to be a hard-hearted nut to crack.

'. . . and this woman said that I'd never fall in love again, not properly, I'd always keep a bit back. Isn't that sad? Isn't the whole point of love supposed to be that you jump in with both feet?' I asked him as we sipped nuclear-hot tea from polystyrene cups in my car.

'Ah dinnae, lass,' he said, wolfing down his third bacon sandwich of the day and dropping bits of fat in the passenger footwell as he surfed through the street's WiFi networks looking for some internet to steal. 'Ha de ye spell "Marylebone"?'

I sighed, reminding myself that emotions were trickier for monkeys to understand than apostrophes. Shoving my tea on the dashboard to cool down, I grabbed Jock's laptop off him to do the bit of every photographer's job they hate the most – spelling – and thought, 'Well, at least he's not the Minicab Rapist.'

The Minicab Rapist is the other kind of monkey. There's nothing about him you can really put a finger on, except all the female reporters agree that if they were waiting for a cab and he came along just as one pulled up, he has the sort of aura which would make them say, 'I'll get the next one, ta. No, really. You have this one. I'm going in completely the opposite direction.' He never, under any circumstances, gets invited to sit in my car, no matter how cold the doorstep is. He just has this . . . quality.

The Minicab Rapist has a long black coat and, aside from his normal bag of cameras and lenses, doesn't go anywhere without what I think of as his rape kit – a separate rucksack into which he occasionally delves to bring out odd items: like handcuffs and duct tape and a camera using old-fashioned film which he will tell you with a leer he develops at home in his 'personal dark- room'. If there isn't some Rohypnol, a pair of latex gloves and a douche in there, too, then I'm a banana.

I try to avoid jobs with him, but I got lumbered earlier this week on a simple inquest. Thankfully it was a pack job, so there were five or six reporters and snappers lurking outside the court waiting for a family statement. I was talking to a friend from another rag about her boy troubles, and she was saying how she wasn't sure what to do about some guy. Uncomfortably aware that the Minicab Rapist was stood next to us, grinning knowingly and listening to every word, I told her that life was short and that if she liked the guy she should just grab the chance. Then she turned to the Minicab Rapist, and pointedly asked him if our conversation was bothering him.

He said: 'Oh no, I find it fascinating. And I completely agree. I just grab women whenever the opportunity arises.'

211

He leered and took a drag on his cigarette while my friend and I stared at him, and then each other, shivering. 'Maybe he's actually a sweet bloke, just mildly autistic or something,' I said quietly, after we'd wandered away.

'Hmm, or maybe he's got Maddie McCann in his freezer,' she replied.

But while the reporters all sense a certain darkness about the man, he must have some kind of charm, because back in the office the sweet-natured, slinkily-fragrant females of the magazine department have fallen under his spell. The Minicab Rapist's main claim to fame is that he took some of the first pictures of Kate Moss back in the day, and reckons he slept with her, too. This old glory so obsesses him that every girl he goes out with slowly morphs under his influence into a version of Kate in her heroin-chic phase.

Now the mag girls are all shapes and sizes and colours of hair. On most newspapers they're super-sleek and glossy, obsessed with the latest Lulu Guinness handbag or Westwood frock, nicking designer togs out of the fashion cupboard and trying out a different celebrity fad diet every week. They spend more on make-up than I do on council tax, and their combined perfumes are strong enough to gas the Kurds.

But at my paper they have fallen victim, one at a time, to the attentions of the Minicab Rapist. They've gone down like skittles. One by one, they've got thinner and thinner. All of them, blonde, brunette or redhead, have grown their hair long, dyed it mousey brown and then stopped washing it. If you walk past their desks you can note the wave of waifs, with his oldest conquests looking like they've just walked out of a Serbian prison camp and his more recent ones kitted out in whatever's in Topshop

212

and smoking like chimneys. It is possible to tell how far through the department he has moved, simply by working out which one looks most like Kate in about 1990.

I was in the ladies' loo on Wednesday when I heard sobbing from the next cubicle. Presuming it was the normal existential angst of working in a newsroom, I ignored it, washed my hands and was about to leave when the sobber unlocked the door, sniffing. It was Linzi or Kelli or Salli, one of the glossy girls, anyway, so I know her name definitely ended with an 'i'. Possibly with a heart drawn over it instead of a dot. I caught her eye in the mirror over the sink and niceness got the better of me.

'Are you OK?' I said, handing her a tissue from the dispenser next to the hand-dryer.

She shook her head and blew her nose. 'Oh, it's Mikey,' she said, sighing.

It took me a moment to realize who she was talking about, and I nearly burst out with, 'Oh, you mean the Minicab Rapist?' but I stopped myself just in time. Rape kits were probably not what she needed to hear about just then.

'He's dumped me and said he's going out with Vicki,' she said, starting to wail again.

I put an uncertain arm around her bony shoulders, having a quick look for needle-marks while I did so. 'There, there, it's all right, you're better off without him,' I said fruitlessly, while she subsided into sniffles. 'Hasn't he got a bit of a track record with most of the girls on your desk?'

She nodded and sniffed. I battled the urge to tell her to eat something substantial. Then she sighed. 'There's just something about him, though. He's impossible to resist. He used to pick my clothes, and order my dinner in restaurants. He really seemed like he cared – he said it was because he knew what I looked best in, and that salads were better for me.'

'Really?' I said, raising my eyebrows.

She went on: 'I asked him about the other girls, I mean I couldn't not. I tried to make a joke of it, and said, "How do you do it?" and he just looked at me like this . . .' She dropped her head like Princess Di on *Panorama* and looked up at me through her eyelashes. '. . . and he said, "It's the baby blues, honey. The baby blues get them every time." Oh God, he has such lovely eyes.'

I stood there, a picture of confusion as she cried again. This was entirely beyond my sphere of understanding. Turning round and walking away would have been rude, but I had no idea what to say.

'Well,' I started, wondering where the hell I was going with this. 'It's kind of unusual for men to tell you what to wear. Or eat. And, you know, you seem bright enough to know that stuff for yourself.'

I thought a bit while she blew her nose. There had to be something I could say that would perk her up a bit, and actually register.

'Look, you've got a job on a national newspaper. You can't do that if you're an idiot,' I said, in the face of all the evidence. 'He's just a rat who shags his way round the office, and didn't love you as much as he loved himself. I shouldn't think he'll be with Nicki for long.'

'Vicki,' she said through the snot.

'Vicki, then. The only thing to regret is that you didn't dump him first,' I said, before finally and desperately calling on *Bridget Jones's Diary* for inspiration. 'What you need is to find a bloke who likes you just the way you are.'

214

Big mistake. With a wail, she ran back into a cubicle and locked the door. 'Note to self: do not channel world's most annoying singleton,' I thought, leaving her to it.

When I got back home that night, double-locking and bolting the door behind me like I do every evening, I dumped my bag at the foot of the stairs with a big sigh and glanced around. The house looked as beaten down and bodged up as I did – paint roughly slapped on here and there over crumbling plaster, a restoration project that needed a lot of love and attention. I walked around, idly picking at the remaining paper and loose plug sockets. You couldn't get Kate Moss to cross the threshold. And I thought, 'God, what a wreck. Who'd take this on?'

Somehow, as my thoughts turned, I realized that when we'd bought it a year before the end, my marriage had been in just the same state as the house: spruced up for public viewing, with ornaments and furniture put in front of the cracks, and problems no one wanted to see, held up by hope more than anything else. Once Fatty had stamped her way into our world the tremors shook all the shit out, including Twatface. I'm left in a life where the flaws are now obvious, and fixing them is the biggest project I've ever had. The house is 150 years old and still standing, so I suppose the structure must be sound. It's just been a bit unloved.

I've started attacking the bedrooms, tearing out the old built-in cupboards, stripping the nasty Anaglypta and discovering the botched plaster underneath. I've learned how to put a new skim of plaster on a wall, paint a ceiling without falling backwards off a stepladder, and put up coving. But in a sense these new skills are hollow compared to what I cannot do: I cannot replace the fuse box or re-fit the bathroom, any more than I could save my marriage, create self-esteem out of nothing or feel more attractive than Fatty.

Then I realized that my self-confidence was probably at an even lower ebb than that of Linzi/Kelli/Salli, who were all so busy subjugating themselves to someone else's whims they'd forgotten who they were to start with. A bit like I did, for a while. Only now I feel like the princess who turned into a frog, or a swan who somehow became an ugly duckling and is scared of her own reflection. At least Linzi, Kelli and Salli all ended up looking a bit like a supermodel.

Jeez, what bloke would like me just the way I am? Cracked and broken and in need of a lot of work. 'Even I don't like me,' I thought, sitting on the bottom of the stairs for a weep of my own.

It annoys me that even at this distance Twatface can still affect me. Sometimes, at a thought or a song or a memory, the tears well up inside and there's no keeping a lid on them. They fountain up and fall down my face, leaving a trickle of make-up behind them and making me feel an idiot for still having tears to spill.

Among my new skills, though, is the ability to rationalize emotion. One day I will shed the last tear. So that means you can never cry the same tear twice, that there is a finite reservoir of sadness, and each time I cry a little bit of the bad stuff leaves me and I'm a step nearer to never crying because of him again.

After a bit I sniffed and wiped my face. 'Are you really identifying yourself with a slightly crappy house?' I asked the floor, sternly. 'Because if you are, you're screwed. A house is not a broken heart.' I stood up and glared angrily around, catching a glimpse of the sunset through

216

the front door fanlight, which I had stencilled with sunflowers a few weeks back. They glowed a lovely gold and made me smile, until I thought about the wiring, the kitchen, the tiles . . . Well, maybe I couldn't do it all. But I could do lots. I had no idea about plumbing or electricity, but I'd learn as I went along, get Dad to show me a few things perhaps, and when there was something beyond me I'd just have to save up to get it done by someone else.

And as for me – well, I have to learn to like myself again, and treat the heartbreak as another task to be fixed. There'll always be cracks, but maybe one day someone will like them as much as the rest of me. Some will pass with time: the divorce will come through eventually, the tears will dry, and each new boy, each flirt, each kiss, will help build me up, step by step. But there won't be nearly as much to be learned, or fun to be had, if I rely purely on another person to do all the work for me. I'm not going to hang around, psychologically in pieces, hoping for some guy to magically make it all better. Life doesn't work that way. No one is going to love me unless I love myself first.

The cracks are there now; I just have to try not to fall through them.

DAY ONE HUNDRED AND FIFTY-FIVE

SOMETIMES a newsroom is the centre of the universe: a Royal dies or a bomb goes off, the phones are going crazy, The Editor's shouting out the intro for the splash from the other side of the office and the words flow, like butter off a crumpet, out of your fingers and on to the screen. Those are the days when you beat the police and the rest of the pack to knock at the door first, and the relatives hand over the family album; when a government press office dreads seeing your first edition drop; when the Prime Minister wants to know what page one is going to be, and it feels like you've a front seat at history in the making.

Then there are the days when it's more like being stuck at a county fair on a wet afternoon. When there's a never-ending display of dull, lumbering beasts, beribboned, primped and poked into being paraded up and down for public approval; it seems like you're up to your knees in more manure than should be physically possible; and the whole thing is run by psychotically avaricious clowns who wouldn't be allowed into polite society.

If you meet someone, at a party, say, and tell them what you do for a living, they generally do two things. First they tell you they never read the papers, aren't the tabloids dreadful, and wouldn't you want to work for a *proper* paper? Then they ask you about what really happened in the latest celebrity break-up, and sit there, open-mouthed, with a canapé halfway to their face, while you fill them in on what Jordan told your friend about her vagina. Then they go and tell everyone else about Jordan's vagina, while still thinking they don't care what the tabloids have to say about anything. People, hey?

Most of them think being a reporter is dreadfully exciting, a glamorous merry-go-round of celebrities, politics and sex, when it's 99 per cent sitting about and waiting for something to happen. In that sense it's a lot like a divorce – one long dribble of nothingness in which you try to keep yourself busy while the passage of time is marked only by flicking elastic bands at each other and a bill of some sort.

When the office is quiet, and strangely full of reporters – who don't get sent out on stories as much as they used to, thanks to budget cutbacks – we indulge in the journalistic equivalents of welly-wanging, tug of war and bear-baiting. They're a series of ritualistic, arcane contests that have been devised purely with the aim of making the instigator feel slightly superior to others, earn the right to shout, 'I win!' and kill time until something more interesting comes along.

They aren't just a way of passing the hours; trained to beat others to the story whatever the cost, reporters have the kind of competitive streak which would make a shark blush. On local papers the most-feared person is the Mum of a Girl with a Pony because if you muck up the gymkhana report she'll have your spleen on a stick by lunchtime. On nationals – where I can't work out if the scum has risen to the top or the good stuff has all sunk to the bottom – the thing you worry about most is the nearest reporter, because you are only ever as good as your last story, which is better if no one else has it. When you're in a race to the door-knock, or a fight with the office chequebook on a buy-up, you have to win at all costs because your job and way of life depends on it. Adrenalin hurls itself around your system so often that you get addicted, and that's why we would all file copy from our own funerals if something interesting happened, and why, even when there's nothing going on, we still compete.

First there's gambling. Ridiculous sweepstakes are by far the most fun, like betting how many minutes late Fifi will be after a showbiz party the night before, or who will get beasted by Elliot first. We also have Cussed a Minute, in which you have to catch Bish on your tape recorder in a stream-of-consciousness swear tirade for at least sixty seconds, without hesitation, deviation or repetition. Then there's Bish Bingo. This last one normally attracts a sizable pot, with subs, reporters and features bunnies all throwing in a pound and pulling out of the hat one of his many stock phrases, then waiting on tenterhooks to hear which he uses first, and thus who gets the winnings.

After that there's the insertion of ridiculous references into copy. 'Trailing lobelia' was one for most of the summer, which was used to describe the supposedly verdant appearance of every two-bed semi, sprawling country pile, down-at-heel squat or luxurious town house that was written about, until Elliot spotted it one day and sent an 'All Staff' email saying that if any reporter used the phrase again he'd fillet 50 per cent off their expenses.

More often it's a case of betting 50p whether one of your amusing tabloid labels makes it into print. 'Peg leg, light-fingered fantasist Heather Mills', for example, is guaranteed to give the lawyer a heart attack and get legalled out long before it sees the page, but last week Buff won a tenner by managing to get 'bungling Nazis' published, which makes the BNP sound like the Chuckle Brothers in an SS uniform.

A lot of fun can also be had with our own office version of Buckaroo. Our health reporter Cubby Fox frequently disappears for hours at a time to 'meet a contact', in the shape of a bottle of Pinot Noir, and other times doesn't even bother to think of an excuse for nipping down to the wine bar for indeterminate periods. The only clue as to where he is, and whether he might intend to come back at some point, is the jacket slung over the back of his chair. The trouble is that the jacket is often in place for hours, days, even a week at a time, although it's a brilliant way of pretending you've just popped to the loo. Bish has given up ringing him to ask where he is, and even Elliot doesn't bother to criticize because Cubby just ignores him. Instead, every time a reporter passes Cubby's chair they pick up a piece of office detritus and poke it in a pocket. It might be a paper clip, a Post-it note, or an expenses form, but they can add only one piece at a time.

He went down for a drink on Tuesday lunchtime, leaving the jacket on his chair, and went straight home from the pub, by which point four reporters had added something to the pockets. His wife rang mid-afternoon as I was walking past his desk, and when I answered the phone to her and she asked me where he was I looked at the jacket and said: 'Oh, um . . . gone to meet a contact.' 'It's amazing what journalists get away with when their wives aren't in the game,' I thought, as I put a stapler down one of his sleeves and went back to my own desk.

He met another contact on Wednesday, and again didn't trouble the office with his presence afterwards, and by then his coat looked like the Michelin Man's bomber jacket. It was already the longest-ever lead time for an office joke, but then Thursday dawned. Every morning the sports, pictures, features and news desks have a meeting with The Editor to talk about what stories they have, which very conveniently gives the rest of us a nice quiet half hour for a snooze, a smoke or what's known as a 'Conference Quickie' – an alcoholic drink to quell the shakes from the night before, or a cup of tea for the seriously unwell. Cubby had shambled in and announced the need for a heart-starter before conference was even called, and was still in the pub when it was over and The Editor kicked the execs back into the newsroom with strict instructions to rip the newspaper up and start again.

Bish stalked over to the reporters in a foul mood. 'Where's the bluddy health ed? His flamin' page two lead's been shat out again by The Editor.' We all kept our heads down. Bish picked up a phone and stabbed a number out, rolling his eyes and muttering about mobile reception in pubs.

'Cubby, it's yer boss. D'you remember? The poor sod who keeps you in a job. I wonder, if you can spare the time from your busy schedule of buggerin' about, whether you could trouble us with your presence in the orifice? It's that place with little white boxes called computers, which we use to write words down and print them out on bits of mashed-up tree, and then fold them together into what we like to call a newspaper, and then sell copies to raise the funds to pay your bar tab. Your machine's due for its thousand-word or six-monthly service, whichever comes first. Now get yer bluddy arse out of the pub and back up here, pronto!'

He crashed the phone back into its cradle and stalked off, stopping by Cubby's chair to shove an empty packet of Woodbines into the top pocket. Bridget quietly got her Bish Bingo list out of her top drawer and announced she had scored two. I insisted I had three from that one rant alone, but was soundly beaten by Harry Porter, who already had two on aggregate from an earlier bitch at the coffee machine, and swept £4.75 in loose change out of the sweepie mug and into his pocket with a cackle of glee and a solemn promise to buy us a packet of biscuits with it.

A few minutes later Cubby was back, tie askew and lips stained a fetching shade of Merlot. Bish spotted him, wheeled his chair back from the news desk and barked down the room: 'CUBS! Approach the bench. And bring some batteries, I've a new arse-kicking machine I want to try out on yer.'

Very much aware that Bish would tear further strips off for perceived slovenliness, Cubby picked his jacket up and threw it on as he hurried the length of the office. Untold numbers of drawing pins, biros and micro cassettes were flung in every direction, scattering across desks and whirring over reporters' heads as Cubby ground to a surprised halt. Leaping from his seat, Bish – who had won by virtue of being the last to add to the load – bellowed out 'CUBBAROO!' and the subs led a round of applause.

Gingerly going through his pockets, a stunned Cubby pulled out spiral-bound notebooks, plastic canteen cutlery and bits of used tissue, and piled it all on a desk in front of him. Agog at the size of the hoard, he turned to us and said: 'Whathefu . . . ?' Tearfully we explained the game he had never realized we played, as his scowl deepened. 'Even in all my years of journalism,' he said, putting his nose in the air and turning on his heel, 'I have never before witnessed such utter bell-endery.' Shuffling in dudgeon towards the news desk, his mood was barely lightened by the fact Bish was now so highly delighted with himself that he couldn't be bothered to deliver a bollocking, and cheerfully told Cubby just to rewrite the lead.

Other times we can't even think of anything interesting to do, and we bet on which raindrop gets to the bottom of the window first, or what time the paper will go off-stone – an esoteric printing term from the days when we used to produce newspapers by banging two rocks together, since when not much bar the technology has changed – and Bish tells us to go home by growling: 'Day bugs fall out.'

Things got so bad at one point this week that we actually had a staring contest, but had to declare it a draw because we were all so zombiefied by boredom no one was capable of blinking any more. I flicked a rubber band at Porter as he leaned back in his chair, rubbed his eyes and said: 'Oh God, this is so DULL!'

'You moan when it's busy,' I pointed out. 'Make your mind up. Would you rather have peace and quiet or constant stress?'

He straightened up and rested his chin on his hands as he gazed around the room. 'Fuck knows. Neither. How many cardboard drink holders have you got in your tower now? It's getting out of control.'

The Tower is a good indicator of how boring life has been over the past few months. If the reporters are all in the office we get through so much tea and coffee that the tower of drink holders in the middle of the desk, which we add to every time someone gets a round in, grows exponentially, like a triffid or a lawyer's bill. This week we had to split it into two and move it on to the floor, where it now resembles the Petronas Towers in Kuala Lumpur.

'Dunno,' I said. 'Sixty?'

'Nah, more like eighty. In a single tower,' said Porter.

The betting fever took hold and before we knew it everyone had chucked in 50p and made a stab at the figure. Porter said seventy-two, Princess chipped in with a ridiculous forty-seven, Nancy guessed an inexplicable thirty-five, and Bridget reckoned sixty-eight. Even the work-experience girl had a pop. Cubby, who was refusing to partake in our silly games on principle by this point, was persuaded to adjudicate.

He counted under his breath while we all tried to put him off by shouting random numbers in his ear. Then he counted again, just to be sure. The tension mounted unbearably until Cubby solemnly announced: 'It's sixty-one, morons.'

'GET IN!' shouted the work-ex girl, grabbing the £3 as the rest of us began to complain he couldn't possibly have counted right, and was he sure he wasn't at least one out . . .

'And yer all fookin' sacked!' bellowed Bish from the other end of the newsroom, glaring at us over the top of his computer screen. We scrambled back to desks and chairs, uncomfortably aware that we probably all ought to find some stories. The threat of sacking is waved over reporters' heads so often you'd think we'd become immune, but no – it just makes us paranoid.

Tania Banks, looking supercilious from behind her own screen, from whence she, too, had refused to play (not that we had really asked her), said: 'You really all ought to be more like me, you know. I give Bish at LEAST ten stories a week, even if I don't think he'll like them, so he knows that I'm *always* busy and *always* keen.'

Nancy rolled her eyes at me, and I grimaced back. Even though we hate Tania, and we know Bish thinks she's a suck-up, the fear kicked in. It was only the worry that an enemy might get more stories in which made us keep our heads down for the rest of the day and start bashing the phones to get some leads.

DAY ONE HUNDRED AND SIXTY-FOUR

ON Saturday a few of us piled into Greenwich to watch Porter try to kill himself by setting off fireworks in his back garden. I was in the kitchen still wrestling with why we were all so competitive, while Porter was outside wrestling with oven gloves and a set of Poundland instructions written in Chinese.

'Maybe we're just children and we only understand things if one person's beating someone else in the egg and spoon race,' I ruminated.

'Yes, or maybe we just need more fresh air and sunlight,' said Bridget as she picked up a bottle of Ernest & Julio with a look of distaste. 'Who in the name of arse brought this?'

There was a brief scream from outside, and then Porter, trailing smoke, rushed in and shoved his face in the sink, which was filled with ice and cans of Stella.

'You all right?' I asked, having a sip of the piss Bridget had handed me in a glass.

Porter lifted his face up, dripping with water and looking crazed and wild-eyed. He grabbed me. 'ARE MY EYEBROWS STILL ON?' he demanded in a panicked tone.

I peered at them – he's receding so there's not a lot to see of him, hair-wise – and said: 'I think so. Although you do smell a bit burned.'

'Fucking Catherine wheels!' he shouted, before storming outside to try again.

'Personally, I think journalists just have a twisted psychology,' Bridget told me quietly as we followed him into the garden for the big display, which consisted of a box of rockets and a freezing cold barbecue of sausages that had been dropped on the ground at least twice. 'And I'm sure you're not supposed to let someone with a mental age of six near fireworks.'

'Ooh, Porter, have you got any of those ones which squeal?' I asked him excitedly as I grabbed the box off him for a look-see. 'You know, the ones which corkscrew round and go "wheeeeeeeeeeee!"'

He swore at me and grabbed it back.

'Oh, that's a shame,' I said sadly. 'My dad used to tell me they were the hedgehogs that had crawled into the bonfire to hibernate, and I could never decide if it was really awful and I ought to save them, or really brilliant because it was so much fun when they died.'

Bridget looked at me. 'You're so screwed up,' she said with a sigh.

Maybe we're all just children. Maybe we need to try harder to be grown-ups. Or maybe it's just a reaction, the same as at a country show, to being surrounded by so much shit that sometimes the only thing you can do is sort it into varieties, grade it by quality, texture and odour, and award points in order to get some kind of handle on things.

Much like writing a secret diary about one's divorce. Somehow all of this makes me feel a little calmer, and easier in my mind with the fact the world's been turned upside down – which isn't something I ought to feel calm about, but that's nevertheless what I'm striving for.

God knows when I'll be able to declare it done with, though. It feels like I've been getting divorced for years when in fact it's just over five months. I wouldn't be surprised to wake up one day and find a decade had passed, with no change to anything beyond my becoming an old woman. I long ago stopped responding to texts and emails from Twatface, finding it simply wound me up and made me wonder why he was doing this, that or the other. When I didn't hear from him I was fine; but after a day where we'd had contact I would spend the night tossing and turning, thoughts spinning round my brain like demented bats in a belfry all hunting the same elusive fly, until I fell asleep exhausted as dawn broke.

With only a few hours' light sleep every night, week after week, it felt like my mind was splintering apart. I could get through to the weekend if just one or two other things went wrong, but if there were three or four I'd be a tearful, depressive heap by Thursday afternoon and just climb under the duvet and stay there. The boss shouting; a difficult phone call or email from Twatface; a long drive on a pointless job; no money and a bill coming in – it's normal, everyday stuff we all have to deal with at times. But with the weight of separation already on my back this weak, flimsy edifice of mine would shatter under the addition of just one too many extra problems.

We're paying lawyers, I reasoned, so we should get our money's worth and let them do the nasty haggling that just causes upset. And since then I've slept a little easier and been able to devote my attention to work and the house. Except I'm starting to realize that the lawyers don't seem to be getting very far, a fact which seems to have also finally penetrated Twatface's brain.

I had this email last night from Princess Flashy Knickers:

<From: Knickers, Princess Flashy, 8.08 p.m.
To: Foxy
Ha ha. Twatface has been in touch to find out if you're ill/had a bereavement/are for some other reason ignoring his texts and emails other than just not wanting contact. I told him you're fine.>

Now, on the one hand this makes me want to bang my head on the nearest wall and scream, 'Leave me aloooooone!' And on the other, I feel like punching the air and doing a little dance and singing, 'He's noticed I'm ignoring him! Victory! I win!'

Then the fear kicked in – What did it mean? Why did he email Princess and not me? Is he worried I'm ill? Maybe he wants to win me back? Does he miss me? What's he up to? Has his lawyer made him write it?

I've been worrying for a while that the way things are going with this divorce, the recession will be over before it gets settled. That means the house valuations and everything else could be defunct, and if the price of the house goes up I can't get a mortgage and I'll lose it. I am absolutely, 100 per cent and 360 degrees, not going to lose my house, even if it is a hovel. It's MY hovel, it was my inheritance that bought it, my work that's making it better to live in, and it's the principle of the damn thing. I simply will not give in and let go of the house, any more than I'd let Banks have my byline.

Keeping myself occupied while the lawyers enjoy their expensive logjam is not getting me anywhere. It's frustrating because no one seems to do things quite as quickly and to the point as journalists. We can beat the police, we can track an entire family's movements and dates of birth, fashion a four-word headline to encapsulate a thousand-word story, and in my case we can apparently get married and divorced in the space of a very short time indeed. Everyone else clocks off at 5 p.m. and does things in a far more roundabout way. Journos go straight for the jugular, no messing.

There are times when nothing happens in every walk and wail of life. When it happens on a newspaper the bone-deep paranoia and infighting with which you're surrounded every day leads you to worry that you'll lose your job, that life depends on finding a story and climbing over the twitching corpses of as many people as possible to get to it first. You hit peaks of nailing story after story, and then slide into troughs where nothing works and everything gets spiked and all the doors are slammed in your face. The trick is realizing when you've bottomed out, and then pulling yourself back up by your bootstraps. I need to find a way to apply the same do-or-die outlook to my divorce – I can't ignore it, hope it sorts itself out or, perish the thought, let the other guy win.

Maybe divorce – and life, come to that – is a bit like a fingerprint. Full of ups and downs and whirly bits, but each one is completely individual. There aren't any rules about what there should or shouldn't be, and it's daft to rate yours against someone else's. All you can do is navigate the peaks and troughs the best you can. And all I really know is this job. I'm not sure whether I'm a round peg in a round hole or if it somehow shaped me, but I know how to write, how to persuade someone to do what I want, and how to beat the opposition when I have to.

All I want is my house, and my life, and to say 'I wiiiiiiiiiiin!' as loud as I possibly can – even if it is the most pointless, painful victory in the world.

Nope. There's no way round it. If I'm going to get what I want, I'm going to have to talk to that twat.

DAY ONE HUNDRED AND SEVENTY-SIX

THEY say that worry makes you sick; but seeing as it also makes you thin, who really cares?

The real problem is not feeling ill, or losing weight, but everything else which follows along behind the worry, like some kind of unpleasant medieval entourage of maladies. The teeth which ache all the time from unconscious grinding, the infected bits of skin down the side of your fingernails where you've been gnawing at them, a constant sense of dissatisfaction and, above all else, the 2 a.m. cold splinter of fear which wakes you up with a gasp and the belief that you are absolutely, totally and utterly screwed.

With me the fear is mainly money. It never used to be – I'm not one of those who cares how much I have or how much everyone else has. So long as there's enough to pay the bills and buy a new pair of shoes when I fancy, then all is right with my world. But having never bothered with more than a mild concern about not spending more than I earn, it is now the central preoccupation of my entire life. Faced for the first time with one salary, one enormous mortgage and a house which would have been turned down for a role in *The Money Pit* over budgetary constraints, my days are now a round of own-brand baked beans, trying to make a tenner last till Friday and pressing my nose sadly against the window of the shoe shop.

I count, constantly. All day and all night, over and over

again in my head. 'That's £32 for the leccy, and £26 for the gas. Round it up and let's call it sixty, then I've got to put some petrol in the car, that'll be £40, and I ought to try and put something aside for the insurance next month, say another fifty, and the mortgage is £980, let's call it a grand, so that leaves me with . . . right. Well, if I eat a big lunch at work I won't eat when I get home, maybe I could manage the £25 for those blue shoes, but I promised Princess I'd go to the cinema with her Tuesday, that's another £15. Ooh, look! I've picked up a pub receipt from the floor, that's an extra tenner, lovely.'

They say that money makes the world go around, but it makes mine grind to a complete stop. What I can and can't afford, where I can and can't go; it defines me now, in a snide, niggly, cheap little way. I have developed a hatred for money; it has almost as much influence over my happiness and well-being as the divorce, with the added issue there's no end in sight to the problems it causes me. It squats like a toad in the middle of my life, too fat to get around and too oily to climb over.

My first job on a local paper earned me the princely sum of £7,000 a year, and it felt like I'd won the lottery. Eighteen and still living at home, I blew every penny on awful shoes, crushed velvet leggings and purple nail polish, while my friends were off at university getting used to Pot Noodles. As the years passed and my salary crawled its way to the unimpressive plateau of being a Fleet Street hack the figures increased, but then so did the rent and the sheer number of shoes. I've never again had so much money as I did when I was on £7,000 a year, back in the days when I never worried about a thing.

After I fell in love it seemed I had even less to worry about. Twatface earned less than me at first, but I didn't mind in the least if there was just one present at Christmas or I didn't get flowers like my friends did. I was too independent to be comfortable with someone spending money on me, anyway. We had each other, and that was all I wanted.

As the years went by his salary overtook mine, but we still took it in turns to buy dinner and split everything half and half. Occasionally he'd be struck with insane generosity and buy me a present. I was thrilled with the gifts not because of their value but because he rarely bought any, and that was what made them special. Meanwhile I did the normal girly thing of buying him clothes and shoes and books and toys whenever I'd been to the shops on my lunch break, and he could expect a dozen Christmas presents.

He always said he was broke, and his bank account statements proved it wasn't a lie. Several times he asked me to help him get his finances straight, and I'd tell him he should try limiting himself to £50 and making it last the week, taking the Tube rather than cabs – and he'd listen and smile and nod, and not change a thing.

I never understood how people could go to war over money, argue, kill, move heaven and earth just to get a bit more. I was always of the opinion that money can't make you happy, but debt can make you miserable. At first Twatface made me feel like a millionaire, with more love than sense and the feeling that the world was ours for the taking. In fact it was all hokum, and we were living on borrowed time, the heart's version of a Ponzi fraud: dreams, built on lies constructed on a wish, in which you repeatedly invest until they suddenly collapse and expose all the loans you took out on the never-never.

Now it seems like there's a mortgage on me as well as the house, a huge pit of emotionally negative equity which, if I'm terribly lucky and slave and cry and work for years, I might just about manage to claw my way through so I can be back at zero, and start again in a whole new pyramid scheme of pain and misery with someone else. What a wonderful thought.

Twatface, as with so many other things, was the opposite to me: life was all about money, and everyone always had more than him. He never wanted to spend, queried each bill, and niggled about everything; he was always tight about 'our' spending, but when it came to 'his' money he was carefree, spendthrift and never saved a penny. After we married I scrimped and hoarded everything I could, and that's how we bought our place. We still split everything down the middle, although it was beginning to irk me that I was earning a third of the household income and paying half the costs. Before I realized 'we' had problems, we started to argue about money.

I'd do the weekly shopping and he'd stamp and shout about being asked for a contribution and say he was broke. He started to hide his bank statements. When I found them, ferreted away at the back of the bureau, they showed trips to ATMs three or four times in one night, getting out £100 a time. 'How the hell do you spend £300 on a night in the pub?' I'd ask, and he would yell at me for being 'controlling'.

Just as we split he had got that huge inheritance of his own, which we had earmarked for renovations and a baby. At the time I thought that if we had a child he might cut down the nights out, and we could have a joint account, so I could save some of our money. I roll my eyes now that I was ever that stupid.

These days, extreme financial anxiety has replaced a husband as my regular bedfellow. Every night after I climb under the duvet there is a moment of dread as I stare at the bedroom ceiling, which needs replacing, listen to the house creak itself to sleep, and think about how much money I owe and what I'd do if I lost my job. When Twatface and I took on the house it was with the cushion of two salaries and the knowledge that one of us could support the other if something went wrong. We could always go on holiday, and one day we knew he'd look after me while I raised the children and maybe wrote a book or something.

And that of course was just the moment when all that safety – all the security of a partner and marriage and a future – flapped its wings and flew south for the winter. There is now no cushion, no backing, and absolutely no plan, just a tightrope and a horribly long fall on to spiky bits if it all goes wrong. No one will support me, and my independent spirit is terrified to find what being on your own really means. Every night I try to think about the size of the problem, and every night I realize it's so big I give up, switch off the light and grind my teeth fitfully till morning.

And if, at the same time, every story you touch turns to dust, and nothing you work on goes anywhere near the paper, and Bish comes up behind you, pats you on the shoulder sympathetically and says, 'Yer poor, storyless fook,' in a pitying tone, it really doesn't do much for your state of mind. All I could do was sit at my desk, squeezing pus from the side of my finger and noting the white flecks in the nail, which meant that yet again I was not eating properly.

In-between trying to rustle up something which might get my name in the paper and save my job for another week, there's the never-ending background worry of divorce. The legal letters have slowed from a trickle to the occasional, unhappy drip, with no movement forwards, backwards or even sideways. Last week Maurice felt 'compelled to mention the matter of costs' which, he reminded me with a giggle, were 'continuing to rise'; but he didn't say a figure, and I was too depressed to ask.

So instead the letters limped on, Twatface demanding money off me and me demanding money off him, both of us spending and achieving nothing except grey hairs. It had been months since I had spoken to him, but the time had come to bite the bullet. I realized that if I wanted the house, and I did – it's the last bit of that dream I had which I'm absolutely not going to give up – I was going to have to fight him for it.

So one morning after the post had brought another desultory 'no change' letter from Maurice, I seized the twat by the horns and rang the person who, for the moment at least, goes by the name of husband.

'Hello, you!' he said in tones of great excitement. 'How are you? I haven't heard from you in ages!'

Taking a moment to swallow the bile which rises every time I hear his voice, and wonder quietly to myself how he can treat an estranged wife who hates his guts as if she's some long-lost pal ringing to see if he fancies a pint, I bit back the angry retort it was choking me not to utter and instead said in polite, clipped tones: 'Fine, thanks. And you?'

'Oh, you know, work's a bit shit. The boss is being

pretty horrible at the moment, but then he is a lunatic. So what's going on with you? How's your mum?'

I rolled my eyes. This was going to be a ridiculous conversation.

'Never you mind. What's going on with the lawyers? Maurice says he can't get any answer out of yours. Don't you want to get divorced and lumber off into the sunset with Fatty?'

'MY lawyer won't talk?' he burst out. 'She keeps telling me that YOURS won't answer letters, and frankly it's getting ridiculous. Honestly, you can't hold this up as much as you might try to, I can't afford to keep hanging around like this, you know . . .' He ranted on for a bit while I gnawed the inside of my face off in order not to scream at him.

I took a deep breath and reminded myself to be polite. 'Look, I've told Maurice to pull his finger out. Your high-priced ice queen is spinning you a line. And even if they're both being a bit rubbish, all that's happening is our bills are going up.'

'Yes, well, I suppose so,' he grumbled. 'I still think you're trying to stall it, though.'

'Oh, stop being such a twat! Why the hell would I do that?'

'Well, you don't talk to me any more, or email, and if you did we could have sorted it all out.'

'No, all that would have happened is we would have shouted at each other and got nowhere. At least this way we've got nowhere quietly. Look, why don't you just tell me what you want, I'll tell you what I want and we'll tell our lawyers.'

He took a bit of persuading, and my lip took a lot of biting, but eventually he said no, he didn't want the

239

house and was happy for me to have it, if I could afford it, and he was prepared to walk away without asking for any extra cash to buy him out.

'Considering you owe me half the deposit, that's very big of you,' I sniffed.

'Well, you get it back this way,' he said, annoyingly. 'What about you, anyway? The lawyer says you're demanding my inheritance, that's not right.'

I sighed. 'I've done no such thing. We bought the house with my inheritance, which you're benefiting from—'

'I'm walking away from it!' he exclaimed.

'You weren't until now,' I pointed out. 'Meanwhile you've got a six-figure sum sitting in your bank, and if you bung me something completely inconsequential you wouldn't notice, like £5,000 or something, I can afford to start on the kitchen and we'll call it quits. It doesn't mean anything to you and it makes a big difference to me. The alternative is I won't be able to take the house on, and we'll have to put it on the market, and the divorce will have to wait until it gets sold. It could be months. Is that what you want?'

He hummed and hahed, and I thought I had him until he said the lawyer had told him we could go in front of a judge to decide how much of the inheritance was fair. My lip was drawing blood by this point.

'Going in front of a judge will take another three months or so, and cost thousands more, all to argue over £5,000,' I pointed out through gritted teeth, as reasonably as I could. 'What's the use in that?'

'But if I do that, the house price will go up in a few months and you won't be able to get it,' he said, somewhat slyly. 'So it's in your interest to take the house now, and leave me the money.'

He had me in a corner and he knew it. There was nothing I could do but bite it down. I don't care a damn about his money, I'd rather not touch a penny, but I wanted to punish him. He should be made to pay in some way for being such a ratbag.

And that in itself makes me feel greedy, and bitter, and vicious, and I'm none of those things. I hate money, and I hate arguing about it, and I hate haggling with my own husband. The whole thing sticks so deep in the back of my throat I feel like a cat bringing up the world's biggest furball.

'Fine,' I growled. 'You leave the house and I'll leave your poxy smegging money.'

'Well, now I'm not so sure. I mean, after all, I'm basically giving you a house.'

'Oh, for . . . you're not *giving* me a house, you're walking away from a massive mortgage and a renovation project. All you're giving me is a lifetime of debt and a headache. Stop being such a fucking TWAT!'

I immediately regretted losing my calm, and took a breath. We were close enough that I didn't want to ruin his mood now. He sighed dramatically. 'I'm doing you a favour. I could make you fight me in court, and I can afford to pay the lawyers, which you can't. This way you keep a house which will have loads of equity in it in a year or two when the market picks up, and I'll keep my money. So basically we're even.'

This was just too much to bear. It was the kind of cracked logic that used to drive me demented when we were married. 'You have a big PILE of cash; I have a big HOLE of cash. The fact that those two things are both worth the same figure does NOT mean we are even; it means I'm several hundred grand in debt. And the house isn't going to earn any money unless I can find the cash to do it up . . . oh, for goodness' sake!'

I took another deep breath. 'Look, fine. I want the house, you want your money. Let's both tell our lawyers we've agreed that's reasonable, and then they can write it down in a financial settlement and we can get the decree absolute. All right?'

'Fine,' he said. 'I'm glad you've seen sense. Can I come and get the bed?'

'The *what*?' I asked, surprised.

'The bed. It's mine. I need it because I'm moving house.'

He was obviously setting up home with Fatty. 'You want the *bed*?'

'Yes.'

'Our marital bed?' This was beyond belief, even for him.

'Yes, it's mine – I bought it.'

'Are you fucking joking?'

'There's no need to swear – it's my furniture.'

'Have you asked Fatty if she wants to sleep in the marital bed?'

'No. I'm sure she won't mind.'

'I'm sure she bloody *will* mind. It's the bed you spent five years shagging me in – when you could be bothered.'

'Well, I need it,' he said, bullishly.

'Are you moving in with Fatty? With *our* bed? You haven't actually told her it's ours, have you? You've just told her you've got a bed somewhere. Jesus!'

Why can't he be a normal kind of shit? Gamble his money away, find a prettier, younger bird who's bright enough to insist on a new bed, and then cheat on her too, like all the other rotters in the world? Why does he have to find one bigger than me, ask me to organize their

242

holidays, demand I give them my bed, and then be faithful and decent enough to move in with her a few months later? What did I do to deserve this kind of weirdness? I feel increasingly unhinged every time I speak to him, and am starting to feel I must be as mad as he always said I was.

Yet it wouldn't do to upset him when this agreement has yet to be rubber-stamped by the lawyers. 'Look, I don't want the bloody bed anyway – it's just some cheap IKEA tat. But I doubt Fatty would want it if you explained. Why don't you ask her, and if she wants it by all means come and pick it up. If she doesn't, I'll chop it up for firewood, OK?'

'OK,' he said. 'Can I ring you again? You know, for a chat?'

'NO!' I said, banging the phone down in the cradle.

I went and looked at the bed, an ugly, orange pine boxy thing we'd had ever since moving in together in our first flat, about six years earlier. After we bought the house we would lie in it and talk about what kind of built-in wardrobes we wanted, and what colour the walls should be. Later I lay and cried in it, sometimes waiting for him to come home, and sometimes trying not to wake him with my tears. But the whole time, if I'm being honest, I thought the damn thing was bloody uncomfortable, and I never really liked it. Come to think of it, he'd had it at university, so his previous girlfriends had been miserable in it, too. Grabbing the car keys I drove to the nearest IKEA and bought a new, metal bedstead with knobbly bits, brought it home and put it all together.

Rather than give in to the urge to chop Twatface's bed up and have a bonfire while I danced around it naked, swigging whiskey, I carefully put all the bits in the back bedroom, because a bit of me knew he'd cause a fuss if he couldn't get it back, and he was easily stupid enough to refuse to agree the financial settlement purely on the basis of a ten-year-old pine bedstead worth £150 that his girlfriend would never sleep in.

And now that bitch thought she was going to clamber in it, did she? Well, we'd see about that. I took the slats, held together with bits of cotton, which formed the base the mattress was supposed to sit on, and pulled out two out of every three bits of wood. They'd bear her weight, but not for long. Then I dug through the bag of nuts and bolts and pulled out a few handfuls, so the damn thing couldn't even be put together properly, and threw them in the bin. I chopped up the slats, and that evening sat by the fire, feeding them into the flames one at a time to keep the chill out of the living room, because I was trying to keep the heating bills down. 'Loads of fun and it's completely free,' I told myself. 'If he tries to shag her in that bed it'll break.'

Then my phone rang; it was Twatface.

'Hello,' I said. Tell me he hasn't changed his mind, I asked the universe.

'Hi. Look, you were right about the bed. Fatty doesn't want it. So, you know, chop it up if you want.'

I sighed.

He went on: 'And, er, thanks for, you know, sorting all this out. It was the right thing to do, I'm glad you rang. Anyway, goodnight.'

He rang off and I lay there, grinding my teeth. He has no worries at all. He has a pile of money and can start a new relationship just like that. I have a hole of money, my teeth are worn down to stumps, and the thought of a boyfriend makes me break out in a cold sweat.

At least if I make it through all this then I'm bound to be a better person, right? I at least know exactly how much money is coming in and going out every month, which I never did with him. There's no one shouting at me about how much I spend in Sainsbury's while simultaneously complaining the sausages aren't organic.

There's just me, now. Ha, for better, for worse; for richer, for poorer. Everything is going to be a struggle, but somehow, strangely, I'm certain it's better like this.

DAY ONE HUNDRED AND EIGHTY-EIGHT

WHEN parents lie to their children, it's with the best of intentions: Father Christmas won't bring you a present unless you're good; if you eat your greens you'll grow big and strong; if you do that any more it'll fall off. They insist none of these falsehoods are really wrong, and that white lies are perfectly acceptable so long as: a) the child will be better off believing them, or b) the adults get a giggle out of it. I was told Santa was a clean freak who would refuse to enter a messy bedroom, and on one memorable occasion was made to believe I would only get my Christmas presents if I stood on my head and clapped my feet. I was at it for ages, while Grandad manfully kept a straight face and gave me helpful hints.

But every lie follows a continuum: there always comes a point where it's impossible to maintain the deception, and you find yourself in the quicksand of crushed disappointment.

It's the kind of realization that trains you for the disenchantments of adulthood. But alongside the kindly-meant deceptions of youth are greater untruths which are passed down the generations without being questioned, and which make you grow up slightly twisty. There's being told that 'big boys don't cry', which just sets lads up for a lifetime of emotional repression, and the belief that little girls must wear pink and play with dolls, even if the most fun they ever have is playing with their brother's Lego.

Somehow or another the message is driven into our heads that it is more important to be attractive than it is to be bright, and that pretty people are better human beings.

Well, the gossip pages prove the best-looking people on the planet are among the most screwed-up, and Faceache tells me that almost everyone who was terribly pretty and popular at school is now fat, ugly and working somewhere grim. I think that if everyone loves you as a teenager then life seems to come easy and you never need to try; teachers mark you slightly higher, the opposite sex chases you, and consequently you learn nothing. The misfits, outsiders and dweebs, the ones who struggled with NHS glasses, acne and unrequited love, have to strive to flirt, be interesting or funny, and as such have the corners rubbed off and get a few street smarts.

But not crying, and the colour pink, and being pretty are mere rubble around the ancient moss-covered monolith of the Greatest Lie of Childhood, a house of sod built on the pillars of You Must Find the One, Happy Ever After, and You'll Just Know. It's these teachings about love that are handed down via fairy tales, books and films, which mean that when you fall for someone you presume you MUST get married and it MUST last for ever, that once you've Found The One you can stop striving. They don't allow for the possibility that maybe the relationship will have a finite course to run, that love is fragile, or that marriage is something you need to work at every day. Cheating is common – just open any newspaper – yet everyone blithely promises not to do it, as though by saying so you can ensure that it doesn't happen, like saying 'white rabbits' to ward off bad luck. A healthier attitude might be to expect temptation – anticipate it even   work hard to overcome it, and qualify for some kind of prize if you do.

I talk a lot about Twatface's failings, and it's only natural, because divorce is about as polarizing as Marmite on a magnet. It's an attitude that is necessary for my survival, if nothing else. But I'm starting to find that what goes along with it is a greater pragmatism about matters of the heart, which means that I can see my own mistakes in a way I couldn't when I was making them.

We fell in love, fine, but we got married because I believed that was what you did when you loved someone, and he went along with the idea. It didn't cross my mind that being a husband or a wife is a job, and it's something you should only do for the rest of your life if you have the aptitude for it. Twatface plainly didn't, but I do think he wanted to try, at first. I should have known better maybe, assessed his character a little more before tying myself to it. But I was young and stupid, and I thought that the things we had in common outweighed all the things we didn't, and the differences just made life more interesting.

After we got together I learned to eat tomatoes and drink dessert wine, developed a love of absinthe and a loathing for Bob Dylan, heard my ovaries tick for the first time, and became part of someone else's family; all things I never thought likely before. Of course there's bad stuff, too, and I also learned to distrust and fear the person you love the most.

I never thought, for a second, that it would end. I never thought there'd be a day when he wasn't my best friend. Yet the marriage lasted only a little over a thousand days, and while I'd argue on my deathbed he bears the greater responsibility for its demise, I know that maybe 30 or 40 per cent of the problems were down to me. I stopped doing all the things you do when you're a girlfriend and trying to get a guy to like you: I didn't wear make-up at weekends, I cut my hair short, couldn't always be bothered

248

to shave my legs, spent all my time nagging him about the things he did that I hated, and generally wasn't much fun any more. I was miserable, but I didn't know why, and it didn't occur to me that he might be miserable too.

As a result, while he might have wanted to try at first, he didn't feel the need by the end. He stopped taking me out to dinner, stopped caring what I thought of him, wasn't bothered if he trod on my toes. Even the class thicko could work out that the first woman who came along who was more of a laugh would turn his head.

I realize now that the point at which the ring went on is when the work should have begun. Maybe we get it all the wrong way round, and should actually be boring and plain and dull when we meet someone, and then save up all the effort and sexy underwear for after we've caught their attention. Which, of course, we'd somehow have to do while looking like a spod.

So if we both stopped working at it, who's to blame? Who made whom miserable first? No single person or thing is at fault, but both of us and maybe neither, because when we were growing up we were filled with stories and messages which told us that when you've Found The One there's nothing more to aim for beyond healthy children and old age.

And, of course, part of the lie is that if you can dance with a guy then you are destined for each other, you're subconsciously in sync, and it will all, magically, work out fine. If you find someone who can waltz you round the floor like Prince Charming did to Cinders then he's The One, that's the rule we all secretly believe. The first time I danced with Twatface was in a friend's flat, after dinner, a couple of weeks after we got together, to an Andy Williams' song. We were both a little drunk, but each seemed to know exactly where the other would put their feet, and I remember thinking it was just perfect. The song we danced to was played everywhere that summer, so of course it became Our Song and was the first dance at the wedding. We were drunker then, but it was still fun, except that over the following years we stopped dancing altogether, until it got to the point where we were such a bad pairing that if he took me in his arms I sighed inwardly and tried to wriggle away as quickly as possible before my toes were stamped to mush.

Seeing as I've spent the past few months drinking, the only dancing I've done recently is barely deserving of the name. So when Fifi demanded I attend the cricket club's Christmas party I didn't stop to wonder if there might be dancing. Instead I donned my normal groupie uniform – short skirt plus tit top – and went with her to some dive bar in Stockwell, where two dozen handsome yet oafish louts had spent the whole day on the sauce.

We walked into a dark and gloomy hole with a live band playing in one corner. The bar was closed off to anyone not with the cricketers, so it was kind of empty, while at the same time quite full. Half a dozen guys waved at us – the recently-turned twenty-one-year-old Porky initially looked a little perplexed on seeing me. Then I could see him thinking, 'Oh, it's that pissed girl' – and Beamy got us a drink. I watched while Fi did the rounds of the boys, pecking cheeks and squeezing biceps or bums while cackling loudly. There were the normal crew of shaggers and misfits, some new faces I hadn't seen before but who Fi seemed to know, and hardly any females in sight.

After a couple of drinks the band kicked in with something loud and raucous and Fi and I took to the floor, and there began the longest night of dancing I've had since the school disco of 1988, when I won a seven-inch single for knowing all the moves to 'Superman' by Black Lace. I danced so long and so fervently that Fi – a professional partygoer – had to have a rest, and people started bringing me ice, which I just put in my bra. At one point I was in the middle of a circle of cricketers – Raffles, Bazzo, a bunch of others I couldn't put names to – and danced wildly with each of them in turn. One grabbed me and spun me round, and I noted only that he was tall before we both threw ourselves into the music, somehow managing to pull off moves you only normally see in films.

He and I kept dancing like dervishes until the music died and the ugly lights came up, and there I was in the middle of the floor with one leg wrapped around his waist, my head thrown back, and a hand in his hair as he bent me backwards over his knee. 'Hello,' he said. 'I'm Paul.'

Finally exhausted, I threw myself on a sofa and knocked back an icy drink. Paul joined me and said he was visiting his brother Raffles for the week and lived in Leeds. 'That's nice,' I said, and squinted at him blearily while thinking he was quite cute. Then he completely blew it by firmly placing one ham-sized hand on my thigh, uninvited, and making me feel like a pig carcass on a butcher's hook. I was offended, inexplicably so, seeing as I had just been literally wrapped around him, and to shake off the hand I stood up, swallowed a burp and dragged him back on to the floor.

By 2 a.m. my feet were killing me, and I'd spent maybe four hours spinning around in heels, throwing myself over every cricketer in the room, but mainly my new pal Paul. On my way back from the loos Fi announced she was off in a cab, and I told her to wait for me while I said goodbye to my dance partner. With a coat in one hand I tracked him down to the bar and said, 'Well, 'bye then,

251

nice to meet you,' and gave him a peck on the cheek. He tried to grab me for a deeper kiss but I ducked it and headed out to the taxi.

'Sooo,' said Fi as she leaned back in the seat and we rumbled up to the Old Kent Road and home, 'why are you here?'

'Well, Dad says they found me under a gooseberry bush . . .' I said, thinking only of my aching toes. God, I'm getting old.

'I mean, why aren't you goin' 'ome with that faberluss man?'

'I can't do that, Fi, I've only just met him. Besides I'm still married.'

She looked at me in disbelief.

I rolled my eyes. 'Yes, well, all right, I know I already have . . . but it's . . . I don't know . . . just too odd to be doing with that when you know you've got a husband somewhere, even if it's not a marriage any more. Married is married, ' I explained. 'Anyway, he grabbed my leg.'

The disbelief on her face went all the way up to eleven. 'You're insane,' she said, shaking her head. 'You were dancin' with him! Really well! And he's 'andsome and fancied you, and it's been ages since you had a shag, izzeht.'

'Fi, I don't judge men by how long it's been since the last one,' I said snootily, and completely believed it until the next morning, when I woke up and thought, 'Oh, arse.'

Back at work, and in an idle moment I turned to Faceache and had a trawl for my Cricket Boy. 'There he is,' I told Princess Flashy Knickers, turning my screen round so she could see his profile picture. 'What d'you think?'

She looked critically at the tall, handsome man and then said: 'Tell me again why you didn't shag him?'

'I'd only just met him!'

'Are you aware we're in the twenty-first century? You don't need to meet his parents first these days. And you said he was a really good dancer. You know what that means.'

I grumbled to myself for a bit, and then she said: 'Why don't you make a friend request? He might be back down south and you can meet him again.'

Horror shot through me. 'I can't do that! Oh my God, what if he can't remember me, what if he didn't like me, what if he says no?'

Princess rolled her eyes. 'Well, poke him, then.'

'POKE him? Are you insane? I'm thirty years old, for Christ's sake!'

'Oh, look, just bloody poke him, and then he'll poke you back, and then you can be friends, OK?' she said huffily, turning my screen back round and throwing the mouse at me. 'Click on it! Go on, bloody click on "poke"!'

'Princess Sophia Flashy Knickers Waddington, I am absolutely totally and not, no how, never and no way going to use poking as a method of flirting!' I cried, as she forcibly positioned my fingers on the mouse and moved the cursor over the 'poke' button.

'Do it!' she growled.

'No! I can't! I won't! What if he wants to get married? I've still got a husband! Oh Christ, no! He might want his bride to wear white! I can't! Gaaaaaaah!' I screamed back, until she brought her fist down on top of my hand and the screen popped up with a message: 'You have poked Cricket Boy.'

Silence fell. 'OhshitwhathaveIdone?' I whimpered.

Princess sat back down in her chair with a satisfied air. 'There. Don't say I never do anything for you.'

It sounds ridiculous, but I was genuinely as scared as when you like that boy at school when you're eight, and are terrified he might find out. I sat, wide-eyed and softly sweating with fear, for ten minutes until I got a message. 'Cricket Boy has poked you.'

'OH. MY. GOD. Princess, he's poked me! He's poked me! Now what do I do?' I demanded, all of aflutter.

'Make a friend request,' she said patiently.

'I can't do that! Oh no, never! I shall return the poke, there, I can do that, that's easy. Look, I did it all on my own.' I clicked and looked proudly at Princess.

She stared at me quietly, then turned to Bridget and said: 'You'll have to take over. I can't deal with this any more.'

The afternoon wore on, with Cricket Boy and I in a poke frenzy, and each refusing to be the one to make a friend request. It must have happened six or seven times, on each occasion driving my colleagues further into despair, until finally I had the message, 'You have a friend request,' and I leapt from my chair with delight. Everyone else was so thrilled their torture was coming to an end they threw their hands in the air with relief, and a sarcastic Mexican wave went the entire length of the newsroom.

Even Bish joined in, and then said: 'What were all that about?'

Bridget and Princess breathed out. 'Thank God for that,' said Bridge. 'Now, will you shut up?'

'Yes,' I said quite chirpily, clicking on 'confirm friend'. 'But, you know, I'm not used to this flirting business. This is all a bit weird.'

'Only the way you do it,' grumped Princess.

I sighed. 'Yes, but the point is you guys are used to it,' I said, waving a hand at the screen. 'Internet etiquette and when to poke or not to poke, dancing with someone in a bar and going home with them if you like them. I've been with one guy for the best part of a decade, and last time I was single we didn't have poking. We barely had email, for God's sake. This is all new and strange, and I don't get it. It's like being a Tudor peasant suddenly dumped in the middle of the M25 with a Bluetooth head-set and a laptop. It's freaking me out.'

Bridget looked at me. 'You didn't flirt with Twatface after you were married?'

'No, I suppose not,' I said thoughtfully. 'Maybe I should have.'

And I should have danced more, too. Next time – if I get a next time – I'll try to keep on flirting and shaving my legs, and won't leave the nice knickers at the back of the drawer. And it would be nice – although I know the thinking behind this is as much of a fallacy as Father Christmas – if my next lover was someone who could whirl me round the floor like Cinderella and make an effort to avoid my toes.

Just then my screen flashed. 'You have one new message.'

'Hello, Cinders!' wrote Cricket Boy. 'How're your feet?!'

DAY ONE HUNDRED AND NINETY-FIVE

'SOME clever chap – apparently there was one, once, like, ages ago – said that all beliefs were a matter of faith, right; so that means believing in Father Christmas is just as valid as believing in God,' I theorized to the bar at large, pleased at myself for sounding so intellectual despite being horizontal on a manky sofa, with an inflatable beehive on my head.

'Yes, but right, that's bollocks, isn't it?' said Bridget, who was on her hands and knees under the table looking for a 20p piece, using the light of her mobile phone.

'Why? Santa's probably got a slightly bigger following than God, and at least he hands out presents once a year rather than all this guilt and afterlife crap,' pointed out Porter from a precarious bar stool.

Bridget banged her head on the underneath of the table in her outrage. 'People live their entire lives based on their faith, you know, and do nice things with it as a result,' she insisted, lifting her reddened face into view and puffing her hair out of her eyes. 'Found it. Where's that sweet machine?'

'Yes, but, OK, there was this other bloke who said that faith is just the way you hold on to an idea that you've already arrived at by logic,' I continued.

Buff, who was lying on the floor trying to drunkenly text a hooker he did a buy-up with two weeks ago, after which he had announced, 'She's not that bad, y'know, for a fifty-year-old brass,' decided to butt in. 'How can you have faith in something that's logical?' he said. 'That's like trusting that something which already works is going to work. It's ridiculous. It's not like the sun coming up in the morning is an act of faith, it's a matter of astrophysisis . . . isis . . . cisic . . . it just happens.'

'My phone's dead, I can't see a bloody thing. Was it on the left or on the right?' wailed Bridge from a darkened corner of the dingy bar.

'Look, you know what I mean,' I said. 'The point is, right, that . . .'

'Seriously, where's the bladdy machine? I've lost it!' Bridget howled a semi-octave higher.

'. . . that I was trying to make before I was so rudely interrupted by Bridget's quest for another jelly baby – IT'S OVER THERE BY THE BOGS, for God's sake, woman, it's the same place it's been in all night! – is that faith defies logic, by definition, otherwise it wouldn't be faith. QED.'

'But you can lose your faith and retain your logic,' pointed out Porter, tossing peanuts into the air, one at a time, and looking surprised as they missed his mouth and bounced off his nose, chin and then an eye. 'Ow.'

'Soooo,' I said. 'And this is the point I've been trying to get at for the past half hour, right, if you lose your faith and then deduce there is a Santa or God or whatever, it's not faith, it's deduction. If I work out whether to trust Cricket Boy not to do the same as Twatface, is that actually trust?'

There was a thunk and a mechanical grinding noise and Bridget came back, chewing joyfully. 'Got the last one,' she said happily, plonking herself down on the sofa and upending the dregs of a bottle of Number 17 Reserve port into a beer glass. 'Your problem with Cricket Boy is not whether you can trust him, it's when you're going to get your leg over.'

'Exactly. You're not about to get married after a couple of pokes on Faceache, for Pete's sake! Christ, women are mad!' grumbled Buff. 'Besides, if ever there was an argument that there could not possibly be an intelligent creator it's Bish. I mean, look at him. Who would design that?'

We all regarded our news editor silently, as he lay quietly and near-horizontal in an armchair, tie askew and shirt undone, paunch spilling forth, with a plastic flower sticking out of one ear and the words, 'If found, inform police' scrawled across his forehead in marker pen. He snored softly, a Christmas cracker paper hat somehow still perched upon the thick brown hair he insisted was his own.

'Proof, if ever any were needed, that life is a chaotic system,' said Porter definitively, brushing the nuts from his hands and standing mostly up. 'There's no way you can explain Bish unless all of life is completely random. And that means you need to stop fretting about stuff you can't know, and just shag this bloke and see what happens.'

'Really?' I asked, pulling the beehive from my sweaty head and giving it a scratch.

'Really. It's a traditional method which works perfectly well for the rest of humankind, so it's good enough for you. You don't want to buck tradition, it'll only bite you on the arse if you try. Right, I'm off home. The Minicab Rapist has already left, right?'

'Ages ago,' I assured him, knowing full well the photographer in question was lurking outside, waiting for someone to hail a taxi so he could ask to share it and bag himself another victim for the darkroom wall.

Riding back home by myself in a cab – having given it twenty minutes for Porter and his would-be assailant to get gone – my inebriated mind turned, as it is wont to when there's no one to snog, to matters philosophical and whether what was traditional was necessarily clever. Tradition tells us to do the same thing, over and over, without questioning it, and in the belief that what's always happened is what should continue to happen for evermore. You see your family at Christmas, you have the same arguments with your folks you've always had; you meet a boy and jump into bed because there's no reason not to. But if we did what's always been done, wronged spouses would stay with their Twatfaces, we'd all be living in the villages our grandparents were born in, and Isaac Newton would never have wondered why apples drop down rather than up.

The real reason we celebrate Christmas has less to do with the supposed birthday of an alleged prophet and is more closely related to the fact that for tens of thousands of years humans have had a big party in the middle of winter as a way of marking the halfway point. The tradition of slaughtering a big fat animal, roasting it, and everyone gorging themselves until they're sick, has its roots deep at the back of our skulls, along with the pituitary gland and the libido and all the other important bits that tell us who we are. If you stripped out the pagan stuff

259

from Christmas no one except the Queen would bother with it any more. And she would soon get bored.

But that's the thing about tradition: after a while it kills the true reason for things, and you forget why you're doing it in the first place, so you tack on meanings that don't have much to do with the cause. Habit inures you to the rut you're in, so that you never question it or try to climb out, which is why I'm actually starting to feel frightened about what will happen when my divorce comes through.

It has been the central pivot of my life for so long that considering what will happen when it's no longer there is like being told there'll be no oxygen tomorrow. What am I supposed to do without it?

And then there's Cricket Boy. It's a safe flirtation with him hundreds of miles away in Leeds. Sometimes we text so much it seems ridiculous, but if I had to speak to him in person or he asked to see me I think I'd take to my heels like Forrest Gump. I haven't even told him I'm married and getting divorced. Are you obliged to tell people up front, like with HIV?

He's just the next boy in the queue, I expect, nothing important or special beyond being Mr Right Now. I need to go through a few different boys, I think, not so much to live it up but simply to heal all the bits that are broken.

Mr Wonderful, were he here right now, would be confronted with someone too terrified to speak to him in person, who would go mental if he left the toilet seat up. The only way I can see to fix that stuff is to practice, over and over again: how to flirt, how to date, how to hold someone's hand or let them meet my friends.

Each chap is a stepping stone to being better at those

things, so that when Mr Wonderful pitches up I don't have to say: 'Hello, nice to meet you, could you possibly come back in a year or so when I'm sane?'

It was all so much easier, last time I was single. Why does it have to be so flipping complicated?

By the time the cab got home I had given up overthinking all this rubbish, which was exactly the spirit in which I had gone out that night in the first place.

One of the more addictive traditions we all hold to at this time of year is that at the works Christmas party you have to get the drunkest you've been all year, or indeed at any point previously in your life, in order to forget it. It's a habit which in Fleet Street turns the festive season from a time of drunken peace and goodwill into a Saturnalia so debauched even Nero would make his excuses and leave.

Earlier that night the female reporters had all squeezed into new frocks and shoes, cackling and gossiping and sharing mascara in the ladies' loos at the office. Our male counterparts had gone so far as to straighten their ties as they waited for us to pile out, giggling, like an advert for hold-it-all-in big knickers, and jump in a series of taxis. Bish had made a proper effort, with a clean pair of corduroys and a fresh packet of Woodbines, while Evil Elliot had decked himself out in a pristine white shirt, black suit, and shoes so polished he could see up his own snooty nose. Tanya Banks, inexplicably, was in a mud-brown tight dress that made her look like a stool sample. I'm not being mean, she really did.

Our crocodile of cabs wound their way to a bar in the West End which used to be trendy and is now slightly run-down, and therefore available at a knockdown rate to the staff of a newspaper whose budgets are always being revised downwards. Despite the 'current economic climate' The Editor had splashed out on a £50 chocolate fountain, a sweet machine which dispensed jelly babies for 20p a pop, and a CD with the word 'megamix' on the side, which was played in a loop for hours while we scoffed the kind of miniaturized food which is always served at these things.

We turned up at the same time as the photographers, who, in their normal monkey fashion, had gathered in a pub over the road for a quick chimp about lenses and a couple of drinks to stiffen their spines before they had to enter a bar without straw on the floor. The fellas had struggled in from their patches all over the country, from Nick the Wop who sat in a corner like Marlon Brando receiving requests, 'On dis, de day of de Christmas pardy,' to Matt the Missile, a photographer so slow and steady and unlikely to get the picture that he is for ever put on overnight watches, sat on his own in the wee hours in a freezing cold Mondeo while everyone else sleeps. I waved at Nick on my way to the bar, and he squinted short-sightedly at me while pouring himself a large glass of Chianti.

'Oo zat?' he said.

'It's me, Nick. You've forgotten your contact lenses again. Want a drink?'

'Nah, mite, I go'wan. Es'cuse me, I 'av to talk to sam people.'

I wandered to the bar, but got waylaid by the Missile, whose guidance systems usually bring him straight up to me before anyone else.

'Hiiiii,' he said to me slowly. 'How aaaaare . . .'

'Oh, hi, Matt, I'm fine. Gosh, you look well,' I said quickly, desperate not to get stuck. 'Oh look, is that Nick waving at you?'

I backed away while his attention was diverted, safe in the knowledge it would take fifteen minutes or more for the Missile to realize he was off-course and do a U-turn, and I had just ordered a couple of bottles of fizz for the girls when Mike the Bike bundled up to me. As a man who spends most of his days freezing in motorcycle leathers on street corners, sucking on a dog-end before gunning his Kawasaki and chasing fleeing celebrities through London traffic or up the motorways, he is unused to the social niceties, and so began shouting in my face about how 'fookin' BRILLIANT' the party was, but how he wasn't going to take any shit off the Wop, 'Just cos he thinks he's the FOOKIN' boss of me.' I stood and looked at him, noted the pupils so dilated they'd spread behind his ears, wiped some spit off my cheek, and asked him politely whether half past six wasn't a little early to be starting on the marching powder.

Just as he launched into a diatribe on the beauties of cocaine, tiny wee Jock Beckett ambled up in his normal Glaswegian fashion and picked a fight with Mike about how he'd managed to lose a TV presenter's bright red Ferrari on a wet day last week, and I was able to escape back to my fellow blunts to get hammered. Someone had brought some unfunny inflatable sheep and wigs, and it didn't take long for us to be drunk enough to find them amusing.

Now at every Christmas do – and Fleet Street is just the same – there are only two rules: 1) You will have to talk to the boss, and 2) You can't get drunk until after you talk to the boss.

If you're lucky, The Editor does the rounds early in the evening but if 10 p.m. rolls around and that still hasn't happened yet, then it's time to move to water if you don't want to wake up to a world of regret the next day. But as I've said before of all the bosses I've worked for – each of whom had only the flimsiest grip on sanity – the current one's not so bad, and tonight was in fine drinking fettle. At around 9 p.m., just as The Editor wandered towards our merry band of idiots for the annual chat, the megamix switched to an Abba medley, which made the boss head to the dance floor so quick the straws were left spinning in our drinks.

Watching The Editor throw a series of increasingly crazy shapes, we realized we'd escaped the drunken talk about How Are Things? and heaved a sigh of relief. Bridget had brought a collection of police contacts to the do, and, after initially trying to keep them as far away from Mike the Bike as possible, had given up, and was just sinking cocktails while chatting up a youthful Scotland Yard press officer.

Valentine Lush, despite taking redundancy and going freelance the previous month, had wangled his way in and got stuck into what was left of the free bar alongside Porter and Cubby. Nancy was bellowing in my ear about her latest date, while I was drunkenly texting Cricket Boy in Leeds, who was demanding a picture of me in my low-cut tight red frock, which I had assured him made me look like Jessica Rabbit in a Wonderbra.

Tania Banks, who had heard Cubby was considering early retirement for the sake of his liver and third marriage, had backed Bish into a corner where she was fluttering her eyelashes madly, and I listened with half an ear as she told him: '... but I really believe the most important role of any journalist is to investigate the scandals in our health service, I mean it's a national institution. And have I told you how much I admired that spread you masterminded last week about the patients' right to choose . . . ?'

Bish, too seasoned a hand to believe that kind of bull or to be happy with someone stood between him and the bar, finished the dregs of his cocktail and grimaced. 'Bluddy poncey drinks! There's nowt wrong wi' stout, yer know. Look, Banks, Cubby's not resigned yet, so give it a rest and let me have one night a year where you don't lick me flamin' arse, all right?'

With that he elbowed a deflated Banks aside, and I was so busy crowing about her putdown to Nancy that I failed to notice a new threat – Elliot.

Once the worry of a chat with The Editor had receded, we'd all happily got smashed and forgotten that Evil Elliot, despite his tendency to snort cocaine off hookers' bottoms in private, avoided alcohol. As such he was not only sober but, surrounded by drunken idiots, in an even worse mood than normal. The Editor can only sack you; Elliot can make your life a living hell. And he was homing in on Princess Flashy Knickers.

She had been having a difficult few weeks with a tummy bug, an ex-boyfriend who wanted to try again, and a massive legal on a story which had come from a previously impeccable, but suddenly rubbish contact on the subject of a minor Royal's fling with a pop singer. This had prompted a deluge of legal letters from barristers so strong that Crow the lawyer had been seen sucking his thumb. Princess did what every reporter in this situation does: she drowned her sorrows, thus making her situation magnificently worse.

I saw her drunkenly lever herself up from a sofa and walk unsteadily towards the loos with a hand over her mouth. Thinking I should go after her and make sure she was puking in roughly the right direction, i.e. not on herself, I put my phone away, only to see Elliot zero in on her like a hungry leopard who's just spotted an unattended fawn in a quiet bit of the Serengeti.

'Sophia, is this wise?' he hissed in her ear as he caught up with her at the side of the dance floor while Abba played for the fourth time that night, and where The Editor, by now inexplicably wearing a long red wig, was gyrating wildly.

'Fnh?' replied Princess, as her eyeballs corkscrewed wildly around her head. I was still several metres away, my feet apparently stuck in treacle as time slowed to a crawl, dozens of dancing bodies suddenly between us. There was no way I could get to her in time, but I could imagine what Elliot was saying as I watched his lips move and his eyes narrow as he bent towards the tottering Princess . . .

'How much have you had to drink? Is this the way you should be behaving in the *current economic climate*, considering the likely size of the legal payout we will be making, thanks to you?' he was probably questioning softly. 'I would have thought that you would be doing all you could to appear professional, rather than an impersonation of Oliver Reed. It's not the sort of thing The Editor would approve of, I'm sure.'

Matt the Missile hoved into view, blocking me off from Princess as he said: 'Would youuuuu liiiike a driiiiii . . .'

Oh God, Matt, not now! Not now! Biting it back, I smiled, gripped his arm and firmly moved him aside as I told him I'd be right back, there was something I just had to sort out. Two metres away and closing, I saw Elliot lean in and deliver his coup de grâce stealthily into Princess's ear, which I caught just as I arrived at her side.

'There are going to be compulsory redundancies, you know. I've been asked to draw up a *list*.'

Princess looked up at him sadly, like a puppy who knows it's been bad. Her chest heaved, her face distended, and a stomach full of mini-sausages, mini-vol-au-vents, and a big pile of brown sludge that may once have been marshmallows dipped in chocolate sauce emptied itself in a technicolour fountain out of her mouth and splattered on to the front of Elliot's pristine white shirt.

All three of us stood and stared as the sludge dripped slowly and softly on to his shiny shoes. Behind me, I heard Porter and Buffy guffaw over the music, and Bish say: 'Well, thank fook it weren't me . . .'

Princess lifted her teary face to Elliot's burgeoning, red-eyed fury and said: 'Oh.' She hiccupped. 'Sorry.'

She put out a hand to wipe the mess away, but Elliot, horror writ on his face as if he were an agoraphobe dumped in the desert, shoved it away. He turned on his heel, put his nose in the air and strode, still dripping, out of the bar, as I led Princess to the toilets to clean herself up.

Ten minutes later we came back out, and Bish stumbled over, clutching a bottle of light ale he'd managed to find, clapped Princess on the back and said: 'Fooking well done, love! Bluddy brilliant, that were.'

Almost inevitably everyone wanted to buy Princess a drink, ostensibly to make her feel better, but more likely to see if they could make it happen again, and she refused to go home on the grounds that, 'I'd just be the drunk girl at the party if I leave early.' I tried to chaperone her for a bit, but was too drunk myself, and gave up entirely after she took a swing at Buffy for throwing peanuts at her.

Meanwhile Valentine and I re-enacted the entire closing sequence of *Dirty Dancing*, including the lifts, which he was very keen on until I realized he was not so much picking me up as just lifting me high enough to rub his face in my boobs.

The Editor was still dancing, oblivious to the drama which had unfolded, along with a variety of secretaries and sub-editors. Even Porter, who never dances, had entered the fray, waving his arms over his head in-between spinning The Editor's squealing secretary around in a series of dizzying loops.

Nick the Wop finished his fourth bottle of red and his final audience with the junior snappers, and apparently decided it was time for the don to dance. The Marlon Brando of Fleet Street lumbered on to the floor to join us all, and then suddenly had his attention caught by an apparently new backside.

He artfully manoeuvred himself until his groin was jiggling alongside this new pair of unknown buttocks, and I watched in fascinated horror as he pressed himself against the target, leering myopically and growling into the stranger's ear: 'Ah don'know who you ah . . . butchu ah fakkin' boodiful.'

The Editor, feeling a hairy hand about the waist and something unmentionable behind, stopped dancing, turned around, and fixed him with a steely glare.

'Nick, isn't it?' The Editor said coldly, just as I grabbed the Wop's arm and dragged him off the floor, while he demanded I tell him he hadn't just done what he had. At 3 a.m. the bar threw what was left of us into the night; Mike the Bike went off to a rave in Highgate, while Nancy and Banks shared a cab home. The Wop wandered into the night singing what he thought was something by The Three Tenors, and an almost-dead Princess finally agreed that it was time for her to go home in a taxi. Bridge, Porter, Bish, Buff and I tried to find a bar but failed, and then, since we were shorn of the most troublesome members of our little band, one of the barmen let us back in for a bottle of port and the final jelly baby while we waited for minicabs to arrive.

The next morning the newsroom was silent apart from the occasional groan and the rustle of greaseproof around hot bacon sandwiches, coupled with the hushed concentration required to apply brown sauce to bread and slurp tea. Even Bish was quiet for once, although traces of marker pen could still be seen on his redder-than-usual forehead.

Porter cleared his throat. 'Why do my knees hurt?' he asked the world at large.

'You were dancing on them for an hour,' I replied, in my usual role of being the only reporter with a perfect drinking memory. 'You thought The Editor's secretary was a bit short for you, and told her so, then pretended you were a dwarf.'

'Oh,' said Porter. 'Did she laugh?'

'Eventually,' I told him.

Just then Princess arrived at her desk, wearing the previous night's tight black minidress and a shamefaced expression.

'Who have you been up to?' demanded Nancy, before Princess shushed her, grabbed her clothes from the previous day, and staggered to the toilets to change and scrub up. We all exchanged looks.

'Who saw her last?' asked Bridget.

Porter replied: 'She was at the bar with the Bike when they threw us out.'

Buff chipped in: 'I saw her outside when we were trying to find a cab.'

'I saw her get in a taxi with Jock,' interjected Tania Banks, primly. 'But isn't he married?'

'Ah, shit,' said Bridget.

Princess spent the rest of the day hiding behind her pride, refusing to answer questions, avoiding Elliot, and scuttling off to the corridor to make calls on her mobile. Jock's a family man, so it's a surprise anything like that happened, although Princess insisted she'd woken up with her clothes on. I suppose it's a tradition at Christmas parties.

We've all done things we'd like to erase – there's a sizable chunk of me which wishes Twatface had never darkened my door – but whatever we are today it's as a product of all those yesterdays, a sum of our parties if you like. They should be the foundations you stand on, not the mistaken beliefs that keep you down in your hole.

They say that some things never change, and it's often a waste of energy trying to stop the waves, whether it's vomit at the Christmas party or the flood washing away what's left of your marriage.

But sometimes, very rarely, things do alter. The tide of faith goes in as well as out, and occasionally brings with it some driftwood or a Cricket Boy you can cling to or do something useful with – like build a bridge, and get over it.

DAY TWO HUNDRED AND FOUR

THAT'S it; I declare defeat. I am over, broken, empty, finished, done. I woke up this morning feeling as spent and faded as a tattered five-pound note that's been passed around between too many grimy hands.

And no, before you jump to conclusions, it's not just as a result of having seven Christmas parties, lunches and/or dinners in eight days, too much wine and not enough fresh fruit; nor is it related to the festive feeling of gloom I always get at this time of year, when I realize I've not done very much in the previous twelve months, and that Christmas, these days, just bores me rigid. This time it is down, purely and simply, to one thing: seven solid, pointless months of Twatface and his unending twattery.

The initial screaming pain which stabbed through me day and night has not gone. It's still there, down at the bottom of my heart, echoing sadly. It is now being suffocated by layers of worry, anxiety, hatred, debt, angst, self-loathing and paranoia. If someone says, 'Anyway, how are you doing? You know, with things?' I can't even summon up the righteous indignation which has kept me upright this far. My outrage has run out of steam, leaving me becalmed on a featureless ocean where bugger all happens, and every day, when it dawns, seems the same as the last.

After spending my last grain of effort on doing that deal with Twatface for me to keep the house, I thought that maybe we'd forced through the last logjam of the divorce and we could get the decree absolute, set each other free and get our lives back again. But he changed his mind after talking to his lawyer, who has in turn peppered my giggling solicitor, Maurice, with a series of demands with which I must comply before Twatface agrees the financial settlement – the final chain still tying us together, and which, until it is cut, is choking both of us slowly to death.

First he demanded I pay £500 for a survey to verify the value of the house, or he wouldn't agree the deal. I told him to fuck off. Then he said he'd bought a sports car, and was broke, so couldn't pay half of the survey, and again I told him to fuck off. Then he insisted on half a dozen estate agent valuations, or he wouldn't agree the deal. I sent him some from three months earlier, and he said they were too old and he wouldn't agree the deal. I didn't even bother swearing at that, just sighed down the phone to Maurice, who said: 'I'll tell him to fuck off, shall I?'

And now here I sit, close to evaporating in despair as sprawled out before me is something called a 'financial disclosure form'. In these unpleasant pages I am expected to map out, via tax codes and pension lump sums and twelve months of payslips and bank statements, six years of my life, so that a court can weigh up all the monies and agree that what the two parties have already decided is reasonable. I hate figures and forms at the best of times, but a big pile of things I just don't understand about Expected Total Outfalls and Cash Equivalent Transfer Values and Taxable Brackets leaves me reeling.

This is my *marriage* – my longest-ever relationship – something built on feelings, which now all comes down, in the end, to bits of paper and boxes to fill in. Where's the bit that says, 'How are you?'

Just reading this form was enough to make me want to slash my wrists. The only thing that sustained me through the deeply unpleasant task was the knowledge that Twatface was infinitely worse at this kind of thing than me, and was bound to be making a hash of it.

How did it get to the point where the interaction of two human beings over the years, their tears and joys and plans and hopes and love and hatred, could be boiled down to bits of paper they can shove in a drawer and forget about? I shouldn't have been stapling tax statements from my savings accounts to this form, it should have been photocopied love letters he addressed to 'The Most Beautiful Girl In The World', the beer mat I kept from the bar we had our first date in, and photographs of holidays and days out and picnics in Richmond Park. That's what it all meant, that's what it was about – not pensions and the hire-purchase on my car, for Pete's sake.

I'd put this form off for weeks, and after struggling with its heartlessness for an hour, I rang my mum for a weep. 'You'll just have to get your head down,' she said. 'It has to be done.'

'Yes, I know, but it's *wrong*,' I sniffled. 'So wrong it makes me want to put my foot through the wall. It's all anodyne, polite, financial crap when what we should really be doing is each saying what went wrong, so that someone tells us off and we learn not to do it again.'

'Well, after everything he's done to you he should have to pay,' said ever-loyal Mum. 'Is there no back page or something where you can get things off your chest, at least?'

I thumbed through the obscene, bald pages, full of words I didn't like. 'There's one here . . . it says, "Bad behaviour by the other party will only be taken into account in very exceptional circumstances when deciding how assets should be shared."'

'Well, he was horrible. That counts,' she said firmly.

'Yes, but I think they mean if he tried to kill you, or ate a baby. He was a git, but he wasn't Idi Amin,' I pointed out. 'I could probably write something. Do you think I should?'

'Do it,' said Mum.

So I sat and wrote and rewrote for hours and hours, and tore up and sweated blood and then wrote again, until I had something which I felt explained eloquently what had happened to my world.

Maybe Twatface will never see it, no doubt the judge will never read it, but I feel better for writing it and it means that somewhere in a court file there will be a record of what really happened to my marriage and the man I loved, once.

It ended like this: 'In law, as the only spouse to have been arrested, I am the only one to have done anything wrong, and our divorce, despite his admission of adultery, is officially "no fault". But I want the record to show that morally and in every other sense this marriage ended principally as a result of his behaviour; that I worked my hardest in the best way I knew how to help him and to make the marriage work; and that my decision to seek a divorce was taken with a great deal of regret for the loss of the man that he used to be. I have no right in law to ask for anything by way of damages for the loss I have suffered, or recompense for the mistrust and lack of self-confidence he has left me with. I have no right even to ask for an apology. But in these respects the law is wrong.'

Which is really so much teeth-gnashing; pointless, worthless and likely just to make you ache unhappily. But I'm a journalist, and if there's one thing that every hack holds close to their heart, it's the foolish belief that if they write something down someone, somewhere, will take note. So I stapled my missive to the form and posted it back to Maurice, and there was a kind of satisfaction in setting it down, in black and white, so it sat in the court's archives. Maybe in a hundred years' time a researcher would come across it, and think, 'God, what a twat! Why'd she marry him?'

Two days later Maurice rang in his usual giggly high spirits. 'Thanks for the disclosure form, but we don't need it. Twatface has agreed the financial settlement because he didn't want to fill his in, apparently.'

'Great.' I sighed, putting my head in my hands and wondering what it was, exactly, that I'd done to the universe that it saw fit to arrange itself in precisely the manner which was most likely to utterly nullify my whole bloody existence. 'Yes, it's brilliant news, isn't it?' chortled Maurice. 'So all that's left is for him to collect his last few belongings. He's sent a list, I'll forward it on to you.'

Within seconds, I had a text from the twat himself. 'I need to collect my things tonight.'

I replied: 'You can't. I'm out.'

He pinged back: 'You can't stop me. I'll break in if I have to.'

'Oh, naff off,' I texted, heading to the pub quiz and a depressing bottle of wine with Nancy and Princess.

I was sitting in silent gloom in the Hare and Billet on Blackheath, listening to them argue about whether Britain's first nuclear bomb was exploded in 1952 or 1954 and whether Nancy could Google it without being seen, when I had another text.

'I shall be passing by the house in half an hour with a big vehicle. Is there no way you can let me in?'

'He's in WHAT?' cackled Nancy when I showed her the message. 'What a twat! Ignore him.'

The next day his list came through: a glittering array of his winter coat, a clothing rail, his bloody awful dog-eared Rothko prints, some saucepans and the spare duvet, with a smattering of books. All of which, because I couldn't stand to look at them lying around the house, I had long ago piled up in black bags in a corner of the living room. I told Maurice that Twatface could pick it all up on Wednesday night at 7 p.m., and resigned myself to a final stab in the guts.

When the hour dawned I cared no more or less than that; I just wanted it over. He knocked on the door, said hello and I silently let him in. He said he wanted to check the loft to see if he had anything left in it, and tromped upstairs to bang and crash about. He came down clutching our wedding album, which he'd found in the box I'd shoved under the eaves when he'd first left.

'I want to take this,' he said, waving it at me.

'Why?' I said. 'You're the one who didn't want to be married.'

'Yes, but I don't have any photographs of you and I'd like some. You know, to look at. You wouldn't let me have any, and I have just as much right to our wedding album as you do.'

'You bloody DO NOT,' I cried. 'That's a record of a happy day which you might as well have pissed on.'

'Well, why do you want it, then?' he said. 'You don't want to be married to me, either.'

'That's not the point. It's going to stay in the loft for the rest of my damn life, but you are not having it under any circumstances,' I insisted, before inspiration struck. 'Besides, we agreed we'd divvy the wedding presents between us, depending on whose side bought them; and my lot bought the album, so give it.'

He handed it over reluctantly, but with a half-smile on his face as though he'd somehow won. 'I do love you, you know. You'll always be my wife,' he said quietly.

'No, I will not,' I said.

'Well, *first* wife, then,' he replied, as I stalked off with the album to put it out of his reach.

And I swear I don't know what happened next; I cannot explain why I felt as I did. But a few minutes later as I saw him slowly taking stuff from the living room to pile up in the hallway, I began to lose patience. He said he was waiting for a cab to come so that he could load it all up, and I snapped at him frustratedly to put it outside the front door, because I wanted him out of the house. He said it was raining, and besides it was still his house, too, and then, as I stood impotently in the living-room doorway and watched him doing it the way he insisted he had to do it, something inside me just broke.

Looking at him standing in what was now *my* home, the place where I finally felt safe and in control and where no one could hurt me, I felt totally violated. The worst person in the world was in the safest place I knew, and it

277

was suffocating. I'd dragged myself up from the bottom of the pit he'd thrown me into, and he had been on my back with every step, dragging me back down. I wanted to finally shake him off and be free of him and all the stupid things he did, to be sure he couldn't hurt me again.

It was like a wave of horror broke over me and washed me away, propelling me forwards to grab a lamp, run to the front door and hurl it into the street. With tears pouring down my face I seized the coat, the clothing rail, his books, and threw them all down the front path and into the air, not even stopping to watch them flutter to the ground before running back to pick up something new. He tried to stop me, gripping my flailing arms, and told me I was mad as I screamed at him, wriggled free and grabbed something else to chuck out of the door. Thirty seconds later Twatface's belongings were lying in a series of muddy puddles in the road as he scampered between them, trying to pick them up before they got soaked, and I tearfully slammed the door with all the force I could muster.

Crumpled in a heap in the hallway, I sobbed and shook and finally just held my head in my hands and screamed. All I could feel and think about was the terror he made me feel, not just in my head or my heart but deep down at the base of my spine and spreading through my whole body. He had been where he should never be, he went where he was not allowed, he hated me and wanted to hurt me, and was not the smiling man I had thought he was. I felt invaded, contaminated, desecrated in some indefinable way, damaged and broken and stamped on – forced to do things I had never wanted to by the person with whom I had once shared the most, and been closest to, and invited into my heart.

I heard a taxi pull up, doors slam, and then drive away, but it still took half an hour for the tears to stop, and another for the shaking to ease. I thought about ringing one of the girls or my mum, but put the phone down the moment I picked it up. How could I explain what had just happened? How could seeing my husband for the last time justify that behaviour? Why had I thrown everything into the street like some kind of banshee? It was all just madness, utter madness.

And now there he'd be, telling himself quite rightly that he married a loon, stroppily trying to dry out his books and muttering about having to get the coat dry-cleaned, moving into Fatty's flat with all the things of his that lived with me for the past six years, and doing what I can't – getting over it. He doesn't seem to feel a single atom of the emotions that have riven me since the bomb went off, and if he does they're a pale imitation of the chemical patterns washing through my brain. Perhaps he went through all the despair months before me, before I knew anything was all that wrong; maybe he was this unhappy a year ago, and never said, just sought solace in anything he could find.

I wish I could do the same. If only I could shag some boy without a second thought, move on, fall in love again, bound through life like an exuberant puppy who takes not the slightest heed of the shit stains in its wake. Why should I tremble at the thought of being on my own with a man? Why should I be a victim, restricted to the same scared routines, like an animal kept in a cage too long who now just goes around and around in circles, looking out of the bars but too terrified even to poke a paw outside?

I was still trying to get my head around this, snuffling and shuffling around, when my phone beeped. It was Twatface.

'I don't know what happened there, but I meant what I said. You will always have been my wife. I'm sorry I wasted your time.'

And that, Dear Reader, is officially the worst thing he has ever said to me.

The fact that we were in love and now we aren't, that we tried and failed, that it didn't last as long as we'd hoped, that he really is that much of a twat and I can be that mental – I can deal with those things. That's easy. It happens to lots of us and I've written that story a million times. But the thought that what is now six years of my life was a waste – that it was all for nothing, earned *nul points*, is over, and now we're back at the drawing board no better or worse for it, and that it can just be wiped away with an, 'I'm sorry I wasted your time' – that offends me. Deep inside, all the way down in the china shop of my soul where there's a single little teacup left in one piece, it causes a tiny fracture to crack its way slowly downwards until the handle drops off and everything is finally broken.

I remember the day when Twatface asked me to be his girl, and I looked at him and thought to myself: 'I don't know what will happen with this guy; it might work and it might not. I might get hurt. But I would rather take the chance, make the leap, than stay safe and never know.' So I kissed him and said yes, and made my choice.

Despite everything that's happened it's a choice I stand by. In our time together I experienced wonderful happiness and a love which made me feel happy and secure. I felt pain and loss and heartbreak, yes, and still do; but the one extreme does not cancel out the other. The alternative to them is emptiness. I would rather feel, and scream, than not feel at all.

Every single thing that happened between Twatface and me – from the first kiss, the first time we made love, the first row, to the last time I saw him, scampering around in the rain picking up the detritus I'd hurled out of the house in despair – counts. Every day, every word, every feeling, meant something. It was not for nothing, it made me the mess I am and taught me a lot about myself and the things and people I hold dear. It showed my truest friends for the rocks they are, and ripped away all the things which weren't built to last until all that was left was me.

It might not seem like much, but that's quite a lot – it's more knowledge than many people get. I'm stronger than I ever thought, and I've survived this far. While I have no idea of the path my life will take after the decree absolute comes through I would rather have had that whole, horrible journey than not travel at all. At least this way I know what *not* to do another time.

It was not a waste. I will make it not a waste – somehow.

DAY TWO HUNDRED AND FIFTEEN

SINCERITY must surely be the most abused, cheaply treated and misunderstood virtue in the world: only those who don't have it lay claim to it, insisting on what nice people they are while those that seek it seem only to find the disappointing opposite in everyone around them.

So people in public life talk about their principles and private lives as though they wouldn't betray both for a fistful of cash, and we poor journalists, who keep a beady eye and a careful note, are called on to fight for things we do not always agree with. No one who says they're being true actually seems to know what it means, and the public who watch us suspect it's a lie even when it's not.

Supposed sincerity is thrown in our faces so often that it becomes almost impossible to spot the truth when it's staring you right in the face.

On Christmas Eve night I pitched up at the family ranch spiky from the start of a hangover after drinking champagne at my desk, as is traditional on newspapers in the festive season. After a few hours of drinking the execs had kicked the reporters out of the newsroom and we'd all scattered to our respective homesteads, leaving the office staffed for the big day by its habitual festive trio of our token Jew, a Jehovah's Witness and a Muslim recruited during the 7/7 terror attacks – after Bish realized his reporters were the wrong colour to get any of the door-knocks we were sent on. Elliot questioned whether twenty-two-year-old Yusuf had the experience to be a reporter on a national newspaper, to which Bish had replied: ''E's brown an' can say "Allah Akbar". 'E's good enough fer me.' Needless to say, the paper produced by those three at Christmas is marginally better than the one a full staff manages to churn out the rest of the time.

I was in a vile mood, not just from the hangover but the never-ending divorce, the upset with Twatface and that turn-of-the-year gloom you get when you're having a rotten time and can't see any prospect of things improving. I barely bothered to string a sentence together in response to well-meaning questions over dinner, and took myself to bed early.

The next morning there was a whole hour of opening presents we were expecting and a few others we didn't really want, forced vegetable preparation, and an argument about politics before we sat down to a lunch Mum had slaved over for hours.

'Well, this is nice,' said Mum chirpily in her paper hat as we tucked into turkey and sprouts in silence.

'It's exactly the same as last year, only without Twatface,' I grumped, insistent as usual on telling the truth, no matter how bad.

'Why are you in such a rotten mood? It's Christmas, for heaven's sake. Cheer up,' said Dad.

'Why?' I said mutinously. 'I'd far rather people just told the truth rather than pretending everything was dandy when it's crap. Christmas *is* crap: it's crap telly, and crap hats, and crap in the shops, and none of us even like turkey, but we sit and eat a hundredweight of it anyway because someone else thinks we ought to.'

Mum and Dad looked at each other. Dad said: 'That's enough now. It's Christmas Day.'

'Huh.' I snorted, like the horrid teenager I become every time I go home.

'Have you heard from Twatface?' asked Mum.

'Got a card from his mum, addressed to Mrs Twatface, would you believe. I nearly put my fist through the wall when I saw it.'

Mum sighed. 'You're so angry. I understand why, of course, but . . . I don't know, you can't go on like this. It's been six months now. Maybe you should, you know, talk to someone?'

'Well, I talk to you,' I said, surprised. 'What, you mean like a therapist?'

'It might be an idea. You know you can always talk to us, but it's a bit beyond our experience.'

I turned it over in my mind. I'd thought about it myself, I must admit, because it had got to the point where my friends were rolling their eyes whenever Twatface was mentioned, and it had occurred to me that once the divorce was through there was going to be the giant triple-headed ogre of Sex and Relationships and Other Men to deal with. That was not a conversation I wanted to have with my mum.

'Well, maybe, but what are they going to tell me?' I asked, stabbing a roast potato resentfully with my fork. 'Let go of my anger, move on? Easier said than done, and besides, therapists are expensive. I've a leak in the roof above the kitchen which comes first.'

Mum said: 'You do know that fixing up the house isn't the same as fixing you, don't you?'

'No,' I said petulantly, 'I don't.'

Although, of course, she was right, and while the house can be patched, heaven only knows how to sort me out. But that's the thing: if you're intelligent enough to realize you might need some help, then surely you're bright enough to work out the answer for yourself. And who wants to hear what they already know? Maybe therapy works for some people, but I'm not sure I could take a psychologist saying, 'He's such a twat, why'd you marry him?'

And besides, a therapist and I would disagree on the topic of fury. Surely, if you are capable of letting go of your rage then it was a worthless anger in the first place? It was really just irritation, unhappiness, or disappointment, and I can let go of all those things quite happily. But if it's proper crawl-up-your-spine-and-spit-flame-from-your-eyes-and-smite-him-God-*smite-him* anger then it's worth more than that, isn't it? I can't let something which has inflamed every nerve ending with righteous ire slip through my fingers like so much sand, and I don't want to, either. It feels like denying the Holocaust.

This was the less-than-healthy attitude I took to the New Year celebrations. Having looked forward to it for the past six months, telling myself that by then I'd have a decree absolute in my hands and could start afresh, I found myself regarding it with a baleful eye because there was still no end in sight. What was going to be new about a year that looked like a miserable continuation of the previous one?

'That's a fine way of looking at things,' complained Bridget as we necked some of Harry Porter's cheap champagne at a party he and his wife were throwing for what

285

seemed like hundreds of people in their two-bed semi. 'How abaht, instead of looking at the past year, you think about the decade? What were you doin' on New Year's Eve ten years ago?'

I didn't need to think. 'I was covering the London New Year celebrations for the first time, and a bloody farce it was, too. My phone kept dropping the signal, it rained, my car got clamped and I couldn't file.'

Bridget rolled her eyes. 'You need to work less,' she said. 'But how about everything that's happened since?'

I thought carefully, and realized I'd spent the past decade having – largely – fun. Fleet Street has kept me gainfully employed, and taught me the delights of eating and drinking on someone else's dime. I have travelled all over the country and a fair chunk of the world chasing stories, fallen in love, experienced despair, grief and heartbreak, marriage, divorce, arrest and brief imprisonment – a story that, if told in the correct manner, with a little bit of spin, can make people laugh and hold an audience captive for a good quarter of an hour. Those ten years seemed to pass slowly at the time, but from this perspective they were packed with drama and incident. Even the tears were things I wouldn't trade. It all made me what I am, and despite the flaws I'm not so bad.

I began to feel a little more positive, and a lot more drunk. When the countdown began and midnight struck, my chest tightened unbearably as the seconds ticked away, and when the poppers flew and everyone threw their arms around each other to cheer and kiss, I let out a breath it seemed I'd been holding since Day 1, when the screaming began. New tears, slow and happy, trickled down my cheeks as my knees gave way and I slumped to the floor, feeling a relief I wasn't expecting, and which is impossible to describe. Finally, the year was over. It was gone, taking with it everything Twatface had done. Never again would he bully or scare me, and nor would he hold me, kiss me, dream with me or love me like he used to. I had held it all in my hands and now it had slipped through my fingers into the past, and I watched it go with a sad kind of joy for everything it had meant and all the love I'd had and lost.

Bridget spotted me and joined me on the floor with an arm around my shoulders, and then Nancy, Buff, Fifi, Cubby, Porter, Princess – and almost everyone else who's held me up this year – got down on their knees by my side, kissed me, hugged me, and in the case of a drunken Valentine Lush, patted me on the head because it was the only bit he could reach in the scrum. They urged me not to cry and to be happy, and I laughed at them as the tears kept falling, and told them I *was* happy – and just glad the old year was gone. I haven't been so happy at the passage of time since I'd been a kid and counting down the days to the next birthday.

When everyone gathered for the wedding I was upstairs in the hotel, anxiously pacing as time ticked away. It didn't occur to me for a moment not to go through with it; I was in the middle of the hourglass, finding it hard to breathe as I slid into the unknown. I got down the stairs, clinging on to my father's arm, through the door and down the aisle, as my heart beat so fast I thought it would burst. I had one thought: that it was better to have loved and lost. Better to say yes, scream it from the rooftops, say fuck it and do it anyway, than to stop and ponder and pick holes in what might happen, and wonder if you ought to say no.

Of course I also told myself that I knew him, and he'd never hurt me; but the fact remained it was a leap of faith, attached only to someone I hoped would help me fly. We came back to earth a bit quick and with a hell of a bump, but the drop was as much a part of the experience as the jump.

My fury at Twatface has been more to do with whether he realized what he was doing. Did he know the things he did would hurt? Did he make me apologize to him because he genuinely thought it was my fault, or because he wanted to believe it? Was he mad or bad, and was everything he wrought really wrong?

When you feel a powerful anger, you can't waste its power. There must be a way to harness it for something useful. Like what? you ask. Oh, I don't know – write a book, maybe. Let someone else know they're not alone. Just shout NO! over and over again until someone hears it, for all the good that might do. All I can tell you for certain is that there was a time when I said, 'I do,' in front of the whole world, and meant it with every part of my being. Just because now every cell screams, 'I DON'T!' doesn't mean that simply by being a negative it's not worthwhile.

There's a poem I read somewhere that talks about the great yes and the great no, and the times you make the big decisions in your life. I said yes to Twatface, not so much because I was certain of the future but more because it was a yes, and it was better to say that than turn away. The same verse says that the right no can drag you down all your life, but poets are idiots sometimes. What the poet should have said is that the wrong no drags you down, but the right one bears repeating if you're sincere.

So here we go, as honest and true as I can be: I forgive Twatface. I can never forget what he did, good and bad, and I don't hold with the namby-pamby Christian thing that forgiveness is a 'Get Out Of Jail Free' card and means your sins are erased. I mean forgive in the sense that I accept it, that I don't demand any more that he be punished. Railing against him is pointless when it can't change anything, and besides it's led me to some good stuff.

Despite it all, if I had the chance I'd say yes again – I'd do it all again, maybe a little louder and harder in places, but I've no regrets. Maybe I'll get the chance to prove that, if I don't stay on my guard too much. Who knows what the next decade will hold?

I'm going to leave the bad memories behind me, and take the good ones with me.

And I mean that most sincerely.

DAY TWO HUNDRED AND TWENTY-SIX

THE call, when it came, was a surprise.

'Oh, hello? *Hello*?'

'Hello?' I huffed, lunging for my suitcase as it passed me on the luggage carousel, which seemed to speed up as it went by, so that as I pulled the bag it ended up being dragged across an old lady's knees and the heads of two small children. I apologized bad-temperedly, manhandled the case on to a trolley, grabbed the laptop bag from the floor where it had fallen and steered the wayward metal cart towards customs. Shoving the phone between neck and ear, hitching my bag on to a shoulder and puffing the hair out of my face, I said: 'Sorry, who's this?'

'It's Maurice,' said the voice, which I could barely hear over the airport tannoy as I fumed through the green channel and looked for the Europcar sign, cursing Mondays while thinking how much I wanted a bath.

'Maurice?' I asked. 'Maurice *who*?' Then it dawned. Maurice the divorce lawyer, the one who thinks everything's funny, and only speaks to me to say nothing's any different to the last time we spoke – except for being inexplicably more expensive. This was just what I needed after landing in Portugal in a rush and on deadline, when the plane was late and I had to file a story by teatime.

'Oh, hello, Maurice,' I said, spotting the right booth and scrabbling in my bag for the printout.

'I just wanted to let you know that we've sorted out the final invoice, your ex-husband has paid his share of the costs, and there's a small overhang which I shall forward on to you with our accounts,' he said as I wiggled my eyebrows at the car-hire woman and handed over the paperwork. I glanced at my watch. It was 3 p.m, and it would take two hours to drive there, so then it would be 5 p.m., and I had to knock on the door, get a chat, and then file by 6 p.m. at the latest, even though I had nothing to write about yet. And I had to call that Portuguese journalist to see if he had anything new for us to use. I wished I was somewhere with a bigger time difference between me and the office. Jesus Christ, woman, hurry up with those keys . . .

'Right. OK, Maurice . . .'

Maurice droned on: 'And once you've settled your account that will be the last of our dealings, and I've sent out copies to you of the consent order and your decree absolute . . .'

I grabbed the car keys being offered, muttered an 'Obrigada', and steered the pestilential luggage trolley towards the doors as I continued to juggle the phone between either side of my collarbone. 'Right, fine. Look, I'd better go, I'm supposed to be working. Hang on a minute – decree absolute?'

'Yes, your decree absolute. It came through a while ago.'

I stopped dead, cases and bags juddering to the floor and hair flopping back in my face as I realized he'd used the phrase 'ex-husband'.

'Decree absolute?' I said again, like a stupefied parrot. 'When?'

'Ooh, a couple of weeks ago, didn't I mention it?'

291

'NO, YOU FLIPPING . . . oh God, no, sorry, look, are you sure? I mean, definitely?'

'Yes. It went along with the consent order because Twatface agreed the financial deal, and then it was all rubber-stamped. Here it is, it was issued on December the twelfth.'

My stalled brain flipped into gear. That had been a week or so after I'd met Cricket Boy. So I'd been unmarried for more than a month, and my new start had happened without me realizing it.

'Right. Well. Good. Thanks,' I said. Maurice said he'd send me the final bill, which should be nearly £3,000 but 'as I am conscious many of the difficulties you faced' which 'arose largely as a result of your former husband's behaviour', he would knock £500 off out of sympathy. I thanked him again, feeling like a charity case, and ended the call.

Slowly I pushed the trolley forwards, looking at nothing while thinking for the first time that I didn't have a husband to complain about. The automatic doors swished open, and I found myself stood in the winter sunshine outside Faro airport, blinking and a bit confused. I wasn't a wife any more.

I had expected glee, relief, the lifting of a weight, maybe a clanging noise. Perhaps even reverting back to being the twenty-three-year-old I'd been before Twatface came along, with a carefree state of mind.

Instead I was just unutterably sad. Sad to have missed it, sad not to have known, sad not to have marked the day somehow, and sad that was, finally, that. When we fell in love I was there, when we got engaged and married I was there; when we split I was right in the middle of it. Each moment was a memory and an image to be treasured or put away until it didn't hurt any more. But the end had come by itself, unnoticed, in the middle of a list of names read out in a court somewhere to a disillusioned clerk. We didn't even say goodbye. It was like hearing someone had died on their own while you were still driving to the hospital; or waking up and being told the surgeon had cut your leg off. Can you do it again, and this time I'll pay attention?

I felt cold and terribly alone, stood by myself on a piece of foreign tarmac. It used to be that whenever I was sent abroad Twatface insisted I text and let him know I'd landed safely, or would be ringing to tell me what everyone else was doing on the story back home, chattering about his day and asking about the job. Now there was no one to ring, no call expected, in fact no one who would notice for a day or two if I didn't answer the phone at all. I had been legally amputated from a person who had been almost a Siamese twin – one I had come to hate, but joined to me all the same, and who had experienced everything in my life for so long I could barely remember what it was like not to have him around, in my heart and in my head. Or on my back, where I'd carried him for years, catering to his every whim like the retarded half of Master Blaster in the Mad Max films.

And now that weight was gone for good. But rather than flying free, soaring towards single life and a new beginning, I felt more like a blackbird who'd smashed into a window it hadn't seen and was lying on the ground with its wings broken. Now what?

I found myself beside the tiny Fiat Shitto which was all the paper could afford these days, unloaded the bags and got in. Mechanically I went through the motions of moving the driver's seat, the mirrors, plugging in the sat nav and programming the route to Praia da Luz where, Evil Elliot insisted, there was someone who had the latest definite sighting of Maddie McCann, even though it had been years since the newspapers had shown any interest in the missing toddler. Then I just sat, staring through the windscreen at the back of the hire car office, brain in neutral, a soldier home from the wars with no one left to fight.

After a few moments I shook myself, muttering, 'Right, do something,' under my breath. I had a story to get and that was purpose, of a sort.

Then it occurred to me that I had always intended to throw a party. There had been one at the start, after all, so there should be one at the end. Grabbing my phone I sent a text round to my mates announcing my divorce and inquiring if they were free on Wednesday – by which time I should have flown back home – for drinks.

I turned the key, and pulled out of the car park and on to the motorway. Sitting alone in the silence between the mountains on either side of the road I began to cry a little, thinking about the wedding and everything that we'd dreamed of, and all the hopes I'd had, which I knew Twatface had shared at first. Then my phone began to beep, and despite the obvious health and safety risks I couldn't help but glance at my messages.

'Oh, honey, FINALLY!' said Fifi. 'I shall be there with bells on! Champers all round!'

'Congrats, you're finally shot of the bastard!!!' from Nancy. 'See you Wed!'

'Thank FUCK,' from Harry Porter. 'I was getting bored. Will there be cake?'

'Oh, good, at last. Don't read this if you're driving, but Dad says check your boiler,' from my mum.

At that I laughed, and with tears on my cheeks while zipping along the motorway at 70 m.p.h. finally felt the relief I'd been craving. My heart cracked a little more, and I almost felt a physical pain, imagining it inflating for the first time in months, and pumping the blood freely once more around my creaking arteries. The sun shone down in my eyes, and what with the crying I could barely see the road, but even though I was far from happy it felt like I was taking the first step back to wherever happy is.

'Ahead, continue straight on,' said the sat nav, and I smiled at it as I leaned over and switched on the radio, wondering if the Shuffle Gods had anything to say to me.

They had Michael Jackson, informing me the sky was the limit but I would have seen nothing until he got through.

I whooped, whammed the volume up, wound the windows down and joined in, tunelessly and full of snot, about the whole world had to answer right now that Michael and I were, indeed, very bad.

Once the song was over I deflated again; but frankly I needed a rest from all the emotion, and my eyes were sunken and sore with sunlight and tears. Within a short time I'd arrived at the address, knocked at the door, called a local journalist to help translate, discovered the sighting had been reported by a blind woman who claimed to be psychic, found another Maddie McCann story about the bumbling local police, got to the hotel and filed while sitting at the bar.

Just as I hit send Nick the Wop arrived, having come on a later plane from a different airport. I greeted him with the news there was nothing for him to photograph, passed him the bar menu, and rang Elliot to inform him he had a slightly better story than the one he was expecting. '*Better*?' he spat. 'What could be better than finding a missing child?'

I rolled my eyes at Nick. 'Well, all right, not better, maybe, but at least it's accurate, which the sighting wasn't – reason being it was by someone who couldn't actually see.'

Elliot sighed at me. 'You've managed to turn a definite splash into an unlikely page thirty-four; congratulations,' he said, slamming the phone down.

'Hey ho,' I said to the Wop. 'Guess what? I'm divorced.'

'Oh, mite, dat's fakkin' bwillant, innit? Lessav a drink, den,' he said, and we enjoyed two enormous steaks, two bottles of red and ridiculous gossip about the reporters and photogs, Princess Flashy Knickers's one-night stand with Jock, and the likely suspects for whom we thought The Editor might be shagging these days. I exchanged texts with Cricket Boy once or twice, me informing him I was drunk, and him replying he was in Greenwich visiting his brother, doing a crawl around my favourite pubs. At midnight the Wop and I rolled off to our separate rooms, promising to meet for breakfast at eight because Elliot was bound to come up with something else for us to do before we could leave.

I was half-asleep in a happy fug of alcohol when my phone beeped. I thought about ignoring it, then heaved myself over, scrabbled in the darkness across the bedside table and brought the phone to my face, squinting at the screen and realizing it was nearly 2 a.m.

It was Cricket Boy again. 'Where are you out tonight, anyway?' he said.

I hadn't told him I was abroad, so he must have assumed I was in Greenwich, like him. I stared at the ceiling, and counted back in my head to the last time this had happened. Let's see, it was the guy before Twatface. No, not him, even. It was the one before that . . . It had been more than seven years, the best part of a decade, since I'd had anything resembling a booty call. Now here I was, finally divorced, my happy-at-times-and-awful-at-others marriage was over, and I seemed to have the attention of a tall, handsome man who could dance me off my feet, and lived far enough away not to represent any threat of a relationship and all the problems that would entail, and he wanted to know where I was so we could hook up for some drunken, torrid, commitment-free shenanigans.

And I was in a different flipping *country*.

I buried my face in the pillow and screamed, briefly. Then I laughed, and texted back: 'Portugal.' He replied: 'Bugger. When are you back? I'm off oop north again tomorrow morning.' I told him I would be back the next evening or the day after, with a sad face, then, when he pinged straight back, informed him it was 2 a.m. and he had to bugger off because I had to be up early. Briefly, I considered the fact that he'd left it till 2 a.m. to text, and I was, therefore, probably just a last desperate roll of the booty dice. But it was welcome all the same, and I turned over, curled myself around a pillow, and drifted off to dream of tall men dressed in cricket whites with grass stains on their knees.

The Wop and I struggled through our hangovers the next day to meet for breakfast and a call from Elliot, who curtly informed us we were booked on a plane home. We headed to the airport, and I got a text from Cricket Boy telling me he had left Greenwich two hours earlier and probably wouldn't be back for another couple of months. 'Damn and blast it,' I thought, 'just my luck.'

DAY TWO HUNDRED AND TWENTY-EIGHT

BACK in the office I learned that one more hack from our team was going to have to go, whether they liked it or not. Dozens more were going in different departments as the bean counters wielded their scalpels, but Bish had managed to fiddle his budget so that it looked like he didn't have as many reporters as he did, and that had saved a few of us. But worse, they would select who to lose using a scoring system – and Evil Elliot was in charge.

The mood among the reporters was depressive. 'Elliot's got a special new Red Pen of Death,' moaned Porter. 'He keeps making notes with it.'

Bridget added: 'I s'pose I could always move back to Oz.'

And Princess muttered: 'I think we can guarantee Teflon Tania will emerge unscathed. Cow!'

We all sat and sighed as we did our work, and I got an early cut for my divorce party. I had intended nothing so much as drinking the remains of Twatface's wine, which I was still finding stashed in hiding places all over the house, and playing country and western music too loudly for anyone else's comfort. But when everyone arrived it seemed they'd all had second thoughts, too, and what had been planned in my mind for months as a raucous bash turned instead into a low-key gathering in my front room, where half a dozen mates in a bad mood shared a Chinese takeaway, and everyone avoided the topic of why we were there in the first place.

We tried not to talk about the redundancies, and after a while I realized no one had mentioned Twatface, or being divorced, or even said congrats and given me a peck on the cheek; they were making polite small talk, which in journalists is just odd. So as I topped up their glasses I made a jokey reference to Twatface's booze, which got nothing but a, 'Mmm, it's nice,' from Fifi.

And then, five minutes later, in a quiet moment, I sighed and said, 'Well, that was a long eight months,' to which Porter responded that he had seen The Editor with a new squeeze in some bar in Covent Garden.

By the time the meal and wine were finished, and everyone declared it was time to go – 'Thank you for having us,' and, 'Well done, you,' kiss, hug, squeeze – several hours had passed at a divorce party which had in no way been a party, and where no one had mentioned divorce. Closing the door behind the last of them, I realized it was all a bit of an anticlimax, for them as much as me. It's impossible to celebrate a negative, and no one sensible thinks the end of a marriage – even an unhappy one – is fun. They had come because they were my friends, and didn't want me to be on my own. But this was the big moment I'd been waiting for, and it hadn't been what I had expected: it had been disappointing.

I had hoped for a sense of dawn breaking after a long, dark night. All I had was the sensation of losing the comforting hatred which had been wrapped around me and kept me nourished for so long. I felt like a baby unwillingly evicted from its warm womb. It was cold and bright and lonely out there, and I was scared as well. I knew I could not, in all consciousness or with regard to my mental well-being, continue to brood on Twatface and our failings any more. Nevertheless, he is going to inform and affect, in my head at least, everything I do from here on in. How do I grow up big and strong, and stop myself listening to what he has to say?

Lying awake in my newly unmarried and unmade bed, I stared at the ceiling and wondered what the hell to do. All the metaphors and problems churned around in my brain as I tossed and turned. I flumped over on to my back, and lay looking at the chest of drawers, where the box which held my engagement ring – and now both our wedding rings – was still at the back of the sock drawer. I sighed and burrowed back through the duvet the other way, and saw the wardrobe, where my wedding dress still hangs in its clear plastic bag, having never been worn since that one and only time. 'Gaaah!' I shouted at the ceiling. 'I'm surrounded!'

And that's the problem. It's everywhere I go – not just the bits and bobs and detritus of married life, but everything I carry in my head. If I'm a newborn, I reasoned, there must be a way to cut the umbilical cord, eat the placenta, bury it under a tree or something. There must be something I could do to turn what had happened to me into compost to promote growth.

Then it occurred to me that I'd considered this before, months ago when it had felt like my marriage was a mouldering corpse laid out in the front room. My rings had cost hundreds, but I'd tried to pawn them and the £50 I was offered hadn't been worth the effort of walking to the shop. I couldn't give my wedding dress to charity, either, for fear of passing the curse on to some other poor cow, and nor could I give the whole lot a decent burial in the garden, because the essence of Twatface with which they were impregnated would probably make my tomato plants turn their toes up and die.

There was only one way to destroy that toxin – the cleansing power of flame. It worked for the Vikings, so why not me?

Next morning I got up, grabbed the dress, ferreted through my socks for the rings, and took them into the kitchen. I decided not to touch the box of wedding mementoes in the attic – I hoped they would bring back happy memories, one day. Scrabbling around in the kitchen bin I managed to locate two plastic takeaway boxes with lids from the night before, an empty tube of Pringles (well, it wasn't empty, but I finished the last stale handful), and a plastic milk bottle, and in the log pile I found a square of plywood and some twigs. Wrapping the cartons up in sticky brown parcel tape to keep them watertight, I lashed the plastic bits together with string to make a raft, the wooden bit tied on top like a platform. Then I stopped and scratched my head, and realized nothing was going to burn without paper under it.

I hunted around the house, but for once had no newspapers to use. Walking into the living room, the first thing that caught my eye on the bookshelf in front of me was my wedding folder, the A4 file in which for a year I'd kept every invoice, email, fax, and detail of our marital plans, from the suit hire to the honeymoon and everything in-between. The vows and readings, the receipt for flowers – and the £200 bouquet I'd refused to throw afterwards, on the basis that it had cost me £200. A receipt for ninety-nine euros for the dress: an ivory silk Chinese frock with hand embroidery I'd found in a shop in the Latin Quarter in Paris on a holiday.

301

Flicking through the folder I ripped out page after page, screwing each one up into a ball until I came across a section that stopped me in my tracks. I had kept everyone's copy of their speech as a memento, and now here they were, the words coming alive under my eyes as I read them and remembered how much everyone had laughed at Barney the best man's jokes, how Dad had made me cry, and the way everyone had been so surprised when I'd stood up and given a speech, too.

Then there was Twatface's speech, the one which he'd put off and not written until the day before, and then only when I'd told him he'd look a tit if he said something off-the-cuff. He'd dictated while I'd written it down for him, occasionally reminding him that he ought to mention the bridesmaids, and that all he had to do was be sincere. So there it was, sitting there in my writing with my words scattered throughout, and I remembered how, because he hadn't done it sooner or practised at all, he'd mumbled and stumbled his way through the whole thing and had made easily the worst speech of the day.

And everyone's words were strangely prescient. Barney telling how Twatface just caused mayhem for everyone around him, and Dad saying he was now a part of our family. I sat on the floor and read, Dad's voice in my head saying: 'My girl gives 110 per cent to everything she undertakes, so I know she will put this and more into her marriage.' Ha, yes, Dad, you were right. I do believe Twatface had more of me than actually existed, which is why I feel so empty now. Then Twatface turned to me and said it was the happiest day of his life.

'And, oh God, here are the vows we wrote,' I thought, eyes filling with tears as my lips silently mouthed the words again. 'I give you this ring as a token of our marriage and symbol of my love for you; through all the adventures we will share I promise to be your friend, your helper and your protector, whether we are rich or poor, sick or healthy, happy or sad. You are the one I choose to spend the rest of my life with . . .'

I cried when I said those words the first time, and I'm crying now because I never thought that one day I'd be writing them here, when it was all over and gone. It was a promise I meant with every fibre of my being and one that I'm proud to say I kept. I stuck to my word when things got rough and even when they were appalling; I was his friend even after Fatty rolled up, and if he came to me for help today, I think I'd give it. I'd have a shout and a bitch, but I would still do what I could for him – although now I'd go only so far as didn't cause me any pain. By contrast he said the same words, and I don't think there was ever a time he helped or protected me from anything. He stopped being my friend pretty early on, and then our fate was sealed. The rest of our lives were never going to go the route we expected, and all that was within our control was the speed at which we travelled to the inevitable destination.

To add to the suddenly obvious predictability of how the marriage had panned out, there at the back of the bookshelf was a pair of miniature silk boxing gloves, one marked 'Bride', the other 'Groom', and joined together with ribbon, which Mum had thought was really funny to tie to the handle of our hotel room on the wedding night. Twatface was unimpressed, I recall, but I'd kept them anyway. If anything should be thrown into the cleansing fire, it was that symbol of two people at war, and of how terrified he'd made me, those times I should have left, but instead had stayed. They and the rings could be my funeral offerings, just like the Norsemen used to make to show how much a warrior had been worth in life. And I suppose that Twatface and I, after all that, were worth little more than three cheap rings and a bad-taste joke about domestic abuse. I grabbed the gloves, along with some of the balls of paper, and went back to my raft in the kitchen.

The paper I tucked under the string which was holding everything together, and then I piled the twigs, in increasing sizes, on top. I took my dress, gazed at it one last time and noted the beer stain and the torn side seam from when Twatface's dad had picked me up and swung me round while I squealed. The hand embroidery was still beautiful, though. I folded it up and tied it on top of the pyre, took the rings out of their box and looped them together with another piece of string and tied them on to the bundle, and attached the boxing gloves, too. I looked at my fire-in-waiting, then out of the window where the cold wind was whipping the snow about. What if it didn't light, or went out? Hunting through the cupboards for an accelerant, I came across a can of WD-40; purchasing it had been the furthest that Twatface's DIY skills had extended. 'Good enough,' I thought, bundling it into my bag along with a box of matches and hoping I didn't get stopped by a policeman. One look and he'd think I was going equipped, no matter what I told him about ex-husbands – and besides, my police caution was still running.

Throwing on a coat and some fingerless gloves, I picked up my rickety raft and walked for a few minutes until I reached the river, praying the tide would be out, so I could get down the steps to the stony beach. The tide was, of course, in. Stood outside the Cutty Sark pub in the freezing cold, I peeked over the railings on the embankment to the waves below and considered setting light to the whole thing and tossing it over. It would be dramatic, if nothing else. But alongside me, amid the expired party poppers and damp silly string from New Year's Eve, were half a dozen tourists taking pictures of Canary Wharf on the other side of the river, and I felt I needed a little more privacy.

The tide was on the turn, but I wasn't inclined to shiver for hours waiting for it to go out properly. My gaze wandered along the railings until it lit on a gate maybe forty feet away from the pub, leading to a set of seaweedy steps being lapped by the tide. Looking nonchalant, I opened this gate and shut it behind me, walking down the steps to a flat bit just above the water where no one could see me.

Hunkering down, I put my raft – pyre, coffin, longship, however you like to think of it – on the step, and sprayed the whole thing with WD-40. Then I sprayed it again, in case it had all soaked in, and then a third time, just to delay the inevitable. Getting out a match and putting it against the side of the box, I tried to think of some words to say. Words had been said over us at the start, but as I searched my head for something meaningful it came up empty. It was the end of an era, one in which I'd fallen in love, got married, been broken and divorced, and there simply were no words to sum all that up. All I really wanted was for it to be done with. Fingers shaking in the cold, I said quietly: 'Goodbye.' Then I struck the match and set it to the paper.

It had so much WD-40 on it that it went up like a bomb. PHWOOOOMP, it went, nearly taking off my eyebrows as I fell backwards off my haunches in an effort to escape the heat. Jerkily I managed to get my hand on to the Pringles tube and lift it off the step, leaning backwards to stop the flames licking up my coat. I threw it out into the air, six feet above the water, and as I watched it spiral down to the waves I worried for a moment that the splash might extinguish my blaze.

The fire sizzled for a second, but then recovered, spitting out flames as the raft bobbed on its takeaway cartons and righted itself. The dress – finally proven to be 100 per cent silk with no nylony bits in it, and I must admit I'd always wondered – didn't curl or melt but burned rapidly to white ash, fluttering away on the breeze, taking with it all the hours of embroidery someone had put into the design. The whole craft rocked as the tide turned and was carried away from the steps, past the pub and down-river, and watching it I thought to myself, 'Well, my girl, if nothing else you know how to build a sturdy ship.' I climbed back up the steps and through the gate to lean on the railings and watch the tide take my life away, sniffling a little as I saw it turn into a soggy, blackened mess. The stink of burning hung in the air, and a grey plume of smoke trailed up to the tourists, who took out their cameras and started snapping, pointing and chattering.

Within a few minutes the dress, papers and twigs were nothing more than a pile of blackness, with little bits I could see cracking off and dropping into the river. It was too far away to be certain, but the flames had surely burned through the string holding the rings – the amethyst he got for our engagement, my thin white-gold wedding ring and his bigger, thicker, silver band he'd got cheap from the market because he wasn't sure he wanted to wear one – dropping them all into the lap of Old

Father Thames, for him to keep or spit up miles away as his mood took him.

It was now down to just a few plastic containers bobbing in the river, and I was uncomfortably aware I was guilty of both littering and pollution. Beating a hasty retreat before the river police could turn up and start asking questions, I turned my back on my raft and rang the only sister-in-arms who would understand what I'd just done – Nancy, mother of two and sadly still stuck in the throes of her divorce.

'Hey,' she said. 'What are you up to?'

I laughed unsteadily. 'I've just burned my wedding dress. It's in flames in the middle of the Thames, on its way to Valhalla,' I told her.

'Jesus Christ,' she said. 'You madwoman! Why?'

Walking back to the house I told her how I couldn't have given away or sold any of those things, and how it had seemed fitting to put them to the torch just as the Vikings had, so that the dead would find peace in the afterlife. 'God knows when I'll be able to do the same,' she said glumly, recounting a tale of festive child-sharing with her ex, involving fights over money.

Then she announced: 'Oh, there's some news on the redundancies too.'

My heart stopped for a moment. The background rumble of joblessness has been too worrying to think about during the divorce, but there was still one hack to be sacked and my work this year probably hasn't been what it should have. My ex-husband threatened to sue the paper, after all, and Elliot has more reason than ever to despise me since I saw his sex tape. Getting binned would put the tin lid on my shitty year.

'I've volunteered to go,' said Nancy, and I felt a guilty surge of relief that my job was safe. I closed my eyes for a second and then remembered to be a friend, and asked her what she was going to do.

She laughed, slightly hysterical. 'I've no idea,' she said. 'I'm in the middle of getting divorced from Knobhead who doesn't pay any maintenance, I'm a single mum, I'm having to sell the house and move somewhere smaller with two young babies. But they're offering me six months' money and d'you know what, it's better than staying in newspapers right now.'

'Really?' I said, slightly hurt on behalf of the trade.

'God yes,' she replied. 'I've loved every minute, but there are days when it's unbearable. The people who sit in corridors have decided newspapers are fucked and are just managing decline. No one's trying to do anything new, to make the internet pay or put some investment into things. Added to which, I've been doing this longer than you and I'm tired of being a journalist. It's stopped being fun, and I'm a mum now – I need to be at home sometimes.'

After she hung up I walked home sadly. I was going to miss having my mate in the office. Val had gone too, and with less staff and more work the newsroom had been quieter and more stressed. I had got used to having my chums around me, imagining they'd always be there just like the paper would always come out in the morning. Except one day it won't, and other people have their own lives to lead.

After I'd got back home I put the kettle on and huffed on my chilled fingers as I gazed out of the back door at the garden, which was covered in a crisp white blanket with not a single footprint in it. It was the best kind of snow; it made me want to pull on my boots and stamp all over it.

At one time it had seemed that my future was all darkness, and I had to feel my way with neither light nor warmth to guide me. But now I realized it was just like the virgin snow, which glinted in that special, weak winter light and makes you squint, and which you know will, in time, strengthen enough to melt the cold away, make the sap pump and draw new life pushing through.

This thought gave me a strange kind of peace. I was free, unencumbered, but stronger for my trials. I had my home, my job, and the paper was probably still coming out tomorrow. My life after divorce was laid out before me, just waiting to be lived, a blank page waiting for me to write a good story on it.

My phone beeped, and I picked it up to read the text. 'Hey, Journo Girl,' said Cricket Boy. 'Fancy a drink this weekend?'

I laughed, then pulled on my boots and went out to make angels in the snow.

GLOSSARY OF TERMS FOR FOREIGNERS AND CIVILIANS

A good line – when working on a major story being covered by all other journalists, exclusives are possible but unlikely. Instead you aim for a good top line to make your yarn stand out from the rest of the pack. Makes for a dramatic headline, but rarely lasts past the top six pars of the story.

Buy-up – a contracted deal between a newspaper and subject of a story for an interview and photographs. Usually involves guaranteed payment for the subject, in return for a promise to provide the legal proof needed and not to speak to other media for a defined period. If either party breaks the contract they can sue the other.

Byline – a line in a newspaper naming the writer of an article.

Byline bandit – someone who sticks their name on another person's copy, for reasons of stealing glory.

Conference quickie – an alcoholic drink taken while the executives are busy in editorial meetings, to quell the shakes from the night before; alternately, a cup of tea for the hungover.

Custard creams – one of the world's finest biscuits. Have one!

Doorstep, door-knock – a job where you have to hang around the front door of someone in the news and try to get them to give you a usable comment.

File copy – the act of getting a story to the office. These days it's all done on email, but sometimes you still have to do it the old-fashioned way, dictating over the phone. Stories are easy, filing is the bit which is difficult – getting the computer to work, driving for two hours to somewhere with reception, and making sense over a crackly phone line when you're drunk.

First edition – the earliest copy of the newspaper printed that day, and the one distributed furthest overnight, with therefore the biggest readership. Most newspapers have up to four editions during the night, on which the late shift can make changes to pick up stories from rivals, and insert late-breaking news, or sometimes a great exclusive they held back so no one else could steal it. Many later editions are produced after people have come back from the pub.

Fleet Street – once the road in which all Britain's national newspapers were based, because it's where William Caxton started printing in the fifteenth century, and was near Parliament and the courts. The first newspaper, the *Daily Courant*, was published in Fleet Street in 1702 – in a room over a pub, of course. As papers grew each one had 'their' own bar in which the staff went before, during and after their shifts. Now it is merely a road connecting the City of London to the West End, filled with shirt shops and bankers. Most of the pubs are still there, and these days Fleet Street is a catch-all term for the diaspora of national print journalists, a tribe of ne'er-do-wells who still pride themselves on their livers and the ability to drink, fight and write, although a worrying number of the young 'uns eat salad and go to the gym.

Front up – the act of presenting a story to its subject for a reaction. Usually done on a doorstep with a tape recorder running, in the hope of getting a good quote or legal evidence if they come at you with a golf club.

Hack – a derogatory term for someone who writes for money. Usually spat out by someone who does not sell, about someone who does. Tabloid journos proudly call themselves such, as did Charles Dickens and Samuel Johnson.

Heads-up – advance warning of a story. Generally done secretly by a member of the public in order to play one newspaper off against another and earn extra cash, or by a friendly copper/friendly journo.

Heart-starter – an early morning alcoholic drink to get the creative process going.

Journalist – catch-all term for anyone who works for a newspaper, from editor to crossword compiler. Never call anyone a photo-journalist, as both reporters and snappers find the idea insulting.

Monkey – deeply insulting term for a photographer, also known as a 'photog' or 'snapper'. Developed because they hang around in packs and scratch a lot. Only news-hounds call snappers monkeys, and in return are called **Blunts** – a perfect bit of rhyming slang, referring to the fact they're for ever getting snappers to do their work for them, or at the least lend them a pencil.

312

News editor – person in charge of the reporters, running the news desk with a couple of minions. Usually a man, he sends journos out on stories, decides what tips to follow up, deals with The Editor, shouts at people on the phone, and has worryingly high blood pressure. Starts early, works late; will stay in the newsroom even if it is on fire.

Off-stone – an esoteric printing term. Metal type was set in a slab known as 'the stone'. When the page is printed, the paper is 'off-stone' and it's time to go to the pub.

Par – paragraph.

Reporter – frontline newshound who spends their life on the road, knocks on the door, sweet-talks the subject, files the copy. Poorly-paid, under-appreciated and generally despised by the public. At parties has to endure accusations of damaging society with simultaneous demands for the latest celebrity gossip.

Ring-in – a caller who rings a newspaper with what they think is a good story. They need to be quizzed extensively before referring them on to the news editor or the Samaritans.

Sent to spike – when reporters wrote their stories on actual paper it was either set on a page or someone decided not to run it. Either way the paper would then be jammed on the nine-inch spike which most journos had on their desks. The practice died out with the advent of computers and too many drunken journo fights but the phrase is still used to indicate a story's been killed.

Snoresheet – a big, boring broadsheet newspaper that old men like to snooze under in the afternoons.

Splash – the front-page story, hopefully an exclusive, in tabloid terms presented with great flair and zing. The more overwritten the splash, the less likely it is to be any good.

Spoiler – to run a story similar to another newspaper's exclusive in order to ruin its impact.

The Editor – do not piss them off!

The Pack – collective noun for a number of Fleet Street hacks all covering the same story. By nature a pack is panicky and can be made to run from one end of a street to another simply by pointing and shouting: 'THERE HE IS!' The Pack generally share their stories with each other at the end of the day after deadline, so any good lines from rivals can be filed for second edition. Usually to be found in the nearest place which sells either a bacon sandwich or booze.

The Reader – affectionate term journos have for their readership.

Twat – mild swear word. Slang for lady parts, but most commonly used to describe an idiot.

Wanker – a self-abuser, an onanist. British swear-word whose use ranges from mild deprecation to violent anger.